How To Get Publicity

WILLIAM PARKHURST

HarperBusiness
An Imprint of HarperCollinsPublishers

HarperCollins books may be purchased for educational, business, or sales promotional use. For information please write: Special Markets Department, HarperCollins Publishers Inc., 10 East 53rd Street, New York, NY 10022.

FIRST EDITION

Printed on acid-free paper

Library of Congress Cataloging-in-Publication Data

Parkhurst, William.
    How to get publicity : (and make the most of it once you've got it /
William Parkhurst.
      p. cm.
    Includes index.
    ISBN 0-06-662062-7 (alk. paper)
    1. Publicity.   I. Title.
HM1226.P37   2000
659—dc21

                                    00-033601

---

00 01 02 03 04   10 9 8 7 6 5 4 3 2 1

To Richard Craven, My Publicist, My Friend

Contents

Acknowledgments

The author is greatly indebted to the following professionals who took the time to share their views, materials, and even office space while this book was being written: Sandee Brawarsky, Richard Craven, Stacey Cohen, Rick Frishman, Diane Glynn, Donna Gould, Barbara J. Hendra, Mike Levine, Kate McDonough, Joan Franklin, John Rockwell, Steve Dworkin, Lori Ames Stewart, Jane Wesman, Jerry Cartwell, Vincent Still, Dan Greenberg, Don Hewitt, Landon Y. Jones, Sharon Johnson, Steve Friedman, "Biker Billy" and Rachelle Hufnagle, Tanya Grossman, and Sarah Parsons Zackheim. My appreciation also to Kathleen Moloney, who edited the first edition and to Molly Katz, without whom *How To Get Publicity* would not exist.

For this edition, thanks to publisher Adrian Zackheim and the publicity department of HarperBusiness—Michele Jacob, Kate Kazeniak, and Stephanie Canarelli. Thanks also to Web designer Joe Notovitz and Internet superpublicists Michael Kaminer and Richard Laermer, who helped me sift through the hype to get to the real magic of e-publicity. Janie Lee of Infocom was a complete pro in providing us with an updated "Bulldog" and great advice for the chapter on directories.

Thanks to Jackie Lyden of National Public Radio and to Emily Hoffman and Leonard Lopate of WNYC, New York; through you

I've gotten a fresh perspective on public radio and those committed to its stratospheric standards.

My gratitude to Laura Gilley and Paul Marcarelli of Parkhurst Communications; the full extent of your research and editorial contributions to this edition can't be expressed in words, so let's just say I know what you did, you know what you did, and may you both get reams of publicity in your very bright futures. Thank you both, and let's go to Cal's.

Steve Oppenheim's years of network investigative journalism and media training contributed substantially to our adverse publicity and broadcast preparation chapters. Thanks too, to Henry Morrison, my longtime literary agent and poker pal. Julie Ross, what can I say but a thousand thanks for your love and understanding. Publicity's loss is social work's gain.

Above all, thanks to Lisa Berkowitz, my longtime friend and editor of this edition. You're the best and you always will be.

Welcome to Publicity

B efore the Internet, I used to tell people that you could follow the steps in this book and easily get $100,000 worth of exposure on media within 20 miles of your home. If you fanned your campaign into the major cities, you could count on national coverage that would increase the value of your radio, television, cable, and print exposure to over $1 million, based on published advertising rates, within about three months. Now, you can get a million dollars worth of publicity in your pajamas. After that, you can really go to work.

The Internet takes publicity to heights never imagined by we who started in the business with IBM typewriters and rotary phones. Until the mid 1990s, mass media communication was a top-to-bottom, noninteractive transmission of information from source to audience. They spooned it out; we slurped it up. "Interactive" meant that you could call a radio talk show or write a letter to the editor. Whoopee.

Along came a bunch of geeks who were lucky to get prom dates, and now the ability to publish (and very soon to broadcast) has been redistributed to everyday people in a way that would be as impressive to Marx as Edison or Marconi. The results are staggering. No matter how large an organization's budget, in the virtual world it is now just one voice among the many. They can put up a Web site, but we can too. Theirs might be prettier, but many of the most elite sites—those drawing the top 5 percent of traffic—are individual, not institutional or corporate.

One of the best descriptions of today's fusion of technology and communications comes from Kenichi Ohmae, the former head of the Japanese office of McKinsey, a major corporate consulting firm. He sees this force as an emerging, invisible continent, rising from the molten depths of creation to permanently change the anthropology of all other continents. The effect of this continent on publicity is to *leverage* each media event into hundreds of other events until it finally rests as a permanent archive.

A *Today* show appearance in 1985 was four minutes of live national television with Jane Pauley—a coup that any publicist could crow about. That same appearance today would be leveraged into a plugged Internet event ("For an excerpt of *How To Get Publicity,* check out our Web site at www.msnbc.com."), then play for weeks on two cable networks, CNBC and MSNBC. It might appear as a promo or a feature on the *Nightly News,* and be made available to hundreds of radio stations.

The appearance would also be plugged ahead of time, often on local newscasts and between programs on the network's schedule.

"Katie, what's coming up on the *Today* show?"

"Possibly great news for women, Stone. We may finally have a real cure for cellulite—tomorrow on *Today.*

A recording artist's forthcoming appearance on a national show is plugged by disc jockeys as a service to their listeners. The simple step of sending an e-mail release to the right program directors generates well over a million dollars worth of exposure before the artist plucks her first guitar chord.

"Jewel's on *Letterman* Thursday night, and the Dave Matthews Band is on *Saturday Night Live.* Melissa Etheridge will be live on the *Today* show this Friday morning."

But can anyone do this? Can you get on national television for your Internet start-up or for your campaign to get more medical care for older Americans? Can you get your own publicity without a network of contacts? In a word, yes. This does not imply that contacts aren't a vital element of a publicity campaign. They are. It's all about building relationships. But talk to any working publicist and she'll tell you that today's media market is content-driven, period. Personal contact is nice, but if you learn what media people need and package it for them in the precise way they need it, you will get publicity every time out, whether you know the person you're pitching to or not.

In the following pages, you'll learn to reach the media in ways and for purposes that you never believed were possible. You will soon know how to expand business or career opportunities, how to promote a cause, how to build and enhance a public image, how to enjoy the satisfaction of increased stature in your home, work, and virtual communities. The only limits that can be put on a publicity campaign are those originating in your own negative thinking

You'll learn how to employ media as a competitive tool in beating a rival to the account, stopping the interstate from passing through your living room, or increasing corporate visibility through coverage in trade journals. If you run a small business or a nonprofit corporation, you can run with the giants on a far more level playing field than in the past, thanks to a seismic media shift from mass to niche communications.

You'll discover how to hold a press conference in person, by real-time video conference, and online. You'll learn to set up a campaign Web site and how to promote it strategically, so that it doesn't just hang in cyberspace like some neglected road sign. You will learn what it takes to appear on network programs and how to travel the well-worn promotional tour circuit taken by plain folks and celebrities alike since the early 1920s, when commercial broadcasting began to flourish.

I'll show you how to maximize the opportunities of your interview, to trade wooden sound bites for the passion that sells your organization, product, or idea. There is advice on focusing your campaign, and guidelines that will enable you to produce materials likely to pique press interest and that will prepare you to express the public side of your personality. Even if you're the most buttoned-up, right-brained thinker in your city, there's a lounge singer inside you itching to escape and belt out "I Just Called to Say I Love You." I can't guarantee karaoke applause—but I will show you how to bring out the performer within.

A waitress in Atlanta used the first edition of this book to become a model, then to open a modeling school. I've heard from a teacher who became a school principal, community leaders who had things built or torn down, professionals who expanded their practices, and a shop owner from Brooklyn who used the procedures to sell customized gilded mirrors. A television journalist advanced to a bigger market by writing a single trade article, and a lot of people raised money for a lot of good causes. But what flatters me most is the response I've gotten from publicity professionals who picked up the book and kept it with them during the scary early stages of their training.

And I can assure you that it is scary at first, but exhilarating. When you watch yourself or your spokesperson on the evening news for the first time, you'll probably pinch yourself and say, "Hey, I did that! It was me!" If you stick with it, there will be a national radio or television network that will be very happy to have you on. You'll cut through cyberspace like an 18-wheeler roaring down a mountain road.

I've done everything that I've described in this book. I've gotten myself on CNN, CNBC, ABC-TV's *20/20*, into *The New York Times*, *The Washington Post*, the *Chicago Tribune*, on talk shows in every major market, and on National Public Radio's *All Things Considered*. And I did it with cold contacts who had never heard of me before the bookings were made.

Does this make me some genius at publicity, an *artiste* with conjuring tricks known only to a handful of chosen souls who pass the secrets on to their heirs at the end of life? I wish. We who do this for a living believe more in the Blair Witch than in publicity genius. In our business, *artistes* flame out in less than six months, usually in less than six days. Those who follow the steps and the rules flourish.

I've also had tons of major market and network exposure in the skilled hands of publicists who did have contacts. Either way, the protocol of publicity was observed without shortcuts.

I've studied a hundred years of American media access. I've talked to the old-time press agents who hung out at Sardi's, smoking nonfiltered Camels while they planted guests on the Ed Sullivan Show or got an appliance displayed on *Queen for a Day,* a forerunner to both Sally Jesse and *Who Wants To Be a Millionaire?*

The publicists of the sixties and seventies also shared their memories with me, recalling parties at the original Playboy mansion in Chicago and the days when Phil Donahue would personally buy you dinner if you brought a celebrity to Dayton. Lately, I've been spending my time with today's Internet publicity specialists, who sometimes conduct whole campaigns in cyberspace.

These professionals all have one thing in common. The great ones love what they do and work very hard at it. In whatever era I've studied, day in and day out the rewards have gone to the publicist who works the hardest. That will never change. Do your research, keep your focus, and you'll do very well.

The Internet notwithstanding, you still have to do a lot of knuckle-numbing labor—stuffing envelopes, collating, running to the copy shop and the post office—and you've probably noticed there aren't any fewer telephones in the world. Yours will be the most important tool of your campaign. A hundred million Web sites won't change what we learned from *Casablanca,* Sweetheart. The fundamental things apply as time goes by.

1

Publicity
What It Is and Isn't

Before you embark on the road to publicity, you'll need a few definitions and a few eye-opening facts.

Publicity is the garnering of free media exposure for promotional purposes—an uncomplicated concept, with many moving parts. *Advertising* is the spending of money for commercial exposure. It's a short message, and it goes right for the monetary jugular. You get what you pay for. If you want to sell your car or get the word out on a dress sale, advertising is your best shot, because the press does not give away time or space that should rightly be sold.

But suppose the car is a 35-year-old Pontiac GTO, and you've thrown a little money into restoring it. Now you have a piece of *Americana*. This is the muscle machine that cruised the main drag of your town faster than anything out of *American Graffiti*. In a car like this one your wife-to-be first admired your muscles through a rolled up T-shirt sleeve where you kept your Marlboros. You've got pictures of you and your buddies in the parking lot of Memorial High getting ready to leave some serious rubber on the asphalt.

This machine saw the rage of Vietnam, the Beatles, Watergate, the rise of cable . . . and through it all the machine was driven and loved by an assortment of interesting people whose snapshots tell a story. This car is no longer simply a vehicle on the market; it's a testament to yesterday. It becomes a candidate for enhanced salability through publicity.

Let's look again at those dresses sitting in the boutique waiting for either moths or customers to take them away. Their only history is that they didn't sell. The shop owner frowns and takes what appears to be her only option—advertising them at 25 percent off and trying to figure out a business where perfectly fashionable attire hasn't caught on locally.

Suddenly, a small item in the newspaper changes the shop owner's whole perspective. The mayor's wife is looking for merchants to donate time and goods for an annual charity fund-raiser at the country club. *Everyone* will be there. The shop owner calls and offers to donate one dress that is *the* haute couture in stylish boutiques from New York to Los Angeles, while offering the rest for a fashion show. The town's most prominent women are persuaded to pose as models; the local newspaper takes photographs; the paper prints the store's Web site, and the dresses move at their original prices within two days.

In both of the examples just cited, an advertising chore became a publicity story because of an *angle*. Whether it's called a *news peg, slant, hook,* or *handle,* the angle is the story's foundation and the pivotal element of a publicity campaign, however large or small.

Angles are derived from the journalist's time-honored news litany: Who? What? When? Where? Why? And How? With varying emphasis, these six questions carry a subliminal, subjective "pricing code" that editors use to determine the timeliness and suitability of an idea.

In Chapter 4, you'll learn more about using the five W's and the H. For now, keep asking yourself *who* you are, *what* you're doing, *when* you're doing it (if applicable), *where* you're doing it, and where people will be affected, *why* it matters, and *how* you get it done. Observe news stories to see which of these building blocks lead the emphasis and which are excluded altogether.

If you look closely, you'll be able to see angles all around you. Take a notebook and begin jotting down angles as you see them in broadcasting and print. Work at spotting the news and feature value of ordinary objects and events.

Sometimes, you'll notice that there simply is no realistic angle. The dresses might be so ugly that no town councilwoman would model them in a fashion show, and the car might be a rusty nine-year-old Hyundai Excel with bald tires. In such cases, advertise and be done with the project. It's the most efficient way out.

The entries in your notebook that point out nonstories are as vital as the ones that analyze legitimate news angles. It's wonderful to exercise your imagination, but no one can create a publicity story when there is insufficient Who, What, When, Where, Why, and How. The press can be lured, coaxed, and occasionally seduced into doing you a favor on borderline ideas, but blatant manipulation is out. Media people have a keen eye for a story; when one isn't there, badgering them will only alienate them.

Tens of millions of dollars' worth of media exposure is given away in this country every day. That statement has the unsettling ring of a matchbook cover land deal or an online special on Elvis autographs, but it's true.

There are 4,793 commercial AM radio stations; nearly 6,000 radio, television, and cable talk shows; 5,682 commercial FM stations; and 2,017 noncommercial FMs, of which 600 are National Public Radio member stations. There are 1,589 operating television stations wired to 11,800 cable systems serving 34,000 communities, 5,000 of which originate programming in their own studios.

The average American home has a television on for 7 hours and 15 minutes every day. Eighty-eight percent of the U.S. public relies on television for its national and international news. We have 1,699 daily newspapers; countless weekly newspapers, insert supplements, and shoppers; and more than 5,000 magazines.

And, as you may have noticed, there are over a hundred million sites in cyberspace. The Web is creating a new wireless presence everywhere we walk, fly, or drive. Soon we'll have it on our beepers and cell phones, in our cars, and probably on our wrist watches as well. We'll all be publishers as well as broadcasters, writing internationally syndicated columns and running our own versions of *Larry King Live, The Howard Stern Show,* or *Oprah!* from home.

What all this means to civilization is something for mediaphiles and behavioral scientists to debate. What it means to us is that we have an opportunity to prosper from the expansion; to employ this new medium as a tool for personal, professional, and financial growth.

People believe that producers and editors are too busy to take telephone and e-mail pitches, and that their feature ideas spring exclusively from their staffs—but they're wrong. Assignment editors and producers know that hard news such as Congressional budget votes or nuclear test ban treaties aren't enough to sustain ratings and subscription levels. They need a large supply of human-interest stories, and usually they don't object if these stories are punctuated with promotional tie-ins in the form of plugs.

The small number of people who profit from their industry knowledge would like you to believe that contacts are everything—that no one gets on *Oprah!* without an in of some kind, and that a *Dateline* segment comes from hanging out with the producers. Untrue.

Most feature material, and even some hard news, focuses on workaday citizens going about their business. They don't have clout, but they do have a story to tell. Corporations and special-interest groups might control real estate and politicians, but they have never controlled the press. It is ours. As difficult as this notion is to grasp at times, it is critical to our process that you remind yourself of your right of access. The press is open to the public—and will probably be interested in what you have to say.

Public relations (PR) is the genus of publicity, the parental umbrella of media- and image-centered activities that include speechwriting, policy statements, preparation for journalists' questions, online and offline newsletters, the syndication of prepared articles, and the submission of prepackaged radio and television features.

PR people are media mercenaries who espouse a particular product or cause. In the 1970s, television viewers became familiar with the image of the company spokesman trying to keep *Sixty Minutes* away from the door, blocking the camera and attempting to intimidate Dan Rather. These days, we're more likely to see that person inviting Stone Phillips inside and taking the questions, looking the interviewer in the eye, and firmly stating that the arsenic that seeped into the community's drinking water was someone else's fault. They are carefully coached for this task, and rightly so.

The press has its own excesses and the advantage of being able to edit tape. In cases where an investigative piece assaults a company unfairly, the result can be disastrous, with exonerating litigation taking years. And, once false rumors arc from TV to the Internet, you have major problems. A strong case presented by a spokesman who is as comfortable under the heat of the lights as the reporter is a more democratic defense and far less expensive.

Not that public relations people are up there with Mother Teresa in terms of good works, but they are sometimes the victims of a snide uttering that something "sounds like a lot of PR"—an implication that those in the field are launderers of the truth. To avoid this soured image, public relations departments in corporations are now called corporate communications departments. Most PR people, if only for pragmatic reasons, won't lie to the press or represent a client who asks them to do so. Maybe they'll spin the message, but they won't lie to the press.

Spokesmen for silicon breast implants, gun manufacturers, and tobacco companies are more visible than their counterparts in less controversial industries. In times of assassination, natural disaster, rumors of war, and every type of public crisis, the spokesman we see translating jargon into English in front of all those microphones is a public relations person doing a job.

Personal Publicity: Misconceptions and Realities

Our focus in this book is on personal publicity, where you have something to say, you're excited about it, you take it to the media, and you benefit from the exposure. Besides the misconception that contacts are the be-all and end-all of the process, here are a few other misconceptions:

You need a super sales personality.   No way. High-powered hypers who think they can bulldoze their way into the green room of a talk show get a backstage reputation that works against them. Polite sincerity, conviction, and an understanding of the show's programming needs will carry you all the way.

You need to be a communications expert.   False. You need to listen to the radio, watch television, read the Webzines and Internet columnists, and newspapers and magazines in both online and offline editions, but you need no special media or communications expertise.

You need charisma to appear on television.   Untrue. The charisma that got you your job, dates, sports trophies, or a part in the school play is enough. Naturally, you'll have to work hard on developing your public side, but unless you want Katie Couric's job, charisma is not something to worry about.

You must have something newsworthy to get exposure.   Interesting, yes; newsworthy, no. If you're doing something that actually makes hard news, you'll know it without making so much as a phone call. The press will camp on your lawn until you come out. Otherwise, anything interesting will have an audience.

You need a public relations or communications background to target your campaign through the nation's talk-show matrix.   That wouldn't hurt, but a few reference texts from Chapter 30, available in most libraries and on the Web sites we provide at the end of every chapter will do.

You need a sophisticated writing style.   The clear use of language is imperative, but the intricacies of advanced creative writing can actually be a hindrance. Journalists have discarded slickness in favor of a straightforward writing style that minimizes adjectives and florid construction. If you forgot your grammar after high school, you'll either have to bone up or find a friend to help you with the written materials. You'll need access to a basic computer and an eye for detail. There can be no errors, cross-outs, or other tip-offs to amateurism.

You have to know about camera angles, makeup, and other techniques. Watching television carefully is more important than possessing any of these skills. We'll show you the basics of studio presence in future chapters.

You need public speaking experience. In publicity, oratorical speech is not necessary; somewhat more polished conversational speech is what you'll be aiming for. You're *supposed* to have some fear of speaking in public—everyone is terrified at times. Apprehension generally evolves into a major asset. So will your VCR.

Publicity is not a panacea. Many people subscribe to a mistaken belief that shouting loud enough and long enough guarantees the success of a project. You should know some truths regarding publicity's limitations:

Publicity will not make you a star. Pick any star of any kind— Kevin Spacey, Pavarotti, Gwyneth Paltrow, Jack Nicholson, Ricky Martin or Ricki Lake, Julia Roberts or Julia Child. They made it because they made it. Most celebrities have a drive the rest of us can't begin to imagine, with talent to match. They have to work *every day* at catching their breaks. Publicity is a tool that will take you to the people in a position to buy what you're selling. Only they can decide if they want you to be a celebrity and, if so, for how long.

Publicity will sell nothing unless people want it. You may choose not to believe that point—quote P.T. Barnum and Donald Trump as you hold your *Blair Witch Project* cassette—but somewhere along the way, you'll come to believe it. Something has to click for people to buy.

Publicity has nothing to do with stunts. The word *publicity* is often coupled with the word *stunt*, but that alliance is about as contemporary as rotary phones. Today's PR professionals generally ignore stunts, because they do not work. They can also backfire, leaving the client with an embarrassing set of negative clippings that linger in the collective subconscious for years. They are best left to experienced specialists who understand how to make them work.

One final note on what publicity isn't. It isn't—or need not be—expensive. Occasionally, one encounters a sleazoid who says, "For a couple of grand in cash, I can get you on the show. Money talks in this business." It happens, but not very much. Radio, television, and cable exist under the scrutiny of the Federal Communications Commission, the government agency empowered to yank their licenses. The Federal Trade Commission (FTC) is empowered to prosecute broadcast or print enterprises if anything doesn't look good. There are sanctions, guilds, and codes of ethics everywhere. Your campaign won't cost you much, and it won't include bribes.

Follow the procedures and you'll see a couple of hundred thousand dollars worth of media exposure for little more than petty cash. Stay with it, and there will be no way to measure the value you'll create for yourself.

Let's get started.

SITE SEEING

Each chapter of this book ends with a select group of Web sites or e-mail addresses that I feel exemplify the lessons of the text. I promise to keep these lists relevant and brief. Many of sites will appear in more than one chapter.

Public Relations Online Resources, www.webcom.com.   A fine site from Impulse Resources Corporation that features a strong buffet of public relations associations, people finders, online publications, and other services.

Public Relations Society of America, www.prsa.org.   Probably the major association of marketing-oriented public relations firms. This site and its links serve as a magnificent guide to how the big PR firms work.

Planned Television Arts, www.plannedtvarts.com.   When it comes
to sleeves-rolled-up publicity in every corner where it can be
found, there's nothing like the staff of PTA, a division of the
megafirm Ruder-Finn. They do tours, radio and video satellite
tours, and Teleprint Conferences (TM), a forum where they hook
up serious decision makers with key journalists. On the other end
of the spectrum, they are among the world's best at negotiating the
slippery slope of getting live interviews with morning disc jockeys.

Michael Kaminer Public Relations, www.mkpr.com.   A young
"wired" firm representing many of the key players in New York's
"Silicon Alley." Michael's Web site, designed by Roger Black,
stands out as a gleaming example of what's possible in site design.

2

Getting Started

Until the sun goes dark, publicity will be a seller's market. Media people know they will perish if they fail to keep pace with the new ideas that come to them through publicity pitches. Some will greet your calls with the enthusiasm of a cat being hosed, but that's because their rich bosses pay them about the same as prison inmates, they have 150 e-mails to check, another 200 pieces of regular mail, and, if they're lucky, a part-time assistant. But they need you and they'll listen to your pitch. It's just a matter of getting started.

If you're not yet online, you can still use this book. Thousands have used it the "old way" with great results. Even today's most Net-savvy publicists spend most of their time in the nonvirtual world of phone pitches, envelope stuffing, and "snail mail." But the Internet is here to stay, and it has forever changed publicity. To keep pace, you have a PC, a modem, and a basic ability to cruise in cyberspace.

Internet publicity is niche marketing. To paraphrase Bill Gates, you have to ask yourself where you want to go today, go there and nowhere else. In this book, our Internet focus will be online media with an enduring presence steeped in traditional journalistic standards. We'll emphasize straightforward communication with online editions of established newspapers and magazines, e-newsletters from recognized companies, trade associations, and nonprofit organizations, broadcast news Web sites, and other media sources with a reputation for fairness and accuracy.

Chapter 5 provides guidelines for dealing with online chat rooms and newsgroups. Approached properly, these virtual communities can be a powerful publicity tool. But if you don't know what you're doing, you're flicking a cigarette lighter over an open gasoline can, for newsgroups are also sources of unconscionable innuendo and rumor. In all cases, we assume you practice the emerging code of conduct known as "netiquette": you don't spam or send unwanted attachments; you keep your e-mail brief; and you don't enter chat rooms under false pretenses or with inappropriate commercial plugs. Cyberspace is about people, not technology. It is a vast network of living, breathing ecosystems, each with its own balance and mores.

Before your campaign begins, you'll need to spend a few hours taking notes. Whether you use the latest laptop notebook from Compaq or Dell, lined yellow paper, or an old-fashioned steno pad, the scribbling you do now will be crucial to your success later. You've been consuming television, radio, and print media all your life, but its promotional essence probably lurks below your radar.

There's a code to learn, and once you know it, you will be able to create publicity anytime, anywhere. It's not a secret encryption so much as a magician's conjuring trick with the sleight-of-hand performed in full view of the audience. Except for breaking news, all that you watch or read in media is publicity-driven. Ignore the high-gloss promos that show the Action News Team charging into peril. Forget the oversold image of the print reporter in a parking garage waiting for a source. That's not how it happens.

Journalism is still a noble calling, and, in a time of crisis, we sleep better knowing Wolf Blitzer is out there somewhere digging out the truth for CNN. But, as a culture, we're more interested in Madonna than Moscow. Feature and lifestyle pieces sell the tickets. And that material comes from publicists.

You're about to take on the exercise of watching television, listening to the radio, surfing the Net, and reading as much as possible, to find the publicity behind media placements. You will observe media with a clear view of why the heads are talking and why the features appear. Consult your cable guide for TV talk shows and start taping them.

Using the yellow pages, or a search engine, go online to visit the site of your nearest major AM talk station. If you have RealAudio or Real Player software (available free of charge at www.realplayer .com) you can listen to enough radio to keep you busy for weeks.

Talk radio has gotten a bad rap. People think they're going to be interviewed by right-wing lunatics in camouflage who step outside during commercial breaks to draw their sidearms and shoot down the government's black helicopters. Instead, they usually find these interviews to be the most stimulating and memorable of their pub-licity campaigns, even if the host is conservative. G. Gordon Liddy and Oliver North do shoot down helicopters, but only if they're known to be carrying liberals.

AM talk radio hosts skew to the right and the callers seem to have far too much time on their hands, but by and large, you'll be very impressed with the interviews you do on these air waves—and you *will* soon be doing them. Notice that their in-studio guests all have something to sell.

Weekends on AM are highly specialized. You'll find real estate and veterinary programs, a national call-in show for cancer sur-vivors, another for HIV-positive patients. There are even dentists with talk shows, a phenomenon about as probable as Ken Starr singing karaoke, but, hey, that's what makes America great. Now scan around until you find an all-news station.

"All day, all night, all news. . . ." ALL PLUGS. There are medical features with doctors talking about the new diabetes medication from Pfizer, business features where the guest just happens to have a book out. Every news station has a gadget guru, a shrink, a travel editor who talks about Delta's new mileage program or that over-looked vacation spot. Get the picture? This stuff doesn't come from investigative teams prowling the city in trench coats.

If you're not a Republican president of the United States, you're unlikely to appear on Rush Limbaugh's radio show, but check it out anyway. Listen to the articles he quotes, the books he praises or trashes, the gadgets that attract his attention. Maybe he steps out of bed, opens the mail, and ad-libs. More likely, his focus is fortified by staffers who deal with publicists they've learned to trust.

If you've been listening to album rock on FM for the past 20 years, you may find your Blue Oyster Cult replaced by Gen X and Y talkers who came of age listening to Howard Stern and "Morning Zoo" teams. They have their own take on sports, talk, and news. It should be about sex, something traditional talk radio hosts think should be outlawed, and it should be on FM. A generation raised with the Huxtables and *Family Ties* knows radio in no other form. Next on our tour, ladies and gentlemen—radio's Gold Coast, the morning drive personalities.

Listen to Don Imus and Howard Stern, along with the clamorous format in every major market known as the "Morning Zoo," "Morning Crew," "Jack and Jill," "Scott and Todd," or "Mickey and Minnie." If your idea of a radio show is Garrison Keillor crooning a ditty on *A Prairie Home Companion*, this experience will be like waking up next to a pit bull.

Imus can be heard on AM as well as FM. His core audience— middle-aged men with a lot of money—is among the most coveted in broadcasting. "The I-Man" first caught industry attention in the sixties with a contest to find a look-alike for black activist Eldridge Cleaver. He created another clamor in the early 1970s when he called McDonald's on the air and ordered 1,200 hamburgers to go, supposedly for a National Guard unit.

Today, *Imus in the Morning* has become an important stop for political leaders, serious authors, and sports figures, all hawking books, CDs, movies, and, often, their personalities as they run for public office. Like Walter Winchell in the 1940s, Don Imus can send a book to *The New York Times* best-seller list just by talking about it on the radio.

Howard Stern's listener demographic profile is younger and more diverse, his audience enormous. Every young stand-up with a sit-com to push or an actor with a movie coming out wants to do the show. Stern belches on the air and can't seem to let a day go by without asking a woman to take off her top. He is like the first season of *The X-Files*, or the early *Seinfeld* episodes. It can take a while to get into the show and the repertory company that is imitated in every major market, usually with little success.

Stuttering John seems to have roamed in from hell as he sticks his microphone into the mouths of celebrities to ask them rude, inappropriate questions. He's become fond of identifying himself as a representative of CBS, accurate as far as it goes, but let's just say that Edward R. Murrow wouldn't get the joke. There's Jackie the Joke Man and two Garys, the longtime producer and "Gary the Retard"—enough said there.

Robin Quivers, Stern's cohost, is a rare female in a prominent place on morning radio, and rarer yet, an African-American. Stern has a street-level take on some of the nation's key social issues, especially race. His conversations with "Gary the Retard" may not be up there with Bob Edwards' long-running baseball banter with Red Barber on NPR, but there is an illuminating sensitivity to the exchange. He has homeless people on the air while most of us just avert our eyes and pass them by. Of course, he has them on to play "Homeless Jeopardy," so he probably won't be earning a Medal of Freedom award from Congress any time soon. But Stern is as fearless as he is inappropriate, and even if Robin's news analysis makes you wonder if either of them has ever actually *seen* a *New York Times*, the listeners are there and they love it.

You're unlikely to be a guest on either of these shows, but you'll certainly end up on their clones. Stern and Imus set the tone for hundreds of local morning disc jockeys, many of whom will be glad to have you on.

While you're researching Imus and Stern, list the guests and what they're plugging. From the guy who had both his wife *and* his mother take their tops off for Howard to promote an independent film to the source book for "Homeless Jeopardy," everyone on Howard's show has something to sell. No matter how unconventional he may get, Stern follows the code. He'll give you your plug.

Switch to NPR, the blissful noncommercial alternative where the air is fresh, the hearts are pure, and no one's crass. The first thing you'll notice is that the meat company being investigated by Congress for gassing innocent ewes seems to underwrite half the programming but okay, they pay for the privilege. You put on Ray Suarez and "Talk of the Nation."

"And Ray, Mother Earth Soap is made with a no harsh chemicals, no pesticides, and no dolphins were killed. Your listeners can check out our Web site at www.MotherEarth.com or call for free recipes at 1-800-Mother Earth." Cool.

Even if you already listen regularly, visit the sites of National Public Radio (www.npr.org) and Public Radio International (www.pri.org), the system's two principal networks. You can hear just about any public radio program online. Terry Gross has a wonderful mix of musicians, writers, comics, and reviewers on *Fresh Air*. And what are they doing? Pushing books, CDs, anthologies, and upcoming HBO specials.

Well, you say, I'll just take my public radio business over to *Car Talk*, the funniest show on network radio. Every car manufacturer wants to be goofed on by the "Tappit Brothers," Tom and Ray Magliozzi. Their outrageous, long-running on-air pleas to Jaguar to provide a test vehicle was a bouquet of welcome and priceless publicity that coincided with the company's campaign to rebuild an image.

Whatever you're selling, you'll need to check out African-American and Hispanic programming. If your school Spanish isn't enough to get you through the morning, get some help because whatever you're promoting, you're promoting to Hispanics, America's fastest-growing ethnic group. And they have bucks to spend. When you check out your local Spanish station, notice the commercials play in both Spanish and English. And notice that all the big advertisers are there.

On the Web or on the air, rap and hip-hop stations are well worth visiting. These stations are major players in the music business. The democratic power of the twenty-first century is right there listening to music you might not understand, but you *will* recognize the advertisers. Adult African-Americans spend a lot of time with community-based talk radio, which you can find in real time on the Web or through the yellow pages. During the O.J. Simpson murder trial, these stations were a principal source of information about the racial subtext of the drama.

Now, start to watch television, paying close attention to what is actually being sold and how the topic of the interview keys into it. Most morning TV talk segments run between four and seven minutes, with the host discharging the plug responsibility at the beginning and end of the interview.

Note the graphics below the chin of the interviewee that sometimes mention a book, organization, or movie. This lettering is often called a *Chyron* after the company that pioneered readable computer-generated graphics, or a *lower third* because of its place on the screen. It quickens the pace of the interview by telling viewers who the guest is—an attorney, author, or business consultant for example. The Chyron will help make you more interesting to the viewers.

You should soon start to wonder if *anyone* goes on the air just to talk. The comic has an upcoming series on Fox, the singer is going to be at the Trump Mega Dome through May 24, and you may rest assured that the head of GM isn't on the *Today* show to talk with Matt and Katy about Chryslers. Even the guy wearing the pig nose outside with Al Roker is pitching half the time. He wants to sell bacon and dance with the Incredible Edible Egg.

Television talk used to end by 6:00 P.M. Now, the shows run 24 hours a day. Notice that *Rivera Live* is usually a panel of shouting lawyers in several cities. If they don't have books out, they're building careers. Larry King these days has either celebrities or newsmakers. Look for the plugs. They're there.

On ESPN, every professional athlete on the planet seems to be wearing Nike's boomeranglike "Whoosh." There are upcoming card signings, CDs, cookbooks, deodorants, exercise machines, and "Great Moments" highlight footage video packages for only $79.95. After a game, the athletes are trained to provide sound bites, win or lose. It's good public relations for the team, which gets at least as much of its revenue from television as fan attendance.

If you've never seen *Oprah!*, you've missed a force of nature. She seems to walk right out of the TV to embrace each viewer, and say *and mean*, "I understand. I've been there." Oprah doesn't pitch anything. She *falls in love*—with a book, an exercise program, or an idea, and like her longtime theme song says, she's every woman.

We've seen her overweight, too thin too fast on a liquid diet, thin the smart way with a trainer and her chef, both of whom had their own best-sellers. When she ran in the Marine Corps Marathon in Washington, D.C., we went on it with her, and when she said she "fell off the wagon" and put a few pounds back on, you could hear refrigerator doors open at night all across America. You have not seen daytime TV until you have seen *Oprah!*

Most of us don't get on *Oprah!*, but you will get booked on local talk shows and noon newscasts. It used to be easy to tell network from local programming. Diane Sawyer was national, the guy who looked like Drew Carey was local. Today, satellite technology has blurred the lines. The local weather person talks to the national weather person live, Tom Brokaw thanks the local anchor by name and proceeds to offer a live rundown of what's coming up on *NBC Nightly News*.

Your local newscast is probably called *News 9 at Noon*, *News 4 Chicago*, or *Action News at Five*. Whatever they call it, there is probably as much feature material as hard news and we know where that material comes from. Your local talk show will have a name like *Good Morning Waukegan* or *Charlotte Today*, and will be a moving catalogue of things for sale.

Cable eternally welcomes celebrities a tad past their time in the sun, especially if they have something to sell on the Home Shopping Network, QVC, or other channels. If you came of age with a huge crush on a particular actor or singer, an on-air conversation with that person can be a superbly uplifting experience. Just get the Visa out, because you're going to have to make a purchase to do it.

Read every newspaper that serves your community—dailies, weeklies, special-interest publications, shopping guides—anything that might be promising to your campaign. Now read the same newspapers online and notice the difference; often there's more to scan and download online. At times, your sole exposure will be in the online edition of an offline publication.

Scan the big newspapers—*USA Today, The New York Times, The Washington Post, The Kansas City Star, The Boston Globe*, the *Seattle Post-Intelligencer*—online.

To get a sense of the unfolding world of online media, check out some of the "Webzines," columnists and other sources that cover the unfolding world of online media—www.wirednews.com; www.mediagrock.com; www.e-commerce.com; www.newyorkobserver.com (very Web-savvy); www.fastcompany.com; www.redherring.com; www.trendstories.com; www.thesmokinggun.com (they post juicy public documents).

When a show says, "Check out our Web site," do so. *Dateline, 20-20, Today, Good Morning America, Biography*—whatever show or network that appeals to you has an interactive site that is often more informative and fun than the broadcast or publication itself. Whomever has something to sell on the network gets reams of free publicity online.

Magazines are an ongoing, comprehensive part of your research. Read them online or offline constantly. Start with those you enjoy most and comb the Net and newsstands for city and county magazines and journals. Go where your message belongs and note the plugs. *Time, Newsweek, Wired, Brill's Content, Forbes*, and other news magazines expand the definition of news to every aspect of our culture while keeping readers abreast of the new technology.

All coverage is important. Even off-peak radio, TV, and cable shows are endowed with clout beyond belief. You'll notice that they have evangelists of every denomination as neighbors in their obscure time slots, whose shows end with a solicitation of some kind. Or, you'll find infomercials pitching real estate with no money down, rock-hard abs, or motivational tapes. There is no such thing as dead time or wasted space in the media. It's all profitable to someone.

SITE SEEING

Here are some Web sites that will help you see the publicity behind the media.

NETWORK TELEVISION:

ABC, www.abc.com
CBS, www.cbs.com
NBC, www.nbc.com

CABLE NETWORKS:

CNN, www.cbs.com
CNBC/MSNBC, www.msnbc.com
A&E, www.aetv.com
HBO, www.hbo.com

TALK RADIO:

Car Talk, www.cartalk.cars. An online edition of the popular public radio program.
Talk America, www.talkamerica.com. The home of the USA Talk Network.
WBZ, Boston, wbz.com. One of the premier news and talk stations.

MORNING DRIVE RADIO:

Howard Stern, www.koam.com. KOAM stands for "King Of All Media." There are many fan sites as well, but start with this one.
Don Imus, www.everythingimus.com. All you ever wanted or hope to know about the legendary "I-Man."

3

Setting Your Primary
Campaign Goal

An ancient pep talk on direction says that if you don't know where you're going, you're probably not going to get there. In publicity, eliminate the *probably*. You need to be very specific about what you want from the campaign, or your interviews will be a mere narcissistic ride. When planning a publicity campaign, the primary goal should be summarized in a simple declarative sentence that spells out everything you hope to accomplish. It's a good idea to list possible objectives and take note of a dominant theme. Here are a few guidelines:

Be realistic. Choose a goal that assumes no grandiose dreams, no big breaks through national exposure. While you can be pretty sure of some form of network distribution in today's climate of niche and virtual media, there are no Hollywood agents likely to scout you for a new Fox sitcom, and there won't be a stampeding crowd waiting to buy what you're selling. Nothing works that way. What you can expect is momentum.

You should pace yourself on the basis of an ongoing media presence with incremental improvement. This is the way commerce works. Most successful actors or comics were around for years before you heard of them. Most products that hit the big time came on the heels of many misses by their creators.

Over the years, we've promoted a number of *Saturday Night Live* books on college radio stations. This gives us the chance to work with the performers and production staff, usually during their summer break. Despite their youth, most of these performers got to the show after years of late nights in comedy clubs, improvisational theater, and high school and college productions. And, although the public scarcely notices, the skits and characters we know best—John Belushi escalating into a rant on "Weekend Update," Bill Murray's lounge singer, the Adam Sandler goofy boy persona, Molly Shannon's Catholic schoolgirl—built very slowly. As they caught on, the network promoted them, making the actors available for interviews and running promos throughout the week. The small steps count most.

Maintain an online/offline balance.   The Internet is a major cultural revolution that is often compared to the advent of the printed press or television, but it's still a toddler, unable to feed itself or you. If you stay in cyberspace too long, you can waste a lot of time and do serious damage to your campaign's timing and momentum. A morning radio personality with two million listeners who won't start the day without him is far more valuable to you than an obscure chat room or newsgroup.

You typically get booked on such shows by getting a producer to read through your press material as she holds it in her hands. However, once you know that producer, you may develop a great online conversational dialogue by e-mail that would take months or years to develop by phone calls or visits to the studio. When to log on or off the Net is up to you. But, as you plan your campaign, remember to strike a balance.

Be very specific.   Treat your primary campaign goal like a fraction reduced to its lowest common denominator. You'll be expected to hold your own on a variety of related topics, but when it comes time to go to the cashier's window for the plug, you should be selling only one thing.

Choose with your personality in mind.   It may be that your firm specializes in the sale of municipal bonds but you're more interested in a lucrative subspecialty, *Fortune* 500 market index funds. Go with the funds that stir your passions. That's what you'll sell best.

Choose with your audience in mind.   No one has to pay attention to you. But if you are able to excite an audience, they will never leave. Let us say that you are excited about no-load mutual funds, and the street smarts that made you successful at selling them tell you to avoid the legalese in favor of a simple starting point: You will tell them how to make more than a million dollars. You maintain your rapport by keeping your topic of discussion at a level the audience will understand. They will follow you anywhere.

Here are a few examples that will help you set your goals with precision:

You're a dentist who just invested in a new laser that eliminates drilling for most patients.

Primary campaign goal: Expansion of practice by promoting drill-free dentistry.

Your goal is short and to the point. You're ready for the next step. Then it dawns on you that most of your fellow dentists at the certification seminar were pediatric practitioners. You begin to picture a campaign that brings legions of children to your office. You love your own kids—but you don't want anyone else's in your chair. So, you make an adjustment in course:

Revised primary campaign goal: Expansion of practice by promoting drill-free dentistry to fearful adults.

You're a 30-year old woman who has been flying since you were 15. Your employer, Kankakee Air Charters, wants to see you out there drumming up new business. You discuss the emphasis of the campaign with the boss and decide that you're more likely to reach potential students than air charter customers. You write up your primary campaign goal as follows:

Primary campaign goal: Increased student volume for Kankakee Air.

Then you start to procrastinate. As you visualize the campaign, you begin to see articles in area newspapers and their headlines: Pert Blonde Pilot Teaches Beginners How to Fly; Prettiest Pilot in Kankakee Urges Everyone to Head Skyward; Woman Pilot Says Learn to Fly Early.

You see the accompanying photograph, which has you smiling from the left seat of a Cessna. You realize that being a woman pilot is a plus, and you plan to use it as a secondary angle, but you have a vague uneasiness about the tenor of the approach.

You begin to realize that you don't want to be only pretty, pert, or an employee of Kankakee Air. You want to fly for an airline, a laurel that befits your training and experience. That's no secret with your boss—everyone who flies wants an airline job. After thinking it through, you agree to speak at schools and go after publicity for Kankakee Air. However, your (personal) notation is now different.

Revised (personal) primary campaign goal: To build a clipping portfolio that will help you in getting an airline job.

Let's say that you're an auto mechanic. Talk show doors will be wide open to you if you can tell people how to avoid getting ripped off by mechanics; how they can do some normally expensive work themselves; how to go online for parts and instruction. You have your own garage, and you want people to bring you their mechanical problems. Whatever it is, you can fix it. Your notation looks like this:

Primary campaign goal: To get people into Art's Texaco.

You're all set, Art. In the next chapter, you'll find out what your booking angles are, then you'll make a press kit and face your public. But right now, something's bothering you. You're losing business to the big dealerships, and you're stuck with a widespread prejudice that American garages can't handle the repair of European or Japanese cars. You believe such an assumption to be nonsense, and you're prepared to talk about it. Now you have an amended notation:

Revised primary campaign goal: To get more people with European or Japanese cars into Art's Texaco for discounted repairs that they formerly thought they had to have done at the dealership.

The primary campaign goal is simply the dominating purpose of your campaign. It is not an ironclad entity; change it when you feel it isn't right. It will neither exclude other goals nor serve as the sole topic of your interview conversation. Take all the time you need to find it, however, because the primary campaign goal is the start, finish, and bottom line of your publicity expedition.

SITE SEEING

Check out the releases of these major corporate sites and see if you can isolate their primary campaign goals.

Toyota, www.toyota.com
Coke, www.coca-cola.com
Pepsi, www.pepsiworld.com

4

Your Booking Angles

Angles are what you have to offer the media—what you have to talk about. Perhaps your primary angle is what you do, perhaps it is what you believe, or how you accomplish your work. Again we turn to journalism's barometric indicators of newsworthiness: Who, What, When, Where, Why, and How, to seek a pattern that applies to your background. Answer the questions under each of the six headings, and a profile of your booking potential will emerge.

Who

- Who are you in your community?
- Did you star in local athletics or plays?
- Did you ever make news that people still remember, such as a rescue or a citation for community achievement?
- Is your family local news in itself?
- Who are you in your professional community?
- Have you done anything that made industry news?
- Who stands to benefit from what you have to say in interviews?
- Did anyone live, die, or make news because they did what you are selling or advocating?
- Who works with you and are they newsworthy in any way?

· Assuming that your story has an emphasis in one of journalism's five Ws and H, do you see yourself as a *Who* story?

What

· What do you do?
· What event are you promoting, if any?
· What is the primary idea or product that you are selling?
· What have you achieved that makes you interesting?
· What can someone learn from you?
· What are the pitfalls of what you do?
· What are the trends that will shape the future of your work?
· What chain of events will occur if something in your field
  does not go according to plan?
· What is the origin of your work?
· Aside from what makes *you* interesting, what makes your
  work interesting?

When

· When did you start doing what you do?
· When were you born?
· When does your product or event become effective?
· When does your own story start?
· When will changes resulting from your work occur?
· When can your audience see you or your product?
· When does the story of your product or idea begin?
· If your audience does what you tell them to, when can they
  expect a change?
· When should a story about you run—or does it matter?
· When does your offer expire and, if it does, when will it be
  available again?

Where

· Where are you from?
· Where do you work?

- Where can your idea or product be seen?
- Where is your project going to be most effective?
- Where is the local tie-in or distributor for your product or idea?
- Where is your event going to be held?
- Where are the people around you from?
- Where did you get your education or special training?
- Are there any additional local people or places that stand to benefit from what you do? If so, where are they?
- Where do you take it from here?

Why

- Why do you do what you do?
- Why should anyone else do what you do?
- Why did you decide to pursue this line of thinking?
- Why do any of us need to learn more about it?
- Why do you make specific claims about your product or ideas?
- Why won't we be better off doing it another way?
- Why should your audience listen to you above any other expert in your field?
- Why did you decide to take your ideas to the public through publicity appearances?

How

- How does it work?
- How do people get it?
- How easy is it for the average viewer in the audience to use?
- How long does it last?
- How good is it?
- How did you get where you are?
- How can someone else get there?
- How long did it take you to get there?
- How long can someone else expect to take getting there?
- How will it go wrong, if it does?

Returning to the notebook, set up your headings and list your angles. Your pattern should resemble the following example.

Primary Campaign Goal: Election to City Council.

WHO:

Julie Anne McGrath, 22 Church St., Madison, NY 42052
Born: Madison, 4/22/67
Attended Madison High, 1981–1985
Pitcher, women's softball team, state championship, 1985
Cheerleader, 1984–1985
National Honor Society, elected May 1984
Attended Yale University, 1985–1989
Yale Law School, 1989–1992
Awarded J.D. degree, high honors, June 1992
Employed at McGrath, Wooten, & Bell law firm, September 1992
    to present, senior partner since 1995
Daughter of former Madison mayor Michael McGrath
Niece of Robert O'Connor, former City Council president

WHAT:

Plan to run for Madison City Council, District 5
Believe in lowering tax rate through bond issues and increase in cig-
    arette and alcohol taxes
Believe in new elementary school for East Side
Believe in saving Harriman Park from urban renewal renovation
    plan currently before City Council
Believe in setting up special prosecutor to investigate dumping of
    chemicals in Woodstock River
Registered Democrat

WHEN:

Will open campaign headquarters July 14
Will campaign through November 7 (election day is November 8)
Plan fund-raiser August 9

WHY:

Time for younger political leaders to become involved in Madison
   electoral process
"Old Boy Network" too comfortable in power
Something has to be done about taxes
Something has to be done about river
East Side must have new elementary school to accommodate
   increased influx of families with young children in area

HOW:

Special investigative committee chair must be impartial, and grand
   jury investigation should follow on river pollution issue
Bond issue will offer investment incentive to citizens of Madison,
   who will be offered first refusal; primary aim is to lower taxes,
   which can be done (see position paper)
Will run a clean campaign with help from young-adult program
Expect endorsements from established political leaders

   Publicity angles come in a variety of shapes and sizes, but they
always fit into one of the journalistic categories. Don't be surprised
if your situation seems not to fit into one or more of the slots. The
important thing is that you now realize that you fit somewhere, that
what you have to say is as important as the words of anyone else, and
that you're now ready to consolidate your angles into a press release.

SITE SEEING

Check out some radio and television shows online and see if you
can isolate the booking angles of the segments.

Oprah!, www.oprah.com.   Oprah's own home page, with links to
   her book club and other interests.
Dateline, www.dateline.com
Today, www.today@msnbc.com.   Because of the NBC and Microsoft partnership, *Today* and other NBC news programs put a lot of
   broadcast content online. An excellent site.

Good Morning America, www.goodmorningamerica.com.   A site
to watch. *Good Morning America* is hungry and, at the turn of the
century, tired of getting beaten in the ratings by the *Today* show
in their traditional playpen, heartland America. So, they're going
with a more newsy edge while trying not to irritate the down-
homers peering over their Mary Engelbreit coffee mugs.

5

Your Internet Campaign

The Blair Witch Project roared into the American consciousness in the summer of 1999, bestowing instant stardom on four previously unknown actors and creating unlimited opportunity for the film's equally obscure producers. Then it fell quickly into parody as local transmission shops and burger joints found the inexpensive production elements grist for easy commercial spoofs. Critics did their share of snickering, and *Saturday Night Live,* on summer hiatus when the film was released, even did a skit on why it didn't do a skit.

But all that came later. During the peak of the frenzy, you may have noticed that no one was laughing at the film's Web site and the brilliant use of the Internet to create an urban legend months before the film's release. As if we hadn't already known, the Web had arrived as a promotional tsunami that has forever altered the way publicity is done. Most of us won't get as far online, but we all need an Internet campaign.

Your Internet strategy begins in the planning stages of your campaign, continues as you do your interviews, and stays on as an ongoing adventure in cyberspace. Most working publicists probably view the Web as an emerging force, too powerful as a cross-promotional vehicle to ignore, but nowhere near in importance to where it's going to be in future years. The real action is offline for the foreseeable future. And, anyone who has done Internet publicity knows

that taking the wrong approach on the Web can be a time killer that
will torpedo the momentum of an otherwise strong campaign.

On the other hand, if you allocate too little time to it, you'll lose
out big time, for no one can deny the presence of cyberpublicity, with
its own language and protocol that gains momentum daily. Whether
e-publicity overtakes offline media or not, it isn't going away. Our
focus here is to give you a firm grasp of the basics, then refer you to
several excellent sites and books to advance your practice.

It began like a black-and-white science fiction movie from the
1950s when a group of Pentagon scientists created an instrument of
Cold War paranoia—a computer network to keep national secrets
from the Communists in case of a nuclear attack. It grew into a
Utopian marvel, especially for marketers. Picture 25 or 30 million
people throughout the world nestled snugly into communities seg-
mented by their demographics and special interests. The cost of
reaching these people is just about zero. There is no postage, no
printing, and no cost for the consumers to get back to you.

And they have money. About a quarter of all Internet users have an
annual income in excess of $90,000, compared to only 10 percent of
the general population. Estimates of median household income vary,
but figure about $65,000. However, as with all Utopian marvels of
1950s science, there's a dark side.

Most of these communities have a barn full of genetically engi-
neered Dobermans trained to come charging at you, barking, baring
teeth, and chasing you right out of cyberspace if you trespass with a
commercial pitch. You would sooner break into an institution for
the criminally insane than visit most of the Net's newsgroups and
chat rooms with a crass invitation to "check out our Web site."

Ask Laurence Canter and Martha Siegel, partners in an immigra-
tion law firm. In 1994, they were among the first to explore the promotional power of the "information superhighway" by flooding the
Net with plugs for their firm. They were soon stalked across cyberspace, deluged with hate mail and death threats, their personal lives
made the object of online innuendo, and their ability to communi-

cate on the Web stifled by hackers. And 1994 was the Victorian Era compared to what can be done today.

Fortunately, there's a protocol for turning the Dobermans into playful pups that will bring you your slippers. You can seed the Internet with links to your site, make enticing directory listings, and craft promotions that bring your audience through your front door. You get it all when you do one thing that 90 percent of cybermarketers forget; find the right virtual communities and become a resource to them. It's not about what *you* want. It's about what *they* need. Understand that and you can get as much exposure as you want for as long as you want. Some initial guidelines:

Focus on the major media first. It is painful to see someone toiling away in an obscure chat room when the content of their publicity campaign is of clear interest to CNN or NPR, *Time, The New York Times,* or *The Washington Post.* Or, sending an e-mail release with an attachment to a journalist when a phone call would have sparked greater interest. Long before you begin chatting and posting, concentrate on building a strong media database consisting of offline editions of online newspapers and magazines, Webzines with real bite, interactive responses to radio and television programs, e-mail pitches to the print journalists who have invited you to submit them, columnists, and sites that count. We address this priceless publicity source at length in Chapter 28.

Use the Net to enhance, not replace good publicity practices. Some say that forums, chat rooms, and newsgroups will eventually be as big as radio and television talk shows. But, as with most areas of e-commerce, *eventually* hasn't happened yet. There's no substitute for a face-to-face meeting to build rapport. After that, it's phone calls or e-mail, depending on the journalists' way of working. Publicity is about relationship-building, which *can* be done by e-mail but is still best achieved in a more personal way, through face-to-face contact or by telephone.

Don't send unsolicited e-mail or attachments to journalists.
The best Internet publicists usually contact a reporter to determine his or her professional interests, then request permission to
send e-mail releases, emphasizing selectivity. As a matter of corporate policy, most journalists delete attachments without opening them, both as personal preference and to protect against
viruses.

Lurk before you post to newsgroups or mailing lists. Usenet
alone is made up of more than 30,000 newsgroups. It's sometimes
a good idea to read the FAQs (Frequently Asked Questions) and
always essential to read the acceptable-use policies of your server.
At the very least, subscribe to a group and converse as an equal
participant rather than an authority or a door-to-door solicitor. In
our office, we usually come aboard as subscribers and ask questions of group members before we post.

In addition to your Web site promotion, which we cover in Chapter 9, and special promotions such as contests (see Chapter 23),
most Internet strategies flow from three very large promotional
venues—announcement campaigns, chats, and online newsletters.

Announcement Campaigns

Announcements are your direct link with the Internet public. They
are posted in two places: with discussion groups, and with the commercial online services such as America Online, Mindspring, and
CompuServe.

The goal of the announcement campaign is to get your message
to people having a specific interest in that topic. Do that and you're
far less likely to be excoriated or "flamed" for a violation of netiquette. When you can identify the appropriate discussion groups,
you can post to them. My suggestion is to choose about 10 to 15
groups to start and take the time to be community-specific in offering your needs.

Posting to Newsgroups

Instead of hypothetical examples, allow me to use our strategy for marketing this book as an example. A couple of years ago, I decided that my best approach to online discussions is to stick with *moderated* newsgroup panels. Usenet is like the hippie communes of the sixties. For about an hour and a half, everything was beautiful in its own way. Then along came human nature. Today, Usenet is a cacophony of a million voices, most reasonable, many very contentious, and some that you hope will never leave their rooms, lest they start shooting at rock stars.

But a moderated group has someone in charge with the authority to block anything he or she feels doesn't fit. The moderator, called a *syops* in discussion groups from commercial online services, is there to cut down on spam, with the soothing byproduct of filtering out a lot of flames as well. You may well thrive in the wild vines of *unmoderated* groups. There's a lot of vigilante types who think they own the group, but you're generally free to post whatever you want, so long as you're not breaking any laws.

More than 10 years ago, we learned that a core market for a book on doing your own publicity consists of professionals with expanding practices. Following the principle of their needs coming first, we've approached professional discussion groups on the premise that media access expands a practice.

But, if we went to Usenet to find all practicing accountants, lawyers, psychologists, dentists, chiropractors, podiatrists and physicians, we'd be working into the *next* millennium. Instead, we narrowed the field to more manageable populations, like dental anaesthesiologists.

Dentists are all doctors, but very few of them become board-certified in anaesthesiology. Those who do can offer medically-based relief for those who experience extreme dental anxiety, a wonderful public service, especially to those over 40 whose early dental experiences predated today's sophisticated pediatric practices. We took the time to learn their issues before posting the following message:

Subject: Media Tips for Dental Anesthesiologists
From: William Parkhurst
Organization: Parkhurst Communication
Newsgroups:

Media appearances help board certified dental anaesthesiologists accomplish two goals; to enhance a practice and gain wider public recognition for the specialty which the public probably believes is an adjunct to oral surgery. Consider offering yourself as a guest on your local television newscast where medical reporters have constant need for practitioners who can talk about new pharmaceutical developments. Local television and radio daytime shows have a large 50+ demographic likely to have strong ingrained fears and are therefore open to treatments that are best done by a board certified dental anesthesiologist. Local station Web sites usually have a listing of talk shows, producers, e-mail addresses and suggested procedures for approaching on topics such as "New Relief from Dental Anxiety" or "New Dental Anxiety Specialists."

Guidelines courtesy of media consultant William Parkhurst, author of HOW TO GET PUBLICITY, a HarperBusiness paperback. A free media access kit from the book is available from Parkhurst Communications, www.parkhurstcom.com.

Only a few years ago, one had to dive through journals to find the principal issues of a profession. Today, it is very easy to go online and learn what issues are important to professional groups. Psychotherapists in private practice need to reach full-fee clients because the HMOs have cut them out of insurance they might otherwise have. However, psychological associations need to reach the public at large, pointing out that domestic violence, bias incidents, hate crimes, school violence, and road rage scream out for more research funding. Understanding these needs means we can make a contribution to their communities.

Sometimes we begin online and cross over into offline publicity. For a book called *Beat Procrastination and Make the Grade*, by clinical psychologist Dr. Linda Sapadin, we posted tips to college radio Web sites during exam time. We then contacted disc jockeys by e-mail, suggested a contest on the most creative exam procrastination stories, and offered Sapadin's book as a prize. It worked very well. You'll find your own way with your own message, but our strongest advice is move prudently, 15 or 20 groups at a time.

Follow-up is vital to any posting campaign. It's important to make sure your announcement was posted and, if so, if your message is part of the discussion. Vary your subject line when cross-posting to a variety of newsgroups; if you say the same thing to too many groups at once, you may activate antispam software that cancels you out.

Your postings can appear in a matter of seconds. However, a major server such as AOL can take five or seven days. Generally, if your postings don't appear within a day or two, you may have a problem. Visit alt.current-events.net-abuse and see if someone is complaining about you. If so, take note of the complaint and respond if you think it's necessary.

Mailing List Postings

I like mailing list postings because they are heavily-moderated. If you get flamed, it's a much higher-grade flame. But, I have to say, we are very careful. It's tempting to mass mail, but we don't. There are thousands of lists online, available through such servers as www.webcom.com or www.liszt.com, but you can find yourself with more angry e-mails than you expected to get in a lifetime if you get too ambitious. As with newsgroups, subscribe, lurk, and be very selective. Again, let's go with our campaign for this book.

Say we've succeeded in reaching dental anaesthesiologists, implantologists, and pediatric and cosmetic dentists, and we did so prudently, without spamming. Now we want podiatrists to know about the book. We'd probably start with the superb server, Liszt at www.liszt.com, and subscribe to 10 lists.

Then we'd move to a fermentation stage where we learn what podiatrists bring to the medical table. Bits and pieces float by and I see all kinds of possibilities. We learn that an infected ingrown toenail can be very bad news if it goes untreated. As I think about what would work for podiatrists, I drift back to my days in television.

I start to see possibilities for a wonderful November or February sweeps month headline. Sweeps month ratings set ad rates for the rest of the year, so local news departments unleash their highest-gloss, scariest news promos. Podiatrists are usually not included. Nevertheless, I sense a strong sweeps news promotion. I hear a voice-over and see a five-second station break piece:

Are Your Feet Killing You? Dr. John Rockwell with Advice That Could Save Your Life—Tonight at 6:00 and 11:00!

Now, I see 10 seconds, between *Martha Stewart Living* and *Rosie!* I picture a sobbing woman saying, "I told her to have it checked out. I wish I'd done more." Next, a quick shot of a rescue team running into a building, or, if the producer is as bad as I think, a funeral cortege followed by a close-up of *our* podiatrist, "People take this problem far too lightly." A stabbing musical riff is followed by a muffled voice-over— "It's just a sore toe, but could it kill you? Dr. John Rockwell with advice that could save your life—tonight at 11:00 on *NewsWatch 5.*"

Well, maybe not. I like to think we're known to have a little taste. But tell me you can't picture it on your local Fox affiliate.

I lurk a little longer and come up with a more tasteful sweeps feature—fashionable orthopedic shoes! I see a shot of the old brown orthopedic shoes that no woman under 80 would be caught dead in, followed by a comic riff this time. We cut to a frowning, attractive woman and a voice-over.

"That was then . . ." Then, a shot of a group of very attractive young women walking into an elevator, wearing striking shoes and short skirts . . . "And *this* is now!" Zoom in on red orthopedic pumps. Next, a young woman who looks straight off a *Vogue* shoot.

"When the doctor said I needed special shoes, I thought, right. I'll wear these like twice. But then he takes out these shoes and I go— what?" Now our orthopedist with an appropriate sound bite about sensible shoes as a fashion statement cutting to sexy, comfortable shoes, followed by a teasing voice-over. "The New Sensible Shoes. Just what the Doctor Ordered—All this week on Fox News 5."

Now, I have the concept and I post this message, remembering the important axiom of brevity and low-key plugging.

Subject: Media Tips for Podiatrists
From: William Parkhurst
Organization: Parkhurst Communications

February is "Sweeps Month" when television stations will be look-ing for good medical features for their local newscasts. For the podiatrist appearing on such programs, there is an added benefit of heavy promotional announcements throughout the broadcast day. This can result in a dramatic increase in potential patient inquiries. But the station won't come to you. You need to propose a feature by e-mailing the program's producers, offering yourself as a spokesman. Your local station Web site will probably direct you to the right producers. We suggest offering a segment on "The New Sensible Shoes—Comfortable and Attractive."

This media tip courtesy of William Parkhurst, author of *How to Get Publicity*, a HarperBusiness Paperback. A free media access guide excerpted from the book is available at www.parkhurstcom.com.

Chats

Remember the dork who used to sit in the front row and interrupt the professor with questions the first three weeks of class? The only thing that shut him up was the first exam. Well, he and every one of those September Einsteins (as I used to call them) is alive and well in America's chat rooms. Chats can be disorganized, clueless, and in terms of reach, insignificant.

But, *mes amis*, this is the Internet, where conventional logic is as long gone as rotary phones. Celebrities do chats all the time. So do authors, politicians, and magazine editors. Why? Because chats qualify as acceptable netiquette. You can reach millions online who would otherwise come at you with scythes. In practical terms, a chat is really another form of announcement campaign.

"I'm from Channel 8 and You're Guilty!: Negative Publicity and What to Do About It," is the subject of an online chat with William Parkhurst, author of *How to Get Publicity*, Thursday, November 5, 10:00 P.M." on New York Chat, www.nychat.com. Free negative publicity guidelines available at www.parkhurstcom.com.

Send on and offline news releases to Web sites, newspapers, radio stations, and your database of journalists. A chat is also a good reason to return to offline media that have invited you back. Be sure to give the event a *hook* in the form of a substantive announcement that you intend to make in your opening remarks, provided you can realistically do so.

The Online Newsletter

Newsletters are easy to set up and maintain online. Using list server software, anyone can subscribe to your newsletter and respond to it. An online newsletter is best composed of several short news items:

Publicity Tips

From: Parkhurst Communications, www.parkhurstcom.com

This Month's Topic: Promoting Your Services on Public Radio

Whatever you're doing, you should be doing it on public radio, which delivers the most upscale consumers in all of broadcasting.

There are three ways you can get on.

In the 1930s, the government allocated radio frequencies for educational purposes, but they remained obscure and largely unnoticed until late sixties activism shone its light into broadcasting in search of airtime for minorities and other groups seen as underserved by commercial broadcasting. In 1970, National Public Radio began broadcasting on a shoestring. Today, there are over 600 public radio stations. For little or no cost, you can be on every public radio station in the country.

Start by appearing as a guest on a local talk show. Virtually every NPR member station has a talk show that is very community specific. National Public Radio's Web site, www.npr.org, has a complete listing of local affiliates. Go to your local station's site for instructions on how to present an idea. If you do well, you have an excellent chance of going national, for NPR, more than most radio networks, pays close attention to recommendations from its member stations.

If you were always good at essays, NPR's top programs, *Morning Edition* and *All Things Considered* invite commentary from people in all walks of life. Contact NPR at 202-432-7000 or e-mail — — —.

Finally, there's commercial underwriting. All local and national programs offer inexpensive promotional announcements in the form of 8- to 20-second underwriting plugs. Restrictions apply and vary from market to market, but it's one of the best deals you can get in radio advertising.

From HOW TO GET PUBLICITY (And make the most of it once you've got it), a HarperBusiness paperback. A free set of guidelines on how to promote your product, services, or ideas on public radio is available from Parkhurst Communications, www.parkhurstcom.com.

Remember to write short, information-filled paragraphs. The Internet is not usually conducive to the direct transfer of an offline newsletter. By subscribing to some of the successful online newsletters, you'll get a sense for the Internet style. Experiment and enjoy. The Net is not going away.

SITE SEEING

If you're not already familiar with the Web, start surfing! It's the only way to really get a feel for what's out there. Some great places to start:

Wired, www.wired.com. *Wired* magazine is an excellent starting point for news of what's happening in the online global village.
ZDNet, www.zdnet.com. A very offbeat and fun site, combining reference, news and product information.
Upside, www.upside.com. A highly recommended site for looking at the Net.

6

Writing a Release

A *release* is a summary of a project, written in a journalistic format. It can, if an editor chooses, be printed or broadcast virtually without revision. In smaller newspapers, magazines, and radio stations, it is not uncommon for a release to run exactly as written by its originating source. In large metropolitan dailies or national magazines, of course, printing a handout in its original form is very rare.

Releases end up in the trash or deleted from e-mail so often, whether they're read or not, that one sometimes wonders about their validity. The paperwork that buries the desk of every media person every day assures that a two-page release mailed by itself, with no supporting telephone call or kit, will not do your cause a lot of good. Hoping publicity will result from such an anonymous approach is akin to picking out the color of the Rolls-Royce you're going to buy when you win the lottery. But this lottery can be rigged in your favor.

Despite its short life in many quarters, the release will always be the most important document of your campaign. When a would-be interviewer agrees to "look at your materials," he will scan the release for less than a minute before making the judgment that will yield, or fail to yield, publicity. Once the interview is agreed upon, the release becomes the spinal column of the press person's preparation.

Almost anyone can write a release. Forget about creativity, education, or long metaphoric treks through the essence of humanity.

Forget about writing as you know it. If you hate to write or fear it the way many dread the dentist, you just might be in the right frame of mind. If you love the creative process, you won't necessarily be left out, but there may be a few things to unlearn. Either way, the greatest difficulty in release writing is a tendency to overcomplicate.

"Kiss"

In your grandparents' day, newspaper editors had a long-standing acronym that they passed along to the earnest, Clark Kent types eager for The Big Story: KISS—meaning Keep It Simple, Stupid. Inelegant perhaps, and no one has used "stupid" as a term of endearment since World War II, but it does sum up your mission as a release writer. A release is a miniature news article and should conform to the journalistic tradition of saying as much as possible in the shortest space with the plainest language.

Of Pyramids and Inverted Pyramids

The New York Times gave us permission to use the following piece, written when Pulitzer Prize winner Thomas Friedman was still in the trenches covering war. Note how he structures his story:

2 U.S. Warships Again Bombard Artillery Batteries Outside Beirut*

BY THOMAS L. FRIEDMAN

Special to *The New York Times*

BEIRUT, Lebanon, Sept. 20—For a second day, two American warships bombarded anti-Government artillery and missile batteries in mountains southeast of Beirut today.

    An American spokesman called it "defensive fire." Maj. Robert

---

* From *The New York Times*, September 21, 1983, page 1. Reprinted by permission.

Jordan, the United States Marine spokesman, said the naval barrage started after the residence of the United States Ambassador, Robert C. Dillon, in suburban Yarze in the wooded hills overlooking Beirut was exposed to an attack from a multiple rocket launcher.

The residence was not hit, Major Jordan said, but several fires were started in the surrounding woods, where the presidential palace is also situated.

Reporters counted at least 40 rounds fired in roughly a 20-minute period by the two ships, the cruiser Virginia and the destroyer John Rodgers. Afterward, the shelling from the mountains on Beirut appeared to subside. On Monday, according to Western military sources, the two ships fired 368 rounds.

The bombardment followed by several hours the first visit by four to six American Marine peacekeeping troops in Lebanon to the Lebanese Army's front-line position at Suk al Gharb on a ridge overlooking Beirut. The purpose, a marine spokesman said, was to "collect information."

A Problem With Coordinates

According to Western military sources, the Lebanese Army did a poor job Monday of calling in the bombing coordinates for the gunners on the Virginia and the John Rodgers, and as a result the Americans almost hit some villages that were not occupied by anti-Government forces.

The marines were believed to have gone to Suk al Gharb to establish firsthand the proper target coordinates. Reporters who were there today saw American and Lebanese soldiers poring over maps of the area.

Meanwhile, efforts to work out a cease-fire appeared to have foundered.

(Continued on Page A12, Column 1)

You can stop reading at any point beyond the lead paragraph and still have the essence of the story. In print or broadcast, editors have to be tightwads with their time and space. They work in shifts of heartburning flux, where they know the complexion of a newscast or edition only at deadline time. Reporters learn to submit stories that can easily be sheared to fit into whatever space or time allocation is available at the last possible minute.

Broadcast stories are shorter, but the format, called an *inverted pyramid* because the weight of the piece is heaviest at the top, remains. A broadcast version of this story might read:

> Two American naval vessels blasted antigovernment military stronghold in the mountains southeast of Beirut today. The attacks appear to have followed an assault on the residence of U.S. Ambassador Robert C. Dillon. Correspondent Frank Carney has a full report. . . .

The Components of a Release

A release is made up of a *lead*, a *body*, and a *conclusion*; in other words, a beginning, middle, and end. At the risk of sounding simplistic, that's all there is to it. It takes practice, but if you bear with it, you'll soon be able to write a release on anything.

THE LEAD

For now, keep it very simple. Whatever you have to say to the public you'll be able to condense into that simple declarative sentence your English teachers told you about. The best way is to take a few examples. *A lead is your opening three or four sentences, and it should summarize your entire message.* Now try your hand at a few leads:

1. You're a financial planner who can take $5,000 of a client's money, invest it in a market index fund, and turn it into over $300,000 in 15 years. Your name is Jennifer Barnes, and you live in Menlo Park, California.
2. You're Bob Carter, an executive at Caller One, a new digital cell phone company that offers customers unlimited airtime

and a reduction of up to 60 percent on long-distance calls, with no annual contract. You want people to know that there's no longer any reason for customers to pay monthly fees and roaming charges or have an annual commitment. Caller One packages it for you.

3. You have a garage full of old household goods—magazines, car parts, lamps, one overstuffed chair, a bed, and other items you thought should be hauled off as junk. But, your wife has convinced you that there is no more junk, only collectibles. So, you're planning a most unusual garage sale three weeks from now. You'll put the goods up for an online auction as well. Your name is Les Hanover, and you live at 323 Laurel Street, Manchester, New Hampshire.

4. You're Judy Wright of Rye, New York, and you want the press to know about your new restaurant, Pasta N Things, a unique concept in dining in that your menu is made up of only pasta dishes—spaghetti, lasagne, manicotti, vermicelli, linguine, and so forth. The address of the restaurant is 101 Woodbine Avenue, Rye, New York. The phone number is (914) 33-PASTA. (Hint: The phone number may or may not be included in the lead, depending on how you decide to structure it. The same is true with the address, although both will certainly be part of the release.)

There are no right or wrong formats here, and if your leads don't match the the following examples, don't worry. Your versions may be even more appropriate, as long as they're short and to the point.

1. According to Menlo Park financial planner Jennifer Barnes, a 40-year-old can invest $5,000 in a market index fund and, by the time he or she is 65, that investment will be worth $300,000.

2. You fell in love with your new static-free, digital cell phone—until you got your first bill. Bob Carter, an executive at Caller-One, thinks people pay too much for their portable phones and he has a solution. Beginning September first, Caller One, a

new division of Silicon Communications, will offer a reduction of 60 percent on long-distance calls, with no annual contract. Carter sees this good news as an outgrowth of two factors: advanced technology and a more competitive market.

3. Like his father and grandfather before him, Les Hanover has always been fascinated by American popular culture. Among his accumulations are an original General Electric Beatles radio his mother gave him when he was in the seventh grade, the Woodstock ticket he bought in 1969, and a baseball that Mickey Mantle signed in 1965. Forty years of Americana will go on sale this weekend, simultaneously at Hanover's home in East Manchester and on the World Wide Web.

4. Pasta N Things, probably the world's first restaurant to specialize in such treats as cannelloni, linguine, spaghetti, and other gourmet pasta items, opens its doors at 101 Woodbine Avenue in Rye on November 21. Pasta N Things is the brainchild of Judy Wright of Rye, who believes her menu will attract pasta fanatics throughout the region.

Those five Ws plus H are the building blocks of the lead, but you don't have to religiously get everything in. If you're feeling adventurous, you have other types of leads you can use, as long as you don't overdo it.

THE QUESTION LEAD

A question at the top of your release can sometimes tantalize an editor into reading further. From the cases we've presented, here are a few examples:

1. How can anyone turn $5,000 into over $300,000? Menlo Park financial planner Jennifer Barnes likes to answer that question.

2. Why do cell phones cost so much to use? According to Caller One's Bob Carter, it's a long story that can be shortened to the tune of a 60 percent reduction in both local and long-distance calls.

3. Can an attic full of discarded magazines and toys turn into a treasure trove of Americana? Les Hanover of 323 Laurel Street is about to find out.
4. Where can a pasta maniac go to indulge in spaghetti, manicotti, vermicelli, and other Mediterranean gourmet delights? They can start with Pasta N Things at 101 Woodbine Avenue in Rye.

You don't always have to answer your questions immediately, but generally it helps.

THE QUOTATION LEAD

Sometimes, a quotation from the principal spokesperson of a campaign will offer an alternative that will appeal:

1. "The middle-income wage earner can and should retire a millionaire," says Menlo Park financial planner Jennifer Barnes.
2. "Portable phones shouldn't cost a lot of money," says Bob Carter, a vice president of Caller One, "and now they won't."
3. "I love my Partridge Family albums and my Six-Million-Dollar-Man costume, but it's time someone else enjoyed them." So, Les Hanover of 323 Laurel Street is having a party—and the world is invited.
4. According to Rye's Judy Wright, "Pasta is good for you and more fun to eat than anything I can think of."

HUMOROUS OR NOVELTY LEADS

These are a little more dangerous for the novice publicist, but you should become familiar with novelty or humorous leads. Watch for them and take good notes before trying it yourself. Again, some examples from our hypothetical case histories:

1. Who's your best ally against the IRS? According to Menlo Park accountant and financial planner Jennifer Barnes, it's your Congressmen and Senators who just passed a new tax break for working Americans.

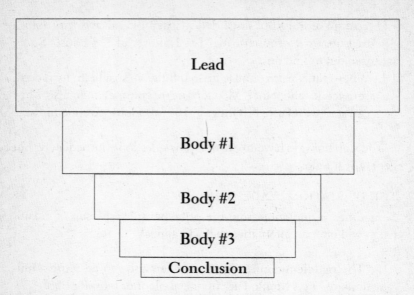

The Inverted Pyramid. The lead paragraph should stress the essence of your campaign in no uncertain terms. Make it simple and direct, highlighting the basic information that you want to convey. Think of it as the only paragraph you have in which to plug yourself. You can then use the following paragraphs to describe the other aspects of your campaign in greater detail.

2. Your cell phone is a money-eating monster.
3. Some would say that Les Hanover's garage is full of junk. Others see collectibles.
4. Pasta freaks can now come out of the closet.

If there are any rules for novelty leads, they would be (1) to avoid the temptation to be excessively cute and (2) to follow with a concise return to journalistic form.

The Body of Your Release

If you're the compulsive type who wants an absolute blueprint for a release form, here it is:

Lead paragraph
Body paragraph 1
Body paragraph 2
Body paragraph 3 (not always necessary)
Concluding paragraph

Some Examples

Before you actually write the release, it's a good idea to list the facts in descending order of importance, then use words to weld them together. We return again to our four familiar cases.

EXAMPLE A

Primary campaign goal: To get clients at income tax time
   Primary booking angle: $2,250 per year like a gift from Uncle Sam

   1. Jennifer Barnes, 71 Tarrytown Road, Menlo Park, California.
   2. Financial planner.
   3. IRAs good for everyone.
   4. Tax advantages of big companies available to everyone for the first time.
   5. Reason for government programs allowing IRAs—to promote savings, which ultimately helps combat recession.
   6. Also helps to combat the effects of an aging Social Security System that's going broke.
   7. Office open Monday through Friday, 9:00–5:00.

EXAMPLE B

Primary campaign goal: To increase Caller One's share in the digital cellular telephone market
   Primary booking angle: Reduced cost of long-distance calls

   1. Robert W. Carter, vice president, consumer relations, Caller One, 153 Cedar Park Lane, Waco, Texas.

2. Antitrust legislation has forced the opening of the new wireless digital telephone networks to competitors for the very first time.
3. Technology enables companies to charge up to 60 percent less for calls.
4. Caller One was recently set up to serve the growing need for economical long-distance calls.
5. The company is made up of more than 500 communications professionals with previous telephone company experience.
6. Caller One uses the most modern equipment.
7. Caller One differs from other "new" telephone companies in two ways: It charges less and the reception quality of the calls is superior.
8. Caller One offers its customers a free telephone.

EXAMPLE C

Primary campaign goal: To sell a garageful of collectibles.

Primary booking angle: An international garage sale in person and on the Internet.

1. A huge collection of 1960s and 1970s memorabilia.
2. Lester Hanover knows he can practically re-create the seventies from the collectibles in his garage.
3. He's been accumulating toys, jewelry, clothing, and movie posters since he was 11.
4. A nostalgia buff even as a kid, Hanover hopes the sale will introduce him to other sixties and seventies "maniacs."

EXAMPLE D

Primary campaign goal: To attract customers to Pasta N Things

Primary booking angle: The novelty of a restaurant serving only pasta dishes

1. A restaurant serving only pasta dishes.
2. Believed to be the world's only restaurant of its kind.
3. More than 35 gourmet pasta specialties to choose from.

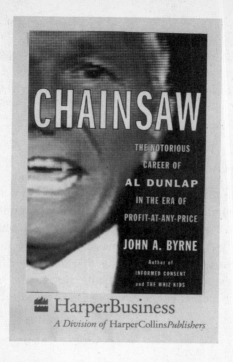

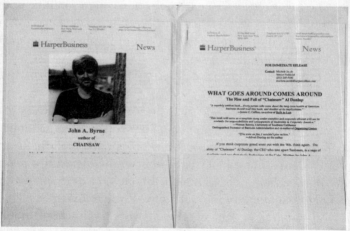

A good press kit should have a release, bio, captioned photograph, and pitch letter. Courtesy HarperBusiness

4. Specialties include Manicotti Supreme, 18 spaghetti dishes, the Cannelloni Adventure, Vermicelli Napoli, Lasagne Fantasy, and Linguine Divine. A special low-calorie section of the menu.

5. Opens on December 11.

The Conclusion

A release's final paragraph or *conclusion* might be a concise summation of your primary booking angle, a final opportunity to reiterate booking contact information, or a parcel of additional information that is relevant but not important enough to have been included earlier. The only rule for conclusions is that they differ from all other paragraphs because of a sense of finality. Review the samples, practice with your hypothetical case histories, and try your hand at it.

Homework

Before you move ahead to the next chapter, where you'll be putting your press release together, practice assembling inverted-pyramid formats and final draft releases for each of the five examples provided.

The Short Bio

A biography on a release is optional, but many current handouts do contain them. For our purposes here, a biography is a brief description of credentials and other key public components of a person's life. Most important, it is a summary of one's life *as it applies to the primary booking angle of the campaign.* If you're trying to sell yourself as an adult long out of school, your high school dramatic achievement award isn't going to pack them in the aisles. Similarly, if you are, like many in today's workforce, a freelancer who wears many hats, be certain to highlight the area of expertise that applies to your pitch:

Stanley Bing
author of
WHAT WOULD MACHIAVELLI DO?
(HarperBusiness; 1999)
Photo credit: John Filo

Creatively crafted press kits can stand out and get to the top of the very large pile of mail that media people receive every day. Courtesy HarperBusiness

Dr. Doreen Carney has been practicing emergency medicine in Waltham for more than 25 years. A 1978 graduate of Bishop Stang High School, Dr. Carney attended Stonehill College and Boston University School of Medicine. She has published more than 25 articles in professional journals and received the 1997 Hippocrates Award for outstanding contributions to the community of Waltham. She currently resides and practices at 4 Crestview Road with her husband, Professor Brian Wallin of M.I.T., and her daughter, Carolyn, a student at Waltham High.

The Format of a Release

Whether it appears on a letter-sized or legal-sized sheet of paper, a release should always be neat and in accordance with traditional format. While there are several ways to do it (and no one will give you a failing grade if you deviate a little), we offer the following specifications for a release.

THE RELEASE DATE

You can either specify that you want your publicity to run on a given date by saying, "FOR RELEASE JANUARY 12, 2001," or use the time-honored, "FOR IMMEDIATE RELEASE." For your purposes, the latter is probably more practical; formal release dates are still in use with the automotive industry, the various government agencies, and in a variety of other settings, but even they are ignored sometimes.

Generally, the press figures, rightly, that anything sent to them is fair game. However, if you've promised a news contact that she can be the first to announce your story, or if other circumstances like the timed announcement of an Initial Public Offering or corporate merger demand silence on the news before a certain date, you must alert anyone who reads your release to this fact by declaring an *embargo date*.

Replace "FOR IMMEDIATE RELEASE" with "EMBARGO DATE: JANUARY 12, 2002." Unless the release contains explosive, news-making information, journalists will then hold your news until the date specified, and your announcement should go as planned.

The release date should go at the top left corner of your release, five spaces below either the letterhead, if you're using one, or the upper edge of the paper. Either capitalize the first letter of each of the three words or put the whole thing in upper case.

THE CONTACT

The simple word *contact*, as in

Contact Kathleen Brown (312) 877-4848, Ext. 321
or kathpr@Chicagpr.com

should appear three spaces below the "FOR IMMEDIATE RELEASE" heading. You should feel free to expand the phraseology to "For Further Information Contact _____

THE HEADLINE

The headline is next, and it should appear about three spaces above the lead paragraph. It isn't necessary to use all caps, but it's a good idea to separate it in some way—italics, boldface, etc.—from the rest of your copy. The headline says something about what you're selling and should be reworked many times before a decision is made. Remember that this is one of life's few opportunities to get away with not using a complete sentence. Read a newspaper carefully to observe the fine art of headline writing before trying it yourself. The headline should be centered.

PARAGRAPHS

Don't waste a lot of time trying to decide whether to indent three spaces or to run flush with the margin and skip a line between paragraphs. You're right either way.

MARGINS

Whatever looks good will suffice as a margin so long as you're consistent.

BOTH SIDES VERSUS TWO SHEETS

For years, our position has been to use a second sheet instead of printing on both sides of a page, but today, many publicists and press people prefer the two-sided release, though it's far from a universally accepted tenet of release writing. Printing on both sides of a legal sheet means that the whole release is in the editor's hands at once.

FONT AND SIZE

Don't get fancy! A release that is difficult to read will be turned over and used as doodling scrap while the reporter is on the phone with someone whose release is legible. A font size of twelve is standard.

LEGAL-SIZE PAPER VERSUS STANDARD

The fewer pages the better. It's better to have a single-page release on a legal-sized sheet than a page and a half on two standard sheets. But there's nothing wrong with either format.

SINGLE VERSUS DOUBLE SPACING

No debate here. Your main body should be double-spaced, with single spacing included if you want to set something off. Quoting a paragraph from a medical journal is an example of using a single spacing within a double-spaced release.

LENGTH OF A RELEASE

Try to confine your release to two pages.

ENDING IT

It is common practice to center triple asterisks (* * *) or triple number signs (# # #) beneath the last line of your release. However, your final sentence is certainly enough by itself to indicate the end of the release.

PAPER STOCK AND COLORS

Black-on-white is still probably your best bet for a release, although you are by no means restricted to it. If your topic is fun, have a little fun with color and the type of paper. Your local copy shop will have a dizzying array of colors and papers to choose from once it's time to make reproductions. Don't choose a flimsy paper, and don't use stock too thick to fit through a standard fax machine.

THE POSTCARD RELEASE

The U.S. Postal Service doesn't object if you use a postcard format to convey your message to the press. Since size regulations change periodically, it's a good idea to check with your local post office before heading to the copy shop. If you have something that can be said in a few lines, the postcard release offers one advantage that is unbeatable: It doesn't have to be opened and is thus more likely to be read.

If you've practiced enough with our case histories and feel you're now ready to do your own release, move ahead to the next chapter. If you still feel a little rough around the edges with release writing, work at it a little longer before moving on.

FOR IMMEDIATE RELEASE

Contact: Jennifer Barnes

(415) 623-0318 or *jbmony@menlocpa.com*

Local Financial Planner Helps "Regular People" Retire as Millionaires

According to Menlo Park accountant and financial planner Jennifer Barnes, the American dream of being a millionaire is more attainable than ever. And the government, besieged by pressure from the strong retirement lobby, is only too happy to help.

"The middle-income wage earner can and should retire a millionaire" says the 35-year-old Menlo Park native who has been helping people plan their retirements since she earned her accounting degree from Berkeley in 1993. Our congressmen and senators, says Barnes, have been under increasing pressure from lobbying groups such as the American Association of Retired Persons (AARP) to maintain a healthy Social Security System throughout the first half of the twenty-first century and beyond.

But saving Social Security is not enough, Barnes says. Our lawmakers are at work making it easier for us to accumulate enough capital for a comfortable retirement through Individual Retirement accounts (IRAs), Keogh Plans, Roth IRAs, government-protected union and corporate pension plans and other measures now before Congress to help people avoid the pitfalls of limited retirement income. However, as always, there's a catch. You have to know your options and, says Barnes, you need to build wealth slowly.

"I don't think people fully understand the power of compound interest and how to make it work for them through the tax loopholes the government has given us as a gift," Barnes says.

If a 22-year-old puts aside $2,000 at an annual rate of return of 8 percent, a conservative long-term estimate by many accounts, the money will compound to nearly $55,000 by age 65. If that same 22-year-old put aside $2,000 a year and managed a return of 15 percent, she'd be worth approximately $715,000 by age 65, and $1.06 million by the time she reaches age 70.

A problem that Ms. Barnes faces daily is either disbelief on the part of her clients, who are accustomed to thinking of legitimate tax avoidance as illegal, or a tendency to procrastinate financial planning. Because she believes an investment portfolio is as essential to a household as insurance policies, real estate, and other long-range systems, Ms. Barnes offers a free consultation to anyone and a seminar on retirement planning to groups of 10 or more. Her office at 71 Tarrytown Road in Menlo Park is open between nine and five, Monday through Friday. Her phone number is (415) 623-0318, e-mail, *jbmoney@menlocpa.com*

FOR IMMEDIATE RELEASE

Contact: Lyn McMillan

(514) 564-4766

E-Mail: *lmcmillan@callerone.com*

Telephone Executive Urges Consumers to Shop Carefully for Cell Phones

"There used to be only a few digitalized cellular phone services," says Bob Carter, Vice President of Operations at Caller One," and now we have hundreds." Caller One of Waco, Texas, is the latest of the freshly minted digital personal phone services that have emerged in the wake of new technology that significantly reduces the interference of earlier portable phone systems.

Caller One™ was established to meet the growing demand for discounted off-peak long-distance calls, a market Carter says has been previously underserved. One of Carter's principal aims is to convince people that such saving is available. People often tell him that his service is "too good to be true."

"People are naturally suspicious of anything that goes against that which they've seen all their lives. Since the nineteenth century, phone companies have been virtual monopolies in this country, but that's all history now," Mr. Carter says.

Caller One is comprised of more than 500 communications professionals with prior telephone company experience. The company utilizes the most modern technology available and plans to continue doing so.

But how is Caller One different from other cellular phone companies? According to Carter, the answer to that question is uncomplicated. Caller One is superior in two ways: It charges less per call, and the reception quality of its transmitting system is superior. Caller One also offers its customers a free telephone manufactured to the highest technical standards.

Information on the new telephone technology is available on Caller One's Web site, www.callerone.net or toll-free at 1-800-555-4921.

FOR IMMEDIATE RELEASE

Contact: Lester Hanover

(603) 622-2232

Sixties and Seventies Buff Plans Internet Garage Sale of More than 200 Collectibles

Who wants to buy a mint-condition Partridge family album? How about an original Woodstock ticket? Les Hanover of 323 Laurel Street in Manchester is about to find out. Hanover, a lifetime collector of 1960s and 1970s memorabilia, has scheduled a garage sale for fellow enthusiasts to be held in his garage on August 11 and 12 between 10:00 A.M. and 6:00 P.M., rain or shine.

The items will also be offered for bidding on e-barter, the new online auction service that specializes in collectibles.

Hanover promises enough albums, costumes, movie posters, campaign buttons, and other artifacts of his youth to keep the hundreds of participants he expects online and in person smiling.

"I don't have Paul McCartney's guitar or John Travolta's white suit from *Saturday Night Fever*, he says. "This is not that kind of sale. What I have is the kind of stuff most kids say got thrown away by their moms when they moved out. I offer them the chance to get it back."

An inventory of items includes an Incredible Hulk Halloween Costume, an original-cast *Saturday Night Live* vinyl record album, and several mid 1970s Superhero dolls, including Wonder Woman, Batman, Robin, and Superman.

From the 1960s, Mr. Hanover offers several Kennedy and Nixon campaign buttons, a General Electric Beatles Radio from 1964, a collection of *Twilight Zone* comic books, and the original Woodstock ticket that Hanover bought, but never used.

If the sale matches Mr. Hanover's expectations, he plans to turn it into an annual event. Inventory may be previewed at Mr. Hanover's Web site at www.goodtimes.net. from May 1 to 5. Bidding begins on e-barter (*www.ebarter.net*) on May 5.

FOR IMMEDIATE RELEASE

Contact: Judy Wright

(914) 337-2782

e-Mail:pastanthings@rye.com

Gourmet Pasta Restaurant to Open in Rye

Pasta N Things, probably the world's first restaurant to specialize in such treats as cannelloni, linguine, spaghetti, and other gourmet pasta items, opens its doors at 101 Woodbine Avenue in Rye on December 11. Pasta N Things is the brainchild of Rye's Judy Wright, who believes her varied menu will attract pasta fanatics throughout the region.

"Pasta is a way of life for those of us who are hooked on it," she says. "And it's actually very good for you, a very healthful food." Ms. Wright disdains the notion that pasta is a threat to a thin waistline. Most of the calories associated with pasta are actually a function of the sauce. With careful preparation and discretionary use of oil, she has developed a "calorie counter" portion of the menu where no entree contains more than 500 calories.

The 35-year-old rookie restaurateur points with pride to her 35 gourmet pasta specialties, which include Manicotti Supreme, 18 variations of spaghetti offerings, the Cannelloni Adventure, Vermicelli Napoli, Lasagne Fantasy, and Linguine Divine. Pasta N Things will be open daily for lunch and dinner and plans to honor all major credit cards. Reservations can be made by phone at (914) 337-2782 or e-mail, pastanthings@Rye.com.

SITE SEEING

Check out the press releases on these sites. Even the big guys write by the rules.

Ford, www.ford.com. Dozens of press releases can be found on this site, from "Live Television Ads to Launch New Ford Focus," to "Ford to Include Standard Trunk Release on Passenger Cars."

Virgin, www.virginmega.com. Updated daily, Virgin's "News and Noise" page is a great example of corporate publicity marketed as music news. Read press releases on the latest doings of the Backstreet Boys and what's new on MTV.

McDonald's, www.mcdonalds.com. This kid-friendly site offers a variety of releases to choose from. Take note that most of the releases are "about" McDonald's charities.

7

The E-Mail Release

Morning radio jocks know their "hipness" will expire faster than a cream pie in July heat if they don't start their day on the Net. Every major newspaper in the country has at least one reporter whose beat is cyberspace. Every magazine, every network talk show has to cover interesting Web sites. Matt Drudge broke the Monica Lewinsky story online, scooping *Newsweek* like a newspaper guy in a felt hat from the 1940s. When the Starr report came out, the world went online to see it. If it's news, it's probably on the Net first. So it isn't surprising that your online news release is a vital component of your campaign with its own protocol and form.

A lot of public relations firms hire specialists to target e-mail releases in bulk. These practitioners carefully prune and guard their media lists. I've talked to a number of them, and I'm about to reveal the secret that separates them from the wannabes. They have mastered selectivity as the key component of an online campaign.

"They know they won't hear from me with superfluous mass mailings," says Michael Kaminer, a former journalist whose firm, Michael Kaminer Public Relations, serves the major players in Manhattan's "Silicon Alley." Kaminer maintains a database of over 5,000 e-mail addresses of journalists and spends hours contacting them offline.

Like all practitioners who could be called *au courant* in cyberpublicity, Kaminer relies heavily on offline communications. Before

he adds a journalist to his list, he typically builds rapport by telephone, asking if the reporter would like to receive material pertain-
ing to his or her specialized interests. How do they prefer to be
contacted?

The maintenance of the database is the work of one full-time
staffer and everyone in Kaminer's 14-person office. When one of his
sources covers a story, Kaminer may well e-mail a thank-you note,
but not before he sits down and writes one by hand. No online trend
gets by Kaminer or his staff, but the secret of his success is that he
maintains the online/offline balance that newcomers often do not
understand.

The reason for this is that the Net is so vast and so fast that we
have come to believe everything we ever need to know or find is on
it. While it is true that there are some fine address services such as
Four 11's Online Directory (www.four11.com) online, your own list
will be culled from personal contact with sources. En route, you are
certain to find list brokers who make some very strong claims. If it
seems too good to be true—you know the rest.

It is very easy to buy into the seduction of having a portal to the
world. There are nebulous services that "guarantee" a thousand or
more "current" media contacts, yours for the push of a button and a
charge on your Visa. Forget that. It doesn't work. Proceed carefully
before you push the button to release your message to a waiting
world.

Sometimes it's a matter of guesswork. Weekly newspapers are
among America's strongest media, but, often you'll find only one
e-mail address per publication. However, as long as there are directories like the *Editor and Publisher Yearbook*, there is no reason to
send your release to an anonymous source. And, for the size of the
mailing of most do-it-yourself publicity campaigns, it's better to just
call the paper and verify the name and address.

Formatting is probably the biggest problem in distributing an
e-mail release. Your message can look fine to you and be an aber-
ration of curls, marks, and horrific indentations on the other end.

This lack of standardized formatting will work itself out in time. For now, it's a good idea to check with a computer consultant on the most current path around the issue. You may need to learn the difference between the built-in software of your Internet provider and Eudora, Chameleon, MCI Mail, Pine, Lotus Notes, and other systems before you push the magic button that moves everything into cyberspace.

Savvy Net publicists compose on a word processing program with a 60 character per line length, and save the file as ASCII text, with hard returns at the end of each line. This will usually help. But before you release it to a large media list, check the text file to be sure it looks nice. While you're at it, check for spelling (a lost art, according to many journalists on the receiving end of e-mail releases).

Don't use tabs. Once you save to ASCII, they're likely to come out as empty spaces that are about as appealing as an actor with missing front teeth. Complete words in capital letters are seen as shouting on the Net. The software built into your Internet provider is unlikely to be compatible with a system devised for direct access, such as Eudora, the longstanding workhorse of Internet publicity specialists.

Once you get through all of that, it's time to compose your release. An e-mail release differs from its hard copy ancestors in length and mission. Where your main release *pushes*, your e-mail release *pulls*. Its job is to *tug* a media source to the phone, a Web site, or, very often, to your press kit. Thus, the standard two-page release is way too long for e-mail.

Your e-mail release can easily be adapted as a posting to online communities. If so, it must be as pristine as a mountain spring, with no commercial calls to "buy," "order," or even "check out our cool site." It is acceptable to direct the recipient to you for "more infor-mation," and to invite them to the site in the signature, below the main body of the release. But know the distinction and work it into your prose, or you will have some very angry people on your case.

An e-mail release should have three components:

The Heading

Think of the heading as an interoffice memo, to and from with appropriate cc's.

To: Paul Marcarelli, Philadelphia Inquirer
From: William Parkhurst, *Parkhurstcom@mindspring.com*
Subject: Review Copy Available, "Don't Know Much About the Bible."
Cc:
Bcc:
Attachments:

Most newspaper reporters and many other media sources will request an attachment on those rare occasions when they want one. Leave attachments out of bulk mailings. On some occasions, such as posting to a corporate internal publication or newsletter, it is occasionally useful to notify recipients of other addresses by completing the Cc field. But for most applications, it's not only inappropriate but an invitation to delete. No one wants to look at a cascade of addresses. Instead, shift to the Bcc (blind carbon copy) field before transmittal.

The Subject Line

The e-mail subject line is your online headline. It should draw the recipient into the main body of the message, but in a very straightforward manner. The subject line for a discussion group posting should be specific to the needs of the group:

Subject: Media Talking Points For Ophthalmologists
Subject: New Software For Screenwriters

When posting to discussion groups, change the text of your subject line often, and never post the same message to the same group twice, or you'll risk getting deleted and flamed for spamming.

Subject lines for journalistic release are less tricky. Come up with one and mail away:

Subject Line: Fear of Public Speaking May Be Inner Ear Imbalance Says New Book
Subject Line: "Greed Is Good" for Young People Says 22-Year-Old Author
Subject Line: 10 Tips For Overcoming Fear of Public Speaking

The Main Body

A bulk-mailed e-mail can be a page, but the trend is a main body with two short paragraphs—enough to fill a screen.

Pasta N Things, probably the world's first restaurant to specialize in such treats as cannelloni, linguine, spaghetti, and other gourmet pasta items, opens its doors at 101 Woodbine Avenue in Rye on November 21. Pasta N Things is the brainchild of Judy Wright of Rye, who believes her varied menu will attract pasta fanatics throughout the region.

"Pasta is a way of life for those of us who are hooked on it," Wright says. "And it's actually very good for you, a very healthful food." Ms. Wright disdains the notion that pasta is a threat to a thin waistline. With careful preparation and discretionary use of oil, she has developed a "calorie counter" portion of the menu where no entree contains over 600 calories.

The 35-year-old rookie restaurateur points with pride to her 35 gourmet specialties which include Manicotti Supreme, Vermicelli Napoli, and the Cannelloni Adventure.

The Signature

After the body comes the signature, which is separated from the main body by a boundary line that is both real and symbolic. Below that line, you can draw a little attention to yourself when posting to discussion groups. Some interpret the signature as a loophole to engage in wholesale plugs. We interpret it as a soft sell, very much like an underwriting announcement on a public radio station. For groups we might say:

Judy Wright offers a free set of pasta recipes from Pasta N Things."
Phone: (914) 337-9970 E-Mail: *Pasta223@aol.com* or Web: *www*
.pastanthings.com.

For a media source, we would take a more conventional path for our signature:.

Judy Wright   Pasta N Things

(914) 337-9970   101 Woodbine Avenue, Rye NY 10534
fax 337-9925   E-mail pasta223@aol.com
Web Site: www.pastanthings.com
For review copies, please state your preferred mailing address.

Here's another example:

Subject Line: "Don't Know Much About the Bible" Biggest Seller in Successful Series

Jesus is descended from prostitutes while Mary Magdalene does not bear out her wanton reputation. The Walls of Jericho may have fallen because the city was built on a fault line, and Eve probably gave Adam a fig instead of an apple.

New York Times best-selling historian Kenneth C. Davis once again calls on his trademark wit and plainspoken style in "Don't Know Much About the Bible," just published as an Avon paperback. This title has become Davis's best-selling hardcover book to date, going into its fifth printing within weeks of its arrival in bookstores.

The new book follows other bestsellers in the "Don't Know Much About" series: History, Geography, and the Civil War. "Even those who think they know the Bible," says Davis, "will be surprised when they learn that their facts are often half-truths and dimly remembered stories cleaned up for the synagogue and Sunday school."

For Review Copies Contact:

Laura Gilley,	Parkhurst Communications
(212) 675-5650	132 W. 22nd Street
Fax: (212) 675-5053	New York, NY 10011
Web Site:	*www.parkhurstcom.com*

SITE SEEING

Start by checking out some wired media:

Online Insider, www.onlineinsider.com. Rather opinionated, techie site, but good for the latest opinions on cyber news events, like the AOL/Time Warner merger.

The Standard, www.thestandard.com. See the "media" column.

Wired News, www.wirednews.com. All kinds of news of the Internet. You can spend hours on this site.

At New York, www.@newyork.com. A great site to learn what's happening in the Big Apple.

E-Commerce Times, www.ecommercetimes.com. As the name says, it's all about e-business. Excellent, easily understandable site with full coverage of the latest online news.

For Online Addresses:

Island Net Media E-Mail Directory, www.islandnet.com
Direct Marketing News, www.dmnews.com
American Business Information, www.abil.com
Webcom, www.webcom.com

8

Your Press Kit

Having done some release isometrics on hypothetical examples, you're ready to try writing yourself up. For some, this is easy. Others find it so excruciating that they call in a friend for a rewrite or editing job, or to do the entire release. All of those measures are permissible, of course, but our recommendation is to do a couple of drafts yourself first. Some guidelines:

- Reexamine your primary campaign goal and booking angle to be sure that each is defined and refined.
- Check to be sure that the facts in your campaign are all there and that they're arranged in an inverted-pyramid style (descending order of importance).
- If you're stuck on form, remember the skeletal basis for any release: Lead + Paragraph + Conclusion. (Remember, too, that too long a release can be a problem, but that one can almost never be too short.)
- If you feel you still need practice and have worked over the five examples in Chapter 5 *ad nauseam*, choose your own examples and work on them. This part of the campaign seems to take a long time, but written materials are the litmus test of journalists. To them, there are those who know what they're

doing and those who don't. Your written presentation puts you on one side or the other.

- Review the five Ws plus H as they apply to your project.
- Without interrupting yourself, write your whole release in a first draft. Don't worry yet about grammar, phrasing, spelling, punctuation, or overall mood of the release. Worry about doing it all the way through without stopping.
- Now doctor up your work with punctuation, synonyms, and other spices of language. You may want to read it aloud or have someone read it to you.
- Do a few more drafts, until you're reasonably sure that it's smooth. Remember, don't be intimidated.
- Give yourself about 10 headline options after you've concluded the main body. Consult a newspaper to see how a story comparable to your own is headlined.
- Resolve to be clear and accurate but to finish this job rapidly. There's still a lot more to do.

The Press Kit

A press kit is a packet of information that offers editors, producers and interviewers all they need to know about you. The release is the centerpiece of a kit but there are other components that complete the packaged version of your campaign.

Not everyone agrees that a press kit is necessary to a publicity effort. If you're out to promote a single local event, a postcard release will more than suffice. Some network shows like *Today* and *Good Morning America* have spelled it out for publicists at association meetings: Traditional kits are too bulky. The worst kits on earth come from the big PR firms. They get into a mind-set of getting everything in to please their clients and therefore accomplish nothing, because they come up with kits bigger than throw pillows, that only a POW would read.

Page 55 unfolds the components of a kit from HarperBusiness, the publisher of this edition of my book. Most campaigns will benefit from a kit that contains a few standard publicity fixtures that you should plan on using.

THE FOLDER

Any stationery store will offer many styles of folders, and you should probably opt for a standard (8½″ × 11½″) in white, gray, blue, or black. You can go paper or vinyl, but avoid the cheaper heavy paper models that look like something you used in a school project. Use your PC to make a tasteful label for the front.

THE LONG BIO

The *long bio* is a one- or two-page biography of your experience. If the information on your release is sufficient, or if you have chosen a "short bio," leave this element out. If you need a page or two to cover your credentials, set it off as a separate component of the press kit. Here is a checklist for the long bio:

- Schools attended, with years of graduation
- Education beyond local schools
- Years married
- Spouse's name and local schools attended
- Children
- Current occupation
- Prior positions if applicable
- Professional credentials that apply to campaign
- Local awards and other listings of civic participation

If you are a physician, an academic, or a member of a profession where a *curriculum vitae* might be in order, submit one, but only if the information would be of real interest to those considering you for an interview. If you are seeking publicity on a professional level, such as in journals, a *vitae* is more than a fine idea. If you're going to appear with the host of an afternoon talk show on the local cable franchise, hide your laurels under the guise of being a "regular person." Impressive professional credentials often inspire fear in interviewers.

A resume follows the same course. If there's an application to your primary campaign goal, use it; if there's not a lot in it that is pertinent to your sales pitch, shelve it.

THE COVER LETTER

The cover letter is a pitch between you and the media source. You're doing the selling. You're telling why you want to be interviewed and, more to the point, why you should be interviewed.

In its ideal form, a pitch letter should be printed out on a single page, geared toward a particular individual or outlet, and written without a lot of hype. The usual practice is to draft a three-paragraph letter, adding the name of the addressee and a few specifics that counteract the form-letter tone that is despised in every corner of broadcast and print.

In many cases it helps for the cover letter and the follow-up phone call to be from someone other than you. You might want to adapt a pseudonym for pitching yourself, or perhaps a friend can be persuaded, blackmailed, or hired to do the phone work. But if you feel that you want to represent yourself, you won't be alone, and no one will laugh at you for doing so. Develop a thick skin in either case. You will get through this fine, but there will be some scar tissue.

THE QUESTION AND ANSWER (Q & A)

Steve Oppenheim of Manhattan's Oppenheim Communications is a former field producer for ABC's *Evening News* and other network programs. His firm now specializes in hard-hitting news stories. Steve and his associates analyze the news content of controversial campaigns, train clients for their media interviews, and produce press kits for a Who's Who of newsmakers, many of whom won't have anyone else doing their press materials.

In the mid-nineties, Steve and I developed a media training program for the Women Campaign School at the Yale University Law School. Would-be office holders heard one thing from Steve above everything else. If you want to be quoted, the Q&A is *the* most important component of a press kit.

I've done dozens of radio and television interviews using Steve's kits and I always turn to the Q&A, especially if I haven't taken enough time to fully prepare for the interview. Only a few years ago, editors and producers were apt to growl menacingly at the notion that a public relations source might be so audacious as to suggest questions. Today, they'll say, "So, where are the sample questions?" Said questions are submitted in two ways: The Q&A that serves as an actual interview, or a list of ten or fifteen questions without answers.

The Q&A usually is set up with questions in bold type or all caps and the answers in italics. A suitable form is both sides of a legal-size sheet of paper, although no one will place you under arrest if you use letter-size. Whether you use two sides of a single sheet or a separate sheet for each side, three pages should be enough. Edit carefully so as to avoid every little clearing of throat, conversational ramble, or other aspect of speech that might not fit into a printed format.

QUESTIONS WITHOUT ANSWERS

To give the kit credibility, be tough and straight. The following are good examples of questions that aren't adoring and self-serving. If you have difficulty thinking up questions about your project, use the following general questions as guidelines:

QUESTIONS FOR _____ on _____

1. What is a _____ ?
2. Why do we need it?
3. What does your _____ do that other _____ s don't?
4. Why did you develop _____ ?
5. _____ , writing in _____ , says that _____ s are a waste of time. Can you defend developing one yourself?
6. What are the special marketing and distribution problems of _____ ?

7. Who is most likely to benefit from your _____?
8. Who are the most enthusiastic boosters of your _____?
9. _____, writing in the *Journal of* _____, says that _____ s such as yours are the wave of the future, and by 2015, _____ out of every four Americans will have one. Are you that optimistic yourself?
10. Your biography says that you attended _____ College. Did your inspiration for the _____ come from your days there?
11. How has this city changed since you were in school?
12. Are there any dangers to _____ that we should know about?
13. Your resume says that in addition to _____ you have a very interesting hobby, _____. Would you discuss it with us?
14. Your wife (husband) is also from _____. Why did you decide to make your home in this community?
15. What's ahead for you?

Notice that questions 5 and 9 are reverses of the same theme. If there is a published source in opposition to what you are doing or saying and you feel you can strongly defend your project, by all means include it in the question.

YOUR PHOTOGRAPH

Today's digital cameras make the photograph easier, but only if you know how to use the technology. Snapshots are out in press kits, but an 8″ × 10″ or 5″ × 7″ photograph, usually a head shot, is a must. Color has become standard, but there is still something very dramatic and artful about black-and-white. Assuming you're starting with a regional campaign, check with your principal newspaper as to what they prefer.

These pictures should be photographed with a 35mm or digital camera, and if you have any doubt about the quality, get a friend or hire a professional. Never scrimp on photos; like printing, they are generally available economically. If you know something about photography and have access to a good camera, all the better. If not, shop around.

The next photographic decision is a head-and-shoulders portrait versus an action shot of you at work. If an action shot best reveals what you're selling with your primary campaign goal, get one. Otherwise, the traditional "yearbook" shot is perfectly acceptable.

THE PHOTO SESSION

If it is the only part of your press kit published, a picture is worth the proverbial thousand words. If your primary booking angle is the promotion of a restaurant, a tool, a product, or some other object, you'll need a photograph of it in the kit. Because your photo is so important, you should visit with several professional photographers for an estimate of both the cost of a photo session and the cost of reproducing the number of pictures you think you'll need for the campaign. The following tips should help you make photo decisions:

1. Before your session with a photographer, decide how you want to look. For some, a head-and-shoulders shot is wonderful. Others are better off in action at work.

2. Ask the photographer to help you choose your best side. Don't be bashful about having shots taken from eight or more different angles and poses. When the sessions are over, you will be shown either proofs or contact sheets. Proofs are preliminary photographs printed on special paper; sooner or later, they'll fade. They exist only to show what an enlarged print of your photograph will look like. Contact sheets are same-size reproductions of whole rolls of shots on single sheets of photographic paper. Usually, you examine the shots under a magnifying glass.

3. If the photographer takes the pictures at your home or place of business, be sure that there are no eye-catching distractions behind you. A sailboat, for example, might be a nice possession to show your friends, but it could be distracting in a publicity shot. Likewise, a book of bathroom jokes might give you a

laugh, but its title visible on the shelf behind you could make you look tasteless.

4. If you're unhappy with the lighting or any other aspect of how you look, reshoot.

5. A one- or two-line caption that describes the photograph should be typed camera-ready and given to the photographer for printing. For example, "Colonel John Zyla with Cookie, his favorite palomino. Zyla breeds and sells palominos at his Grab Bag Ranch in Merrimack, New Hampshire."

GRAPHICS

Your printer can direct you toward many logos, type styles, and other graphics that will embellish your press kit. Check prices very carefully, and avoid a lot of fancy gloss that will strike the media person as too slick.

ON DOING IT YOURSELF

We don't recommend any home-brew calligraphy here, but with the availability of desktop publishing software, and other graphics options that come standard with most home computers, you might opt to produce the printed materials for your kit at home. Just remember that a laser printer or a high-quality inkjet is pretty standard. Even if it doesn't print in color; you'll be glad later when you pick up your crisp reproductions from the local copy shop. Experiment with fonts and style until you find something that reflects the sensibility of your campaign. You might have a friend design a logo and scan it in to your computer. Whatever you choose, try to keep the look of the materials consistent and easy to read.

Summary

Here, then is a recipe for your press kit:

1 two-page release, offset, typeset, or laser printed (If you can say it in one page, all the better.)

1 or 2 photographs (5″ × 7″ is probably easier to work with than 8″ ×
  10″, and the press is used to photographs of this size).
1 Q&A list of questions
1 cover letter, no more than a single page
1 sturdy folder

SITE SEEING

There are many ways to view press kits. Check out the following
sites which contain complete press kits online:

Chrysler, www.media.chrysler.com   All you ever wanted to know
  about Chryslers. Really great kits.
NASA, www.nasa.gov/newsinfo/kits.html   This is an organization
  that has learned to meet the press head-on. Superb press materials.
Intel, www.intel.co.jp/pressroom/kits/news.htm   If you wanted information about Intel, you've got it here!

9

Your Campaign Web Site

Let's simplify this. You need a campaign Web site. You need a domain name. You need not to make yourself crazy.

Nothing torpedoes a campaign faster than the Web Site Shuffle. Should I hire a designer? Which designer? Can I do it myself? What's HTML? They say the worst thing in the world is a boring site. How can I make sure *my* site isn't boring? STOP! Your Web site doesn't have to be the eighth wonder of the world. If you're blessed with a lot of money, hire a designer. If not, don't. There are about 500 inexpensive options.

We did our site with the resources of Mindspring and software from Joseph Notovitz, a very successful designer whose clients include a Who's Who of major corporations. Joe, like all the best Net entrepreneurs, knows that he's in a cutting edge business where today's low roller is tomorrow's high roller. He offers inexpensive instruction and software, an online newsletter, and help when you get stuck. He is endlessly nice. We'll tell you how to reach him and many others at the end of the chapter.

For the record, HTML stands for *Hypertext Markup Language*, the computer code for making language presentable on a screen. A hyperlink can be thought of as a starship taking you through space and time to your destination in cyberspace. Click and go to London

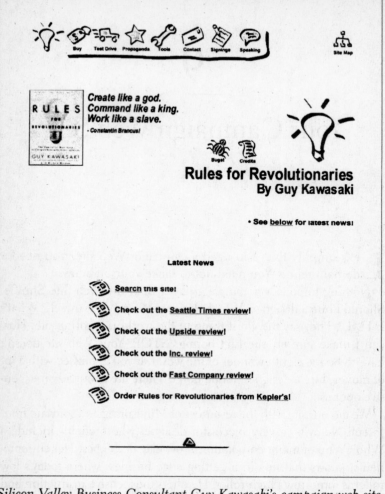

Buy   Test Drive Propaganda Tools   Contact Signings Speaking   Site Map

Create like a god.
Command like a king.
Work like a slave.
- Constantin Brancusi

RULES
FOR
REVOLUTIONARIES

GUY KAWASAKI

Buget   Credits

Rules for Revolutionaries
By Guy Kawasaki

• **See below** for latest news!

Latest News

Search this site!

Check out the **Seattle Times review!**

Check out the **Upside review!**

Check out the **Inc. review!**

Check out the **Fast Company review!**

Order Rules for Revolutionaries from **Kepler's!**

Silicon Valley Business Consultant Guy Kawasaki's campaign web site for his book Rules for Revolutionaries.

or Vienna or San Jose. Or, get folks out there to come to your site, the key objective of Internet publicity.

Richard Laermer is president of RLM Associates, one of New York's leading cyber public relations firms. He's been promoting Web sites for years. To go to a Laermer site launch party is to hang out with Manhattan's Men and Women In Black, the Downtown Crowd. These people are *wired*, babe. They have that big-bucks IPO sparkle. Things are going well for Richard because a great deal of all new business in New York is Internet-related. But, like all savvy publicists, Laermer isn't taken in by the Net's hype and myths.

"The Internet today," he says, "is about rising above the noise. A lot of people online don't *get* it. Those who do get it will do very well. Those who don't just add to the noise." And *getting it* is heavily about knowing what to put on a site. A company can spend over $300,000 on a site design and $50,000 on a launch party and miss a key component of good Web design.

"It's astounding how many sites lack an obvious way to get in touch with live people," says Laermer. "If journalists can't find you, they will not cover you."

Let's assume you don't hang out with the downtown Manhattan crowd and that you don't have a couple of hundred thousand dollars for today's trendiest designer to make your site hot and hip. But let's also assume you're going to make sure every journalist who contacts your site has an obvious way to get in touch with you. Do that alone and you're way ahead.

An updated Web site gives a journalist the story of your campaign, even if he checks in at 2:00 A.M. When I was chasing stories in a radio newsroom, there was nothing worse than an approaching drive time newscast and an unreachable source. I'd be on hold, shuffling copy, watching the clock and hoping I'd be able to get the sound bite on time. If not, I'd pray like an atheist in heaven that the competition wouldn't get theirs either. Nothing's changed. Reporters are always on deadline. They tell horror stories of being on and trapped in a hellish maze of voice mail and Web site links, all leading to no breathing human being. Here's a checklist for planning your campaign site:

Make it easy to find and remember. Cut a hundred corners, but don't skimp on your domain name. A standard registration is just about the only regulated element of the Net. But it can be frustrating because almost any name you select as a first choice was probably taken by some greedy troll between 1993 and 1996. And that troll won't give it to you without a sizeable investment. This is the name you'll be dropping throughout your campaign, so persist until you find the name you want.

Make it readable.   HTML is readable light. A good site is restful to the eyes. Designers prefer Net-specific fonts such as Verdana, Ariel, and Georgia over such standard word processing staples as Times Roman. At the end of the chapter for resources to get you started on a good Web design.

Make it fast-loading.   Most people won't wait for more than 15 or 20 seconds to view a site. Computer-savvy surfers know to turn off their "autoload image" feature for quicker downloading of photographs and graphics. The rest of us tap our fingers waiting for graphics to materialize. Do everything possible to make your site fast.

Make it original.   Your Web site is not a figment of your imagination or an appendage of your home. It is an external display of your wares before the world. Thus, you can hang a likeness of Dilbert on your kitchen wall, but if you put him on your site, you're violating a trademark and breaking the law. Use of trademarked or copyrighted material without written permission will get you sued. There's enough free art and up-and-coming designers willing to work inexpensively to aid in successful site development.

Keep it current.   A site need not be a mosaic of color and moving images, but it does need to be updated regularly so reporters have a reason to return.

Be sure your site is targeted to the reporters it is meant to serve.   If your campaign is going to break news or draw publicity, it should have its own page that is easy to find.

Present an easily understood contact list.   "Gee, I'm sorry, I'm in the shipping department. You need to talk to Jerry, gosh, I can't even think of his last name, but his extension is 348. I think. He's at lunch now and I don't know if he's coming back, but I'll have him call you."

Don't go there. List names, phone numbers, and e-mail addresses of contacts and when they can be reached for comment. If your campaign carries the weight of urgency, there should be a 24-hour line answered live.

Offer accessible press release archives.   Post releases chronologically into a database and create a simple query form so that journalists can move quickly to a given topic. Establish separate fields for the date of the release, the headline, author, text and other pertinent information.

Your Home Page

The home page is your reception area. It sets the tone and mood of your campaign. It should say something about your mission and provide a little history or philosophy about what you do and what visitors can expect when they accept your invitation to explore the site. Your home page needs a beckoning graphic. If you scan in your logo, convert it to a Graphic Interchange Format, or GIF. The human eye does not easily follow a straight scan of print on a screen. Corel Draw,™ Word For Windows,™ Microsoft Publisher,™ and other programs offer inexpensive graphics. Remember to be sparing. There's nothing more amateurish than a home page full of uncomplimentary moving images that detract from the design.

With photos, graphics, and text, you should describe the benefits of the goods and services you'll be showing in depth on subsequent pages. Twenty to 40K is the acceptable range for a basic 14K modem. If you use small pictures with a click-on enlarging feature, you'll avoid a long download.

It is crucial to have links to significant pages on the site. Group them by topic. Otherwise, you can be overlooked by the search engine crawlers.

Your home page should also feature links to other relevant sites, but this can be a mixed blessing. Once you have the customer in your reception area, you don't want him or her scooting off to some other site. Be selective.

Your site should be campaign-specific, with the smallest page count possible. Each additional page should feature a page title at

the top of your Web browser that contains key words. This will help
the search engines find you. There should also be a smaller version
of your home page graphic, a readable page background (white is
good), and it probably doesn't hurt to include your URL address.

Registering Your Web Site

Be polite and patient, persistent and methodical. This is not a process
you're likely to get done in one sitting. Theoretically, registration is
free. Yahoo!, Infoseek, Lycos, Alta Vista, and other search engines will
register your site, sometimes in multiple categories. But, as a practical
matter, you also may want to invest in a one-stop service such as Submit It! (*www.submitit.com*) or Promote It! (*www.promoteit.com*) for the
smaller sites, or to explore the Net's famous marketing device value-
added options. These include bold listings, new links, featured "best
bets" listing, cross-referencing, hot links, and multiple listings. Prices
vary from affordable to exorbitant.

Those who know the registration game generally recommend fill-
ing out the registration forms of the major search engines yourself.
In the mid-1990s, the engines were overrun by "index spammers"
who mass-registered, whether they had real sites or not. To avoid this
indiscriminate registration of sites, they've become very prudent in
checking out new registrants. This takes time.

The key word entry is critical to getting your name around the
Net. It's wise to avoid generalities such as "online marketers." And
remember that you're not writing the neutral descriptive copy of a
press release here. Entice.

Keep a hard copy file of items for later reference — passwords, registration instructions, procedures for changing listings. You may eventually need them.

Links

Any online publicity campaign should include a quest for compli-
mentary links to other sites. Unlike directory registration, the link-

age campaign is a series of pitches to post a link to your site. This is a steady pursuit with a lot of built-in rejection. High-traffic sites spend millions of dollars on radio and television promotion for their visibility. They're not about to hand their hard-won consumers over to you, especially on the basis of an e-mail pitch. If you're a non-profit organization wishing to promote a valid event on the site of a major corporation, you might have a shot at a major site, but the link you make to the company will be offline long before it appears online.

Use common sense. More is not better. Seek offline relationships. Infoseek and Galaxy are excellent directories to search out sites that compliment your campaign. Move gradually through the engines until you reach a large inventory of listings for the professional group you wish to contact. This is sometimes known as a *supersite*. Once there, spend some time finding the right sites and make a pitch for your link. Be prepared to explain why they should take up space on their site, especially a home page, to send their traffic to you.

Find a few sites at a time and do some research. Which of the people behind the site do you need to contact? And is e-mail really the best way to do it? Maybe, maybe not. You might want to shut down and proceed with a good old-fashioned snail mail note. Compliment. You admired the site and feel their constituents might benefit from a link to you. And you, of course, would be happy to reciprocate. But if you're a new kid on the block with no traffic to report and no track record online, don't expect Dell or Wal-Mart to say, yeah babe, come aboard!

The linkage campaign is like booking *Oprah!* or NPR. Anyone can do it, but it's a rarified few who can do it consistently and well. By all means, pursue a linkage campaign, but pursue it slowly.

Offline Site Promotion

You don't need a trendy Silicon Valley publicist to throw a launch party for your site. If you're in New Kensington, Pennsylvania, you'll probably have a better shot at significant attendance and coverage

than you would if you lived in San Francisco, where site parties
have been going on for over half a decade. See Chapter 27.

Your domain name will accompany you throughout your campaign. You'll say it on radio and television, see it in print, hand it out
to people. Be it elaborate or ever so humble, it is the centerpiece of
your campaign.

SITE SEEING:

Take a look at these sites for businesses and events in Westchester
County, New York. They are all doable with just a basic, working
knowledge of Web site building.

Kirkpatrick & Silverberg, www.silverkirk.com.   This is the site of a
   law firm based in White Plains. It is a very good example of a basic
   site that contains all relevant information, including clearly displayed contact information. There is nothing fancy about this site,
   but it tells you everything you need to know.
Inn at Pound Ridge, www.innatpoundridge.com.   A basic restaurant site that conveys the character of the facility, along with all relevant information.
Peekskill Celebration, www.peekskillcelebration.com.   A wonderful, creatively designed site for the annual celebration of the Hudson River, held in Peekskill.

10

The Campaign Strategy

We're now at the starting gate, the point where you make decisions on what type of exposure you wish to use for yourself. Targeting your publicity is equivalent to preparing a battle plan or a political strategy and should be approached with comparable attention to detail.

On or offline, think of four interconnected media strategies—local, regional, national, and virtual. Chapter 28 will deal extensively with national exposure. For now, plan on sticking to the grass roots. That's where even the most illustrious generally start.

Set up a campaign room or corner with a map on constant display. This might sound a little prescribed, even pretentious, but as you progress, you're guaranteed to see the value of having a place to go every time you wish to work on the campaign.

From this point, you should spend a segment of every working day on the campaign. It can't move on a piecemeal basis, for all effectiveness in publicity is based on momentum. Scan the map for its geographical possibilities, bearing in mind that you're looking to sell something to potential customers. Where are these consumers of your brainstorm likely to be? Perhaps most of them are 20 miles from your front door; perhaps they're all over the world.

Start with a city or town in your region that is similar in makeup to your home base, on the assumption that it's better to take an act to New Haven before trying Broadway. Draw a circle around that town and label it with a "1," meaning that it's the first media center you wish to target. Follow a similar procedure for four more towns in your region, bearing in mind that you're better off working away from a big city at first.

If you live in a city, go toward the suburbs for your first appearances. Since our publicity blueprint starts with weekly newspapers and public-affairs radio programs, there is no need to wait very long to target large population centers; but for openers, the congenial tone of small markets will be more conducive to building confidence. That's what it's all about now.

In your thinking, as in the standard dictum of mediaspeak, cities and towns will become *markets*. All population centers are ranked by demographers: New York is #1, Los Angeles is #2, and Flagstaff is #208. Your own first five markets should be chosen on the basis of their access to you and whether your primary campaign goal has any bearing on the needs of the population.

Once you've made these five choices, it's time to find out what media outlets are available to you. The telephone directory is a good start, but you'll need more advanced reference material from your public library. In the extremely rare instance where a library can't help, there is often a local advertising agency or public-relations firm (in small markets they tend to be one and the same) where you can take notes. See Chapter 11 for all the specifics, and Chapter 30 for a list of available reference materials.

Radio

The 24-hour talk stations in larger cities are your "A" targets and probably should not be approached yet. Your "B" stations are local live talk shows in medium-sized cities (roughly 100,000 to 300,000 in metro population), and the "C" programs, your start in broadcasting, are the public-affairs programs you logged in Chapter 2.

The source material will list program directors and public-affairs directors, which can often become confusing. Sometimes, the news director is also the public-affairs director. As a rule of thumb, plan to write to the radio program director in small and medium markets and the public-affairs director in large cities.

Type out the names and addresses of your radio targets (call the station and ask for the program director's name if there's any doubt), making sure that in your best judgment you've listed them in "A," "B," and "C" order. Now you have a master radio mailing list. (Make sure you maintain a file copy of your master mailing list, because you may wish to use it beyond this campaign.) Assemble your press kits, stuff them in manila envelopes or jiffy bags, type the addresses on labels, and stack them in a corner. You're not ready to mail them just yet.

Television

You probably have spent more time with TV during the last 20 or 30 years than you have with any spouse, teacher, lover, friend, or parent. It's more of an appendage than a medium. Thus, you might be a little dazzled by the notion of moving from your living room to inside the tube, but there's nothing to worry about. You're going on television soon, and it will be fun as long as you don't get too ambitious.

For the purpose of compiling your strategy, we'll skip intermediate points in favor of two broad categories.

Television "A" is a daily talk show or combination news and talk show, while a "B" is a weekly public-affairs interview program. If you haven't kept a log of these local programs, take the chute back to Chapter 2 and do so now, for it is important that you concentrate only on the "B" category for the moment. Now compile a list of "B" programs; you'll probably have to do some calling to find out the names of the producers. Once more, put the names on labels, put the kits inside the jiffy bags and the labels on the outside, and put the bags to one side. Again, make sure that you maintain a file copy of the mailing list.

Cable

Generally all public-access cable programs are funneled through the program manager of a system, and the host you see on screen functions as the producer. Repeat the process for cable, bearing in mind that you're looking for local-access shows rather than network offerings. It's often difficult separating them in the tangled web of cable-viewing options. If you're having difficulty here, simply call the cable system, ask for the programming department, announce that you're compiling a list of local talk shows, and ask if they can help by listing some of their more enduring programs.

Newspapers

Local is where it's at. While metropolitan dailies flounder, weekly newspapers have grown up to become healthy, vital adults. In large cities, neighborhood newspapers are snapped up almost before the ink is dry. On the Upper West Side of Manhattan, where I live, we hover around the package room snatching up copies of the *Westsider* or *The Spirit*, the two weekly papers that tell us what's going on in our piece of the Apple.

When I lived in the southern Westchester village of Dobbs Ferry, it was *The Enterprise* and the advertising-rich "shoppers" that carried news of police activity, high school sports, community theater, and supermarket bargains. And when the kids were in school, my wife and I didn't wake up to Imus or Stern, but to a local radio personality named Bobby Lloyd who never missed a school closing, or a zoning controversy in the whole county. And, if you wanted to know which developer was about to stick you with an unwanted high-rise or a tax-supported road so he could build it, Kevin McHale of Cablevision was there to cover it.

The more sophisticated we get, the more we need a village, to paraphrase Hillary Rodham Clinton. File the weeklies as Bs and the dailies as As, but it might just be the smaller publications that give you the coverage.

Look up the editors' names, and make your lists, again stuffing the envelopes and separating carefully. The newspaper scenario is less rigid than broadcasting, where it's virtually imperative that you start small. Our strongest advice is to read target publications and get to know something about who does what on what page. If possible, do the weeklies first. This sometimes presents a problem because there are extreme differences among weeklies; sometimes they're simply not professional enough to be worth your time. Make your best judgment, but stay out of big-city newsrooms until you've had some practice with reporters.

The Booking Sequence

There are no hard-and-fast rules now. It's all up to you. Our recommended sequence of building blocks is as follows:

Radio B.   Weekend shows hosted by lawyers, dentists, and other members of the community who are hungrier for guests than the mainstream talkers. It's easier to get your radio wings this way.

Newspaper B.   (including small magazines)—Weekly newspapers

Cable/Television B.   Local public-affairs programs in any market. They're there to serve your community. Almost any cable system has a show you can get on. Some, like Connecticut's "Exchange" are extremely sophisticated and run all day in a posh, community-minded suburb. Others are dreadful. Some are just a couple of boring heads in front of a potted plant. Unless a show is run by a bunch of unbloomed adolescents who think flatulence is funny, a common occurrence in New York City, it doesn't matter whether a show is "good" or not. While it's on, it's your show. Make your pitch.

Newspaper A.   Daily newspaper profiles

Television A.   Daily talk shows in any market.

You may wish to read the following chapters on interview preparation now, or you might prefer to teethe a little on the "B" media first. Our position is that the best preparation for radio is weekend interviews in small markets; the best preparation for television is local cable; and the weekly newspapers are a wonderful print-interview lab. If you're tired of stuffing envelopes, get your feet wet here. Just stay away from the "A"s for now. Mail your "B" press kits, make your follow-up calls, and go on the air.

SITE SEEING

Parrot Media, www.parrotmedia.com.   Nearly 75,000 media sources and resources.

KCBS, San Francisco, www.kcbs.com.   One of the best news/talk stations in America. Listen in.

Booknotes, www.booknotes.com.   *Booknotes* with Brian Lamb is one of the great long-form interviews.

Broadcasting & Cable, www.broadcastingcable.com.   Since the 1930s, *Broadcasting & Cable* has covered the business of broadcasting. You always know who's doing what to whom and what it means long-term. In the old days, *Broadcasting,* as it was then known, arrived on Mondays to the eager anticipation of executives and on-air personnel. Today, the online edition tells us everything we need to know on a daily basis, at the click of a mouse.

11

Your First Interviews

Whether you're in a one-street prairie town a thousand miles from the nearest Kmart or in midtown Manhattan, the procedure rarely varies. You send a "B" press kit, or an e-mail with an attachment you've been invited to submit, follow it up with a call, and set a date for the interview.

You may discover, to your This-Is-Easier-Than-I-Thought joy, that your mailing results in the station calling you. If it happens, enjoy it. Only in a small town is such a scenario likely to occur. In most cases, media people expect you to make a follow-up call. Don't be surprised if it is not returned. In the media scheme of things, ordinary rules of social conduct don't always apply. The producer who would never consider not calling back in other situations routinely ignores mounting messages in favor of getting the pressing work at hand behind him or her. Editors and producers are on a constant deadline, which sometimes takes precedence over the courtesy of returning telephone calls. Don't take it personally.

Chapter 5 (Your Internet Campaign) covers establishing online relationships with journalists and learning whether they'll respond to e-mail. At the turn of the millennium, both print and broadcast journalists and producers often reported that they responded more quickly to e-mail correspondence, but, unlike expensive telephone lines, e-mail addresses are easy to change and prioritize. Make sure you're sending your e-mail pitch not only to the right person, but to the appropriate e-mail address within the journalistic organization. The only way to do that is to inquire, probably on the phone.

Persistence, then, is one of your first and most important lessons in telephone contact work. When you do get your contact on the phone, don't be surprised if she or he sounds rushed. Get used to that as well and don't let it throw you. Just get to the point quickly and with confidence.

For a little perspective on whom you'll be talking to through the campaign, here's a quick glossary of media titles and what you might expect from those holding them:

Producer.　This is one of the most common titles in the talk field: it can mean anything from a powerful person around the station to a dweeb who runs for coffee. In most local settings, read *producer* as the person responsible for booking the guests on a talk show.

Associate producer.　In major market settings (big cities), there may be two or three associate producers who specialize in the booking of specific guest categories such as entertainers, authors, local community groups, antiques specialists, or cooking segments. For the most part, an associate producer takes your calls and decides if he or she wants to sponsor your idea and book it on the show.

Talent coordinator.　On large network shows, talent coordinators are responsible for preinterviewing guests: that is, having a conversation with a potential guest to determine that person's suitability for a particular program. In medium markets, the title is often applied to a freshman booker, while in smaller towns, the talent coordinator also changes lightbulbs and parks your car.

News director.　There's a reason beyond ego why anyone with this title takes himself seriously. In any setting, the news director has to be the representative of fair journalism and First Amendment rights, a difficult task in a one-horse station where sponsors, tinhorn politicians, and other two-bit power brokers think they can control what goes out over the air. In small radio stations, the news director is the whole department. In large television stations, the title implies a snarling boss (a woman as often as a man today) who commands a fleet of vans, helicopters, remote satellite units, and other state-of-the-art reporting implements. Regardless of the setup, any time you end up with a "news" person, stay as far away from hype as you can.

News producer. You'll meet him or her when you're appearing on combination news and talk shows. The news producer is a line foreman who has to keep rearranging the priorities of a broadcast until (and even after) the show goes on the air.

Talent. The general term applying to people who go on the air, and one of the reasons for an institutionalized ego sense among these folks. Phil Hartman's magnificent portrayal of Bill McNeal in *NewsRadio* was no figment of some writer's imagination. You'll meet him often.

Engineer. The technical person responsible for maintaining logs and equipment to FCC specifications. You won't be writing to engineers, but make friends with them when you can. They tend to have the attention of everyone in the station.

Executive producer. Read that one as boss of the talk show and act accordingly.

Program director. In small and medium markets, this person is the head air personality. In large cities, the job signifies the executive responsible for everything that goes on the air. Television is apt to tag the slot *program manager.*

Editor. The person in charge of reporters, generally in television and newspapers only. In radio, the title usually exists in large stations only.

Reporter. The person a newspaper, television station, or magazine assigns to interview and write about you. They tend to shun overt flattery, but like anyone else are responsive if you show a sincere interest in them. Always play it straight with reporters. Like police officers, they have well-developed ESP and will handle your case in a manner dictated by their professional instincts.

Investigative reporter. A muckraker who is committed to uncovering the dark side of a story. You'll not meet them in the normal course of a campaign, but if you are involved with a more probing reporter and you have something you prefer to omit, see Chapter 21.

Assignment editor.   The person who chooses or fails to choose a reporter to interview you. A very important name to know.

If your "B" material is in one place, or perhaps already mailed, and you choose the "get wet" option of a public-affairs interview, make your follow-up calls (or get some help in doing so) and go on the air. If you would prefer to wait, read through Chapter 20 before moving on.

SITE SEEING

Check out these examples of regional programming.

WNTN, Newton, www.wntn.com.   Solid local radio station in the Boston surburbs.

All News Channel, www.allnews.com.   A great example of a regional cable news channel. There's bound to be one serving your region.

Drug Topics, www.drugtopics.com.   A trade publication for drug-store owners. A perfect niche publication.

Ebony West, www.ebonywest.com.   An Illinois-based black radio network.

On Now, www.onnow.com.   Pick your subject, and *On Now* will find a talk show carrying it on a given day.

12

Making Your Pitch

Getting and scheduling an interview used to be called *booking*, and those who specialized in this high-adrenaline cog of the publicity wheel were referred to as *bookers*. Now, the solicitation of a media source to take action is often referred to as a *pitch*, while the scheduling of an interview becomes a noun, the *booking*. The preferred terminology in corporate communications and at many of the larger PR firms is, simply, a *placement*.

Those who pitch for a living are too busy to worry about what it's called. If a funnel-shaped cloud reaches a thousand feet into the air and it's coming in your direction at 80 miles an hour, do you really care if it's a "cyclone," a "waterspout," or a "tornado"?

The 1990s saw a dramatic shift in how media interviews are scheduled. In the days of rotary phones, publicity was heavily about personal contact. The publicist was forever running off to lunch or a watering hole to hammer away at the contact until he or she said yes. That's still a strong approach to publicity, but today booking is done by voice and e-mail meshed with the live pitch.

You can book an *Oprah!* show or NPR appearance without ever making personal contact with a producer until she calls back and expresses serious interest. Thus, you have a tiered system that demands several separate psychologies of communication.

Even the most experienced PR professionals will often admit that they developed sloppy booking habits early in their careers and that such untidiness, once imprinted, creates problems later. Bad booking habits are sirens that whisper seductive aphorisms about saving time, skipping steps, achieving the same results with half the work.

A problem is that *mouth booking*—the cold solicitation of a media source without prior correspondence—sometimes works very well. But if you're planning a campaign that will take you to networks, through large cities, or to print publications with sizable circulations, and to Webzines and online editions of major media sources, there is a structure as old as a rare French wine. It costs extra time initially but saves many hours once the momentum of a campaign takes over.

Whether you're going for a guest shot on *Aunt Kay's Kitchen* or planning to nail a credit card thief on *20/20*, the most efficient booking procedure requires only five steps.

Developing a Media List Prior to the Campaign

Even though you've been through the reference books and Internet media lists, people change their jobs very often. It's a good idea to make a preliminary check of your more important sources. For example:

"Good afternoon, WFEA."

"I have some correspondence for Mr. Ray Fournier. Is he still news director?"

"I'm sorry, Mr. Fournier is no longer with us. Mr. Dave Peretz is now news director. He's not here, but I can give you his voice mail."

"Thank you. Do you happen to know his business e-mail?"

"Uh, yeah. We all pretty much have the same address here. Dperetz@wfea.com. But let me give you his voice mail."

A little call like that can make a big difference in whether a station makes a booking. You not only have Dave's e-mail address, but a way to pitch everyone else at the station. Press people often discard correspondence for their predecessors but open mail addressed to them.

Even if you're mailing a kit, the pitch letter should be in its own envelope with the addressee's name in plain sight. Some shrewd publicists even write the contact name in their own penmanship, figuring (often correctly) that a personal touch will be more likely to get attention.

The Precall

"Dave Peretz."

"Mr. Peretz, my name is Bob Carter, and I'm a vice president of Caller One. I'm sending along some consumer information on how to save up to 60 percent on cell phone calls. I'm hoping you'll take a look and perhaps consider an interview."

"Sounds interesting, Mr. Carr . . ."

"Carter, actually."

"Sorry. I'm terrible at names. Anyway, it sounds interesting but a little commercial for us."

"I know. That's why I'm focusing on consumer issues. Naturally, I'm hoping to get my company name in, but the emphasis is on saving money in general."

"I'll take a look and get back to you."

Or, you can leave this voice mail:

"Dave, Bob Carter of Caller One and I'm a regular listener to *On The Line*. I'm sending over a kit on how consumers can cut their cell phone bills by 60 percent. I'm proposing a segment with Skip Jensen of the Department of Consumer Affairs, who's worked with us on our consumer kit. Give me a call at 212-675-5650."

Give careful thought to anything you say on voice mail because that could be your only pitch. Any time you call a media company, be prepared to pitch for 10 to 15 seconds and no more. Otherwise, you can expect to be deleted. Like an e-mail pitch (see Chapter 7), a voice-mail pitch needs to be short and very clear.

He'll take a look. That's the whole purpose of the precall. It is nothing more than a brief introduction and a solicitation to watch for something in the mail. Or, if you've received your contact's approval, something online. The precall saves a lot of time, because the source sometimes refers you immediately to a more specialized colleague who is more likely to do the interview. In other cases, you'll be stopped right in the middle of a sentence and politely informed that there is no way at all that this person is able or willing to do the interview.

At the very least, the contact is alerted to a specific piece of mail. Professional publicists who have to work on the telephone daily sometimes either skip the precall or use it as a booking pitch because of a familiarity with the contact. Since you are working out for the first time, the precall is highly recommended.

The Mailing

If you live in a small community, you might want to take a ride and drop your press kits off in a single afternoon. Otherwise, use first-class mail and padded envelopes. The U.S. Postal Service is anything but dainty. The beautiful press kits you've assembled will arrive looking like last November's turkey if you skimp here. Gimmicky deliveries by costumed messengers or using expensive express-mail services are unnecessary.

The Follow-Up Call

Don't wait for anyone to call you. Within five days of your material's arrival, you should be on the phone with a well-planned pitch no longer than thirty seconds in duration. If this sounds like a difficult pursuit, don't feel like a failure. Most people talk too long, become tongue-tied with the brusqueness of many contacts, or hang up the phone only to remember that a critical point was left out.

A well-rehearsed pitch is a possible alternative. Our recommended method is to write out what you want to say, condense it to about 20 seconds, repeat it often, *then* transfer it to notes.

THE FIRST DRAFT

"Hello (Mr./Ms.) _____. My name is Lester Hanover, and I sent you a press release on something you might find interesting. Believe it or not, I'm having a garage sale for weekend car enthusiasts a week from next Saturday. I have an unbelievable assortment of carburetors, body parts, brakes, tires, batteries—in fact, I have enough stuff to build a car from scratch, which I've done three times. I'm wondering if you did get my release and, if so, if you might want to set up an interview."

THE REVISED DRAFT

"Hi, this is Les Hanover, and I sent you a release on a sale I'm having a week from Saturday, more like a party for people who go crazy for cars and their parts. I've built three cars from scratch myself and can give your listeners some pretty good advice on repairs. I'm hoping we might be able to talk about it on the air."

NOTES

Boiled down to notes, the pitch looks like this:

1. Les Hanover
2. Sent release.
3. Giving a sale for car enthusiasts a week from Saturday.
4. I've built three cars from scratch and can give listeners a lot of repair advice.
5. Wondering if we can talk about it on the air.

To be honest, few professional publicists have the need to pitch from notes, but most would agree that for about 15 seconds you have the attention of a contact who's never heard of you. The purpose of translating a written pitch to notes is to avoid the stilted, singsong quality that can cause the receiver to come up with an instant dial tone. The most important step is to practice repeatedly, taking as much time as you need to get your pitch to a natural, confident rhythm.

If you receive a firm "No," be polite, get off the phone, and move immediately down the list. Do not stop once you've started booking. If the response is an "I'll think about it," make a note, wait a few days, and call again until you either hear words of refusal or interpret a tentativeness as a "No" in this contact's response repertoire. Keep calling people and you'll hear the word "Yes" soon enough. When it happens, write a brief note to confirm the interview:

Ms. Betty Chuckrow
Night Talk
WOR Radio
1440 Broadway
New York, NY 10018

Dear Ms. Chuckrow:

Delighted to confirm our interview for Friday, November 23, at 3:00 P.M. I'll be arriving at 1440 Broadway sometime after 2:30, and I'll ask for you on the 23rd Floor. Please feel free to call me at 222-3232 if there's any further information that might be helpful. Again, thanks for your interest. I know it will be a lot of fun.

Sincerely,
Les Hanover

As time passes, e-mail often replaces the postal service as the preferred venue of producers and journalists, many of whom will tell you that they prefer to receive virtual correspondence. But things sometimes go a little crazy in cyberspace, so if you're in doubt, send two notes, one through the Internet and one "snail mail." People still do read it.

The confirming note is a hedge against the all-too-common mishap of showing up and not being expected. Keep a copy of the letter in your files.

While there are many variations in the booking procedure, the structured approach, carried through for a number of hours per session, is the most effective way to get publicity. If you delegate the chore, as many do, take responsibility for your campaign and ensure that the person representing you follows the steps. They always work.

To recap, the five booking steps are:

1. Tighten mailing list.
2. Precall
3. Mailing by postal service or e-mail if invited
4. Follow-up call with well-planned pitch
5. Confirming note

Initially, it's all a haze and you may be tempted to walk away from it and resolve to one day hire your own publicist. Who needs the aggravation? But once you learn to pitch and book, you've learned the most important element of your campaign. You'll soon build a wellspring of confidence and you'll be able to do it for the rest of your life.

SITE SEEING

Fox News, www.foxnews.com.   Fox News is loaded with national and local pitch possibilities.

WFLA, www.wfla.com.   A solid, professional network-affiliated TV station in Tampa. A prototype.

Small Office, www.smalloffice.com.   A magazine for small businesses.

Arizona Family, www.azfamily.com.   This is a great example of local television and online linkage. Powered by Phoenix stations KTVK and KASW, this site is a portal for Arizonans and their state.

13

Looking at Yourself

An interview is a simulation of a conversation disguised as a candid exchange of ideas. True, there is a subculture of people whose professional lives depend on interviews—from talk-show assistants to movie stars—and these sleight-of-hand experts can make it look real, but don't be surprised if your own on-air discussions aren't sonic booms at the outset of your campaign. It takes practice before you can learn to regulate the pressure on your word flow, listen to a conversation's underlying rhythms, pick up the pace here, drop a bit of controversy or gossip there, and come in with the host or hostess for a commercial break at the precise moment of a floor director's signal.

It is the work of master interview carpenters that we see most on television. A skilled interviewer can effect the most sincere demeanor, staring deeply into a guest's eyes while inserting the proper nods and the appropriate questions as he or she plans dinner or replays an erotic fantasy. An experienced talk-show guest can be impassioned to the point of tears, pleading the plight of impoverished children while wondering if there's a bathroom nearby and if the upcoming break will provide enough time to use it.

Does this mean that we're being had every time we observe an interview? Far from it. The situation is artificial; the people are genuine. When Oprah picks a face out of the audience to comment on a guest's work, she's thinking about her topic and her show. But if her gourmet kitchen had caught fire the night before and the trauma dominated her thinking, she would still probably be able to get through the show without her audience knowing her plight. All pros have learned to choreograph interviews with a repertoire of questions and answers that they use constantly. They've learned to tap and project from a reservoir of reality amidst the chaos of studios, remote locations, and newsrooms. Their livelihood depends on making the process look fresh every time. You're going to look fresh every time. You're going to learn some of this magic. It's really easy.

First, you must relentlessly scrutinize your appearance. Get used to looking at yourself. Look at recent snapshots, or have some taken. Scan a full-length mirror. Have a spouse or close friend talk to you honestly about what should change. You don't have to make dramatic alterations, but you do have to take a head-to-toe inventory.

Hair

Is this the hairstyle you really want or is it a comfortable vestige of another era that you've been meaning to update? Play around with it, trying a few new looks before making a decision. Men tend to have a more difficult time here than women, primarily because they're not accustomed to seeking advice from those they trust.

Regardless of the style you prefer, and whether you're a man or a woman, there is one cardinal rule. Hair should be neat and out of your face at all times. The devil-may-care "casual" hairstyle is not only distracting; it is also likely to detract from your purpose in being on the show. When in doubt, lean toward understatement.

Curls are wonderful, but they should be kept trim and on the haircut-to-haircut growth cycle. If they get too long, the scrutiny of a closeup will make it look as if your face were under a vineyard.

Take a compact hair dryer with you to the television station. If this makes you feel vain, remember the danger of weather and what it can do to your hair. Whether you are caught in a rainstorm or are merely the victim of a sticky day in August, an unkempt hairstyle will throw you off, especially when you see yourself in the makeup mirror just before air time. You don't have to show the world you're carrying a hair dryer, but you should never go into a television station without one. There may be only one moment in the whole campaign when you need to slip into the restroom to use it, but that moment will produce one very deep sigh of relief.

If you're bald, can you live with it, or would you prefer one of the many hair replacement options now available? And if you wear a toupee, level with yourself. Does the netting show? Forget what the guy who sold you the thing said about it being the same hairstyle George Clooney wears; George has his own hair and you don't. If it looks phony, get a new one, or, as we strongly suggest, go without it!

Baldness carries its own attractiveness and credibility, and a good cut on the hair you *do* have says you're not apologetic of the fact that nature has taken its course on your hairline. However, if you feel uncomfortable with your head, carefully research noninvasive hair replacement options, but don't go alone! Bring along your most brutally honest friend.

Eyes

Many men who have never appeared on television learn that they must wear makeup, and they wonder if this means eye makeup. It does not. The next paragraph is for women only.

Have you tried anything new in eye makeup lately? Are you satisfied with what you see when you look carefully? Experiment a little and take the best advice that comes down the pike—your own. You have to listen to yourself even though you need friends and their advice. Don't be so self-critical that you lose objectivity, however. Look for what really pleases you and allow yourself to enjoy it. The start of a publicity campaign is a good excuse to visit a department store for a complete facial (but don't go the night before your first appearance!) and an eye-makeup consulting session with a specialist.

We say everything with our eyes. You should practice speaking into a mirror and monitoring your eyes and eyebrows during the conversation. If you're excited about something, do your eyes register the emotion? Practice "saying things" without using words. Know your eyes and what they're capable of conveying.

Do you look at people when you speak to them, and if so, do you hold eye contact for a socially appropriate interval? If you've never thought about that question, you're probably in great shape and there's no need to go crazy with self-consciousness at this point. But you might also have been told that you shift your eyes too much, or that you look away, conveying a demeanor that you don't feel. Now is the time to seek advice and deal honestly in your assessment of the situation. Practice holding, or not holding, eye contact during conversation. If you're a lifelong averter, take the time to learn conversational eye contact through your own practice and in the observation of others in social situations.

What about glasses? Do you think you should switch to contacts for your appearance? You might worry about glasses glaring on camera. In most cases, studio lighting is so advanced now, glare is rarely a serious issue, but you may consider investing in nonglare lenses for your favorite frames. Many people who feel wonderful with glasses feel the need to be without them on television. If it makes you feel better to change to contacts, do so. If you're going to squint or blink to achieve what you consider a better look, stick with your glasses. If glasses are part of the way you see yourself, part of your character, and cemented to your self-image, wear them. Letterman does.

Nose

A lot of people don't like their noses. Don't run out and find a surgeon; just know your nose from varying angles. Probably the most important item to check here is whether your nose tends to shine under the high-temperature conditions of a television studio. If so, you'll have to experiment with powder. If you're not a fan of heavy foundations, try any one of the light transparent powders available. There also are several extremely light antishine foundations that professional makeup artists use that you may want to research. This advice applies to men as well as women.

Nostril hair might need clipping before a television appearance. Check it out.

Makeup

Women who do not know how to apply makeup are a rarity in our society. Rules rarely change for television, but an up-to-date makeup consultation from a specialist is never a bad idea. Otherwise, remember to add enough time in your schedule to keep it all fresh and pay a little more attention to eye makeup than you would for a normal, nonpublic meeting. Are you wearing makeup that truly flatters, or are you trying to recapture a look that age has taken away? If so, what's the next look going to be like for you? Now is the time to experiment and decide.

Men should consider purchasing makeup from a department store or pharmacy offering theatrical makeup, for only there can they be guided in the proper direction. The person selling makeup will take a professional look and offer you some very sound advice. Don't be bashful about this. The person who routinely sells theatrical makeup sees men all the time. If you have to travel a few miles to find this kind of professional makeup distributor, the trip is well worth it. Most towns, however, have someone who furnishes schools and theater groups with professional advice and supplies.

Men should be concerned with only two types of makeup: pancake and corn-silk. A well-stocked drugstore will help you with the selection of a pancake that matches your skin. Take a friend when you go, and carry the makeup with you whenever you're doing television. It is applied with a wet sponge and a piece of cloth.

Even more convenient is corn-silk powder that can be applied quickly and with little trace of a "made-up" look that makes many men feel uncomfortable. Whichever you choose, be sure to use some kind of makeup. You will look better, and all the macho guys wear it.

A lot of people assume that a television station has a professional on hand to apply makeup to guests. Some do and some don't, and even when there is such a person present, there is no guarantee that you'll receive anything more than a cursory dusting. Don't leave makeup to chance.

Mouth

Fear of the dentist is an international pastime. Perhaps you've been procrastinating a cleaning for fear of the doctor's scolding, or because you think one visit is going to lead to a $10,000 investment in caps. Make peace with everything but the cleaning, which is imperative at this point.

Should you bleach? Not necessarily, but if it's something you've been considering anyway, a home bleaching system from your dentist might be a nice, if slightly expensive, indulgence before you begin your campaign. Your dentist can now offer a variety of new cosmetic techniques such as enamel bonding for chipped or seriously discolored teeth, and he doesn't even have to use a needle in many cases. Talk to a number of dentists if you have serious cosmetic problems. The verdict might not be as bad as you anticipate. Technology has given us lower costs.

Women should choose lipstick carefully; bright reds and oranges are distracting, while lip gloss makes light bounce around your face. It won't be your fault. Television studios, despite recent technological advances, still have glare potential.

Chin

Men with heavy beards are vulnerable to looking sinister, especially as the hour of 5:00 P.M. approaches. Kings, princes, and quarterbacks often shave before late-afternoon or evening television appearances, and you might have to do the same.

Check to see where your chin lands in the normal way you hold your head. Practice moving your head around to highlight it at its best.

Your Good and Bad Sides

Actors and actresses aren't kidding when they demand that only their best sides be photographed. Find yours and practice tilting your head in front of a mirror. Whether you are pleased with the prospect or not, you'll probably be seated to the left of a talk-show host, but it doesn't matter. If you know your face well enough, you'll be able to tilt it slightly to your advantage.

Neck

Plan to go light on neckwear. A simple gold chain or a string of pearls is preferable to a junkyard of clanging necklaces and pendants. Men have to choose between an open-shirt look or a jacket and tie, either of which is all right. When in doubt, lean toward the conservative end of the dress spectrum.

Nothing between your waist and chin should distract from the purpose of the interview. Loud shirts, plunging necklines, medallions, or busy T-shirts can throw off your whole pitch. In the event of a novelty campaign, political interview, or some other sharply focused appearance, you might even consider a T-shirt as a powerful means of free advertising, but check out a show before wearing one. You might find yourself bumped prior to airtime if a producer feels that your shirt and the free plug it delivers compromise the show with the public, the FTC, or the FCC. Be guided by good taste.

Weight and the Camera

You will frequently hear that television adds ten pounds to your appearance. Sometimes it does not add any weight, and sometimes it adds more. Make your decision on weight early on and live with it. If you're overweight and not generally inclined to diet, don't make unrealistic demands on yourself. If you enjoy the challenge of a diet and have been up and down the scales a few times, go ahead and lose. In either case, assess and accept. Don't go out on the campaign with any reason to make body language apologies for your appearance.

If you just can't lose the pounds, resolve to be so damned good that no one will notice. By and large, the camera does add weight, and there isn't anything you can do about it. The camera does lie, though. Some people, regardless of their physical excesses or deprivations, experience a miraculous alchemy when the red light blinks on. They look wonderful. No one knows the why or how of this, but anyone who ever spent more than a day around a studio has stories of everyday people who radiate a glow on camera. If you're not in this category, pretend you are.

Legs

Women usually know it and men sometimes don't: Keep your knees together in the course of an interview. Don't fidget with your legs or move your feet across the floor. Put your legs in a comfortable position, feet on the floor, and sit there until you receive the signal to leave the set.

Clothing

Now's the time to shop. Dress to convey the image you want to project. If you're hard at work to right a social wrong and wear a mink to the interview, your outfit will be remembered and your message lost. Watch talk shows again and resurrect your notebook.

Notice that middle-aged people in conservative gray convey an aging, weak impression. Someone the same age in a medium blue looks ready to run a marathon. Call your partner or someone you really trust in for another consultation and consider the following traditionally held views on television dress:

- Extremes of any kind should be avoided—too light washes you out, too dark tends to exaggerate facial features. White shirts are worn nowadays by television anchormen, but they have an army of lighting technicians. In a local television or cable interview, they may not have the expertise to make you look good in white. If the lighting is wrong, the white will glare and the director will shoot you in an unflattering facial closeup.

- Bright reds and shocking pink look better off camera than on the air because they tend to frizz up and sometimes "burn" an image that remains on screen after the director has punched up the next shot. Dark greens can make you look downright scary. Lighter, minty shades can also reflect an unflattering pallor to a carefully prepared makeup job. While some television personalities manage to look good in green, our advice is to avoid it.

- Wear an understated pinstripe if you favor stripes at all. Bold stripes sometimes distort. Those who favor a tweedy, elbow-patched look have to be careful about their choice of patterned sport jacket. Pronounced herringbone or tweeds will appear to jump off your sleeve and into the air when the camera moves. Large-patterned plaids can create a make-believe weight problem or add to a real one.

In short, your color scheme has to be reminiscent of Goldilocks' porridge: not too light, not too dark, not too anything. It certainly must not be too cheap. This isn't the time to cut back on the budget. Tans, blues, and medium browns are especially effective, and you should feel free to choose a cut that flatters you. Make sure that the fit is exquisite, even if it never has been in your life.

Shoes

Scuffed shoes are always out. If you are inclined to allow the luster to dull, you have a little something to unlearn. In most cases your shoes will not be seen, but they should look great anyway.

Media trainers often advise clients not to do television with a brand new outfit that has yet to mold itself to the contours of your body. Personally, I love the feel of a brand new jacket or suit and I don't usually break it in before I go on. The rules above are only guidelines. I know women who dazzle in green, even though we recommend not wearing it. Love what you wear and it will affect every aspect of your campaign. Publicity provides a wonderful excuse to get that outfit that has been haunting your dreams. It gives you a legitimate reason to shop.

SITE SEEING

Image and Media Consultants:

www.beauti.com.   "Internet Connection for skin care and cosmetics."

Prime Point Consultants, www.prpoint.com.   An image consulting service to a number of PR firms.

www.cosmopolitan.com.   A great site for a virtual makeover.

Parkhurst Communications, www.parkhurstcom.com.   We specialize in helping people who write books and have to go on national television. I'd add a third element. They usually don't want to—in the beginning. In the end, their publicists usually have to rope them off the public stage. I say there's a lounge singer in all of us.

Cameron Communications, www.camcom.com.   This New York City agency specializes in all phases of image consulting and media training.

14

Listening to Yourself

You might wonder where radio people find their exaggerated announcing qualities and whether you should do anything to make your voice sound like theirs. No way. They sound like that because professionalism in radio demands the shedding of regional accents; while doing so, they often pick up an announcer sound that is as difficult to escape as the accent itself. You'll sometimes find that radio people announce everything—the taste of the punch, the color of your dress, the falling of a leaf. This you don't need.

Your conversational resonance is far more important than any effort at standardization. If you have a stammer, lisp, or other serious impediment, only a certified speech therapist can help you. There are books on phonetics that will rid you of your accent if you some-day want to do so and are prepared to spend a year or more practic-ing on a daily basis. For now, check out the following hints.

Your voice is a gust of wind that becomes sound by traveling through a vibrating larynx. You can trace the entire path of your voice by putting your finger on your neck as you open wide and say "Aaaaahhhhh," just as you would if a doctor were checking your tonsils. Feel around for the vibration, and you'll have the larynx. The mouth and nasal passages serve as resonating caverns.

Your tongue taps voice into speech in an amazing concert with your teeth and lips. Pay attention to how these articulating organs work together. Notice that your S's hiss through the teeth while M and N sounds find air only after traveling through the nose. Stick your tongue out (preferably with no one else in the room) and try to make an S. Hold your nose while attempting any word with M or N.

Nervousness reverberates through your system from the larynx to the final sounds of articulated speech. When you feel uneasy before an interview, try breathing deeply before going on — not an exaggerated intake but a quiet and slow passage of air. Don't rush it.

Practice opening your mouth wide as you let the vowels bounce around in there. Aaaaaaaay . . . Eeeeeeee . . . etc. Read aloud as you enunciate every syllable. These exercises won't get you voice-over work in New York, but they will accustom you to the sound of your own speaking rhythm.

Chapter 16 will help you develop a media act. For now, listen to yourself in conversation for a while, hard as that will be at first. Do you take too long getting to a point? Do you trail off? Do you retreat when a louder person interrupts? Are you sometimes too quick to interrupt yourself? How well do you really listen? It's homework time again.

Exercise 1

Take every question that could possibly come up for your primary booking angle, and print each one on its own card. Have a friend ask them at random, shuffling the cards before each session.

Exercise 2

Tape yourself during these sessions, and make yourself listen carefully. There's a better-than-average chance that you're going to hate this, but do it anyway. Most people have an impression of their vocal selves that differs dramatically from reality. You might find a regional accent that you never knew about, and chances are that the voice you've always heard is more suave and melodious than that terrifying bray the tape recorder is now claiming belongs to you. It takes time, but eventually

GUEST: SARAH FERGUSON, DUCHESS OF YORK						
TOPIC: *"WIN THE WEIGHT GAME"*				**DATE:** WEDNESDAY, JANUARY 12, 1999		
CLIENT: SIMON & SCHUSTER				**TIME:** 6:30-9:30AM EASTERN		
CODE: 30804				**STUDIO:** DC-SLINGSHOT		

SATELLITE SCHEDULE

TIMES	MARKET	STN	AFL	PROGRAM	INTERVIEWER	AIR
AA) 6:25-30	MIAMI	WFOR	CBS	AM NEWS	JIM & LIV	L
A) 6:33-38	RALEIGH	WNCN	NBC	AM NEWS	SHARON DELANEY	L
B) 6:39-44	GREENVILLE	WSPA	CBS	AM NEWS	JULIE & TOM	L
C) 6:45-50	ST. LOUIS	KSDK	NBC	AM NEWS	ART HOLIDAY	L
D) 6:51-56	HOUSTON	KTRK	ABC	AM NEWS	DON NELSON	L
E) 6:58-03	(5 MIN. BREAK)					
F) 7:07-12	ALBANY	WNYT	NBC	AM NEWS	JIM KAMBRICH	T
G) 7:13-18	WEST PALM	WPTV	NBC	AM NEWS	ROXANNE STEIN	T
H) 7:19-24	JACKSONVILLE	WAWS	FOX	AM NEWS	DAWN LOPEZ	L
I) 7:25-30	CINCINNATI	WKRC	CBS	AM NEWS	JOHN & CAMMY	L
J) 7:34-39	LOUISVILLE	WAVE	NBC	AM NEWS	LORI LYIE	L
K) 7:40-45	SAN ANTONIO	KMOL	NBC	AM NEWS	LESLIE & VICENTE	L
L) 7:46-51	(5 MIN. BREAK)					
M) 7:52-57	KANSAS CITY	KCTV	CBS	AM NEWS	VALISSA & BRIAN	L
N) 8:01-06	(5 MIN. BREAK)					
O) 8:08-13	NASHVILLE	WTVF	CBS	AM NEWS	BETH TUCKER	L
P) 8:14-19	INDIANAPOLIS	WXIN	FOX	AM NEWS	JORDANNA & CLARENCE	L
Q) 8:20-25	GREEN BAY	WLUK	FOX	AM NEWS	CONNIE & PETE	L
R) 8:26-31	(5 MIN. BREAK)					
S) 8:32-37	WILKES BARRE	WBRE	NBC	AM NEWS	MARK HILLER	T
T) 8:40-45	MILWAUKEE	WITI	FOX	AM NEWS	MOLLY OR MARK	L
U) 8:46-51	BIRMINGHAM	WBRC	FOX	AM NEWS	RICK JOURNEY	L
V) 8:54-59	TOLEDO	WTOL	CBS	AM NEWS	PATRICK MCCREERY	T
W) 9:01-06	CLEVELAND	WEWS	ABC	AM NEWS	TANYA & BRAD	T
X) 9:07-12	PHOENIX	KSAZ	FOX	AM NEWS	KATHLEEN DIMICO	L
Y) 9:13-18	ROANOKE	WSET	ABC	AM NEWS	PATTY MARTIN	T
Z) 9:19-24	DALLAS	KDFW	FOX	AM NEWS	JULIA SUMMERS	L
Z1) 9:25-30	WASHINGTON	WUSA	CBS	AM NEWS	CHRIS ENYART	T
Z2) 9:30-45	STUDIO GENERIC				KRISTIN L. CLIFFORD	T

Morning drive air personalities constitute one of the strongest sources of publicity. This schedule is for Sarah Ferguson.

Planned Television Arts, Ltd. of New York

you will start to coexist with the sound of your speech. Be comforted in knowing that those wonderful voices that pitch shampoo or beer are the product of many years of training—and often their owners still cringe.

Exercise 3

Work out a list of adversarial questions, being as rude as possible with yourself and your primary booking angle. If you think there's nothing controversial in your subject matter, consider the possibilities in the examples we know well:

"Mrs. Barnes, don't you think you're denigrating your profession and your position in the community with the blatant commercialism of your press release on tax loopholes?"

"Mr. Hanover, you might call it a garage sale for auto enthusiasts. I say you're a junk merchant without a peddler's license."

"Mrs. Parnell, you're really selling teeth-rotting, sugar-based junk food to raise uniforms for young people, and you're setting a horrible example. Isn't there some other way you can find the money for the Little League?"

"Mr. Carter, the ubiquity of the cell phone has unleashed a swarm of fly-by-night cellular service hucksters. Are you one of them?"

"A restaurant serving only pasta sounds disgusting, Ms. Wright, if I may inject a personal comment."

Most of your interviews are going to be conducted by nice people. But be ready for the rare occasions when insult replaces reason.

Exercise 4

Have your partner ask the questions and interrupt every answer you provide, changing the subject to a totally irrelevant conversational track. Your job is to return to your primary booking angle within two minutes.

Exercise 5

Switch places with your partner and ask the questions yourself. Then repeat the steps in Exercise 4 as you take the role of the interrupter.

Exercise 6

With your partner asking the questions, answer them as:

- A loudmouth with no interest in the subject matter beyond its conveyance of his ego needs
- A super-shy individual who can't get a sentence out without stammering
- A back-slapping comic who makes a joke out of everything
- A pedantic pseudointellectual who turns every sentence into a philosophical treatise
- A malaprop who misinterprets questions and comes up with non sequiturs for answers

The purpose of this chapter is for you to observe. Don't fret about problems you've found. They'll work themselves out in time, if you make the commitment to their solutions. Our purpose for now is to help you know more about the you that others see and hear. Pay as much attention to yourself as possible, stressing the positive. You don't have time to completely overhaul your persona, so make an attempt to isolate what impresses you about yourself (and do allow yourself to be impressed), and you'll soon be able to use these strengths to your advantage.

SITE SEEING

National Association of Government Communicators, www.nagc .com.
Listen to the following stations and check out their Web sites for interview content and format.

WOR Radio 710, www.wor710.com. This station has been talking for about 75 years. A great site for longer interviews.

Bloomberg, www.bloomberg.com. Bloomberg's news and financial reports make it the short sound-bite capital of all media.

Radio Black, www.radioblack.com. A comprehensive guide to African-American talk, urban music, and a whole world of radio you might never have known about.

Imus, www.everythingimus.com. Look to this site as an example of a morning drive personality.

15

Problem Interviews

Most of your interviewers will be serious, competent individuals who are well positioned in their trade. There are exceptions that you should know about. This chapter provides an overview of interviewer types, some of whom should be in mortuary work or another field where they can cause no embarrassment and do no harm. But limelight, even at the most local level, is addictive, and these characters will generally tell you that they stumbled into the radio station or newspaper office as children en route to another destination such as the library, where they hoped to pick up a book on how to stick pins in moths. They got into the business by mistake, and they brag about it. You are about to be part of a lifelong compounding of that mistake.

Not to worry. Anyone with a byline or access to a broadcast transmitter is important to your campaign. Most problem interviewers suffer primarily from insecurity born of vanity and some inner voice that tells them their careers will not, and should not, go any further. You can control the situation by knowing what you're up against. Meet the cast.

Barbie

Her hair celebrates *Brady Bunch* or *Mork and Mindy* reruns. She dresses up for her interviews courtesy of a local boutique that gets a plug in the program's closing credits. Her teeth glisten like Chiclets beneath a shade of lipstick that is a trifle too pink. Barbie didn't get to read your material and confesses just before you go on that she prefers not to know too much about her guests for fear of losing the freshness of the moment. As a result, you're there to talk about saving money on cell phone bills and she thinks the segment is about handling obscene callers or developing a pleasant telephone manner, like hers.

SOLUTION

It's her show, and she can take it anywhere she wants. If you can do it without being too pushy, look for your opportunity to glide toward the plug as gracefully as possible. For example:

BARBIE: "So, Bob, as an executive of Caller One, what advice can you give me on obscene phone calls?"

BOB: "Actually, Barbie, the Caller ID that's standard on most modern cell phones has gone a long way to eliminate the problem. But I'd advise your viewers to talk with a specialist we have at Caller One who knows far more than I about dealing with obscenity. Her name is Helena Reed and she can be reached between nine and five at 555-3535. I've developed another area of expertise, and that is to save anyone with any cell phone up to 60 percent on their monthly bills."

Of course, if you do know something about the topic, so much the better. If not, don't try to fudge, and never be overbearing. Barbie will often misrepresent your product or organization, as she did above. When that happens, try to avoid interrupting her or saying, "I must correct you, Barbie." Simply work in the correction within the context of the discussion as soon as possible. When you introduce a fresh topic, Barbie, or any interviewer, has little choice but to run with it. Meanwhile, you have little choice but to run with Barbie, for she represents thousands of viewers who take her a lot more seriously than we do.

Ken

This guy saw Ken Olin as Michael in *Thirtysomething* and never quite got over the experience. His hair has that eighties abandon, his eyes blaze with puppy dog warmth, and he has the intelligence of a waffle iron. He's there because he's been told he was cute since preschool and now he's over 40, but, gosh, you know, cute's cute. He smiles flirtatiously at the camera and looks right through you. His reaction to your subject matter will vary from inappropriate jokes to feigned interest in all the wrong places.

SOLUTION

See solution to Barbie.

Barbie and Ken

Lucky you when this dynamic duo interviews you together on a local morning talk show. Between making plugs for restaurants that give them free food and boutiques that supply their wardrobes, interrupting each other, dropping names of the eminent community members who greet them at the club, and taking commercial breaks, they will barely notice that you're on the set.

SOLUTION

These folks kind of know they're not Regis and Kathie Lee. They desperately crave respect and, let's face it, they got their own TV show even if only the Almighty can explain it. Give them their due if you can pull it off in a nonpatronizing way. In a world where materialism is often the scorecard of position, their salaries, lecture fees, freebies, ribbon cuttings, and other emcee functions often earn these stooges six figures apiece every year. They've done something right, even if that something happens not to be their jobs. Barbie and Ken want short, punchy answers to which they will respond by tripping over each other to give out the plug information. You could do worse.

The Mini-Stern

This interviewer has a hard time living with the notion that Howard Stern is in New York watching babes take off their tops while *he's* in a radio station between the Sears Auto Center and Wal-Mart, watching Volvos park. He knows that fame is a phone call away, if only he can show Infinity Broadcasting, Howard's network, that he has the stuff.

You walk in on a Monday, the day *Broadcasting & Cable* comes out with its news of major promotions and the happy settlement of salary negotiations. You don't know it, but yours is going to be part of an audition tape that Mini-Howard is, damn it, going to get right this time. He makes no distinction between real interviews and entertainment. If you're there for something as noble as curing diabetes or a fund-raiser for the homeless shelter, Howie Wannabe will be looking for his opening:

"I've got a better idea, Al. Take all the money you raise, rent a big party room at the Hyatt, right? And you have an open bar for the homeless where they can, like come in and drink all night. Then you get them some rooms where they can go in and shower and sleep it off. I like that a lot better than your cause. By the way, do the homeless get a lot of action? I mean, they have nothing better to do, right?

"What?"

"Like, with all due respect the homeless people don't want to go to shelters, especially women. Get them a room at the Hyatt, let them get drunk out of their minds, okay?"

And that's if Mini-Howard likes you.

SOLUTION

Chapter 17 has more on dealing with shock jocks. Be calm. You can't use the logic of everyday interviews if you're trapped in an episode of the *X-Files*. Let yourself go a little, but hold your ground.

"That's a plan that hasn't been tried, Howie, but I really don't think our board would go for it. But what does work is treatment and, sadly, there hasn't been any money for that."

"Hey, Al. I wish you were right, but you're wrong. They don't want to be treated, and they don't want to be helped. They just want to roll around in their urine and gross people out."

"Well, some *are* harder to reach than others but I haven't met anyone who gets up in the morning down there on Elm Street and says, I think I'd like to roll around in my waste and gross people out. Except maybe you, Howie."

My personal experience with morning radio personalities is that they are generally shy people acting out a schoolboy fantasy. If you can do it, give them some of what they hurl at you and you'll be fine. But if they're too offensive, walk.

The Little Limbaugh

Unless you're an ex-president, Rush Limbaugh goes on the air with only his commentary and his adoring callers. But the Little Limbaughs of talk radio live with the reality of guests that they terrorize with rhetoric, hoping to get better jobs. This is not to confuse them with the real stars of conservative talk such as Michael Medved, Alan Keyes, or David Brudnoy, who are contentious but pretty gracious with live guests.

The Little Limbaugh interviewer is just a schnook with fantasies about buzzards and your carcass. Sometimes it's an alter ego thing where the kid who was bullied grows up to kick sand in the face of every adult on the beach. The mike is a power elixir.

In other cases, the Little Limbaugh is a lifelong risk-taker, and you're part of the run. Every decade in the history of broadcasting seems to have produced a brief need for a few of these fire starters; the air waves are littered with their memories.

Whatever the psychology, the Little Limbaugh will insult, lie, distort facts, and generally take whatever measures he deems necessary to demean your case.

SOLUTION

Arguments sometimes make good broadcasting, so you'll have to put aside your biases to determine whether you're dealing with a contrary person or a genuine LL (of which there are very few). If so, excuse yourself and leave the studio.

The Catatonic

Suppose you've been through a dozen or more interviews already and your act is tight. You've danced your way through various lines of questioning, sometimes with difficulty but ultimately with triumph. You've seen it all, you think, until you meet the Catatonic.

The Catatonic asks you a question, then sinks into a coma from which only an act of war can arouse him. You give the usual answer and take the usual pause as you await a follow-up question. Because the system hasn't failed you before, you have no reason to expect what's about to happen. You feel little hairs on the back of your neck standing at attention. He's not saying anything.

The Catatonic is sometimes deliberate, sometimes inept, but always jarring. Mini-Howard and Barbie become comparative love objects as you fumble around for something to fill the ether. They at least talked. You weren't out there alone. They've been around for a long time. Dan Greenburg, the author of the best-selling *How to Be a Jewish Mother*, his first book, recalls meeting a catatonic on an AM talk station in Chicago.

"So, you're from New York, Dan."

"Yes I am, Ed."

What's that French restaurant?"

"Well, there are about two thousand five hundred of them in New York, Ed."

"You know the one I mean."

"Er . . . Lutece?"

Pause.

"Le Cirque? La Grenuille? La Caravelle?"

"Nope." Pause.

Greenburg proceeded to run his considerable knowledge of Manhattan eateries past his interviewer, receiving either a pause or a shake of the head after each one.

"It was obvious to me," he recalled years later, "that I wasn't going to be interviewed until I stumbled on the name of that restaurant. Luckily, I hit it."

Because of the medium's longer programs, the Catatonic is more likely to be a radio interviewer than a television talker or a press person. But not always. Best-selling author Bill Bryson, who has spent much of his adult life in England, nodded politely through the Catatonic phase of our media training, but I don't think he believed he'd see such a thing. But when he got to Minneapolis, he did a television interview from the floor of a mall and found that the interviewer knew nothing of his book, *The Lost Continent*, and proceeded to stare at him, nodding empathetically, but contributing little during a 30-minute interview.

Today's Catatonics can also be found in smaller public radio stations. Five minutes in, you know you haven't stumbled onto the next Terry Gross.

SOLUTION

The Catatonic offers either a wonderful opportunity or the most difficult interview of your campaign, depending on your ability to recover. You're on the guillotine if you're in the midst of "tour glaze," a phenomenon that settles over interviewees like a cast-iron mold. You become so accustomed to the same questions that your answers become rote. You've trained yourself to respond to questions with the concise and punchy answers that are the center beam of virtually all interviews. With a Catatonic, the rules change. You have to take over.

In the next chapter, you'll learn more about solidifying your on-air persona by first developing large blocks of conversation that are whittled to fit the ordinary chatter of your interviews. The Catatonic provides an exception, where you return to large paragraphs of speech.

You're not as bad off as you might initially believe. First, take a second to breathe deeply and get your bearings. If he's going to pause, it is not your responsibility to fill.

The Cable Guy

In the frenzied cable explosion of the 1980s, local franchisees happily committed to the donation of valuable air time to local communities.

Whether it's called *public access*, *community television*, *leased access*, or *local origination*, these channels have become home to some of the worst interviewers in the history of broadcasting. And I love going on these shows because they can be the most fun you'll have on your tour.

Don't get me wrong. This system also produces some very good interviewers—lawyers, professors, community leaders, and young broadcasters on the way up—who outshine their commercial television counterparts. But with them come characters who make Wayne and Garth of *Wayne's World* look like Yale faculty members. Get ready for the Cable Guy, whose name is usually either Josh, Tiffany (they're women at least 50 percent of the time), or Matthew. Let's tune in on Cable 8:

"I hate cell phones, don't you? I mean, what's this all about, people walking around with phones in their ears, like they have to work out their grocery lists and relationship issues on the street so everyone can hear their life stories. Bo-ring. Well, Cable Eight Tonight welcomes Bob Cartwell of Caller One who's here to help us save money on the things, like we really need more of them. Bob Cartwell, welcome to Cable 8."

"Thanks, Matthew. Actually, my last name is Carter."

"Whatever."

"And, well, I kind of like cell phones."

"That's cool. We're in a democracy here, not like Russia or somewhere."

"Actually, Russia's a democracy now, too."

"Cool."

SOLUTION

The Cable Guy's part of your road trip. He may not be the sharpest tool in the shed, but he's no shock jock either. Unlike Ken, who does know the timing and pace of television, the Cable Guy can do a 15-minute riff on his likes and pet peeves, 5 minutes on the weather, and another 10 on his girlfriend before he even gets your name on the air. But, mostly, he's just not well-versed on technique, and if you're a

JANE WESMAN PUBLIC RELATIONS, INC.
928 BROADWAY
NEW YORK, NY 10010
212-598-4440
FAX 212-598-4590

Television Satellite Tour
for launch of **MODE** Magazine
Thursday, February 27, 1997

organized and produced by
Jane Wesman Public Relations, Inc.
New York, New York

uplink -- 10 AM -- Galaxy 6/Transponder 16

all times listed in the Eastern time zone

10:10 AM - 10:17 AM, Sunrise, WAVE-TV, Louisville, Kentucky, tape
10:18 AM - 10:25 AM, News, WLKY-TV, Louisville, Kentucky, tape
10:25 AM - 10:30 AM, News, WMC-TV, Memphis, Tennessee, tape
10:30 AM - 10:40 AM, News, WOOD-TV, Grand Rapids, Michigan, tape
10:43 AM - 10:53 AM, 7 Live, KIRO-TV, Seattle, Washington, live
10:53 AM - 11:00 AM, News, WDIV-TV, Detroit, Michigan, tape
11:10 AM - 11:20 AM, News, WISH-TV, Indianapolis, Indiana, tape
11:20 AM - 11:25 AM, Today's THV This Morning, KTHV-TV, Little Rock, Arkansas, tape
11:25 AM - 11:30 AM, Arkansas Today, KTHV-TV, Little Rock, Arkansas, tape
11:40 AM - 11:45 AM, Noon News, WCHS-TV, Charleston, West Virginia, tape
12:08 PM - 12:15 PM, The Exchange, News 12 Connecticut, Norwalk, Connecticut, live
12:16 PM - 12:20 PM, Noon News, WYFF-TV, Greenville, South Carolina, live
12:20 PM - 12:30 PM, Noon News, WXII-TV, Sherman, Texas, tape
12:40 PM - 12:50 PM, Noon News, WTHR-TV, Indianapolis, Indiana, live
12:50 PM - 1:00 PM, News, WRBL-TV, Columbus, Georgia, tape
1:00 PM - 1:10 PM, News, KENS-TV, San Antonio, Texas, tape
1:10 PM - 1:20 PM, Noon News, WISC-TV, Madison, Wisconsin, live
1:20 PM - 1:30 PM, Afternoon Report, Newschannel 8, Springfield, Virginia, live

#   #   #

Jane Wesman Public Relations   in the year
20
2000

Since the early 1980s, publicists have made effecive use of satellite technology to "tour" clients around the country. This tour schedule is for Mode Magazine. Jane Wessman Public Relations, Inc. of New York good sport, he'll trip over himself to help you with your plug. As the Web expands into digital video, it will be more feasible to watch the Cable Guys before you book them. For now, ask someone you know to tape the show for you.

I happen to be a big supporter of Cable Guy interviews. The more of them you do the better you get, and when the *Today* show calls, you'll be ready.

The Pal

Press people who have deadlines but no air time to fill are adept at an interviewing technique designed to gain your confidence. They smile and nod supportively, encouraging you to say more without actually telling you that they approve. Some of our best investigative reporting occurs this way.

The Pal is a threat only if there are things you don't want publicized. Political people and others in public life know that a chance remark made during an interview can become the basis for tomorrow's headline and perhaps the end of the whole ride.

If you are being interviewed on a topic of little controversy, the Pal is merely making full use of the luxury of nonshowmanship. He or she doesn't have to be on and isn't. Enjoy the technique but don't get overconfident, lest you find yourself tomorrow afternoon saying, "Gee, did I say that? I couldn't have."

SOLUTION

Print journalists are your greatest opportunity for strategic leaking of information in a contentious situation such as legislative issues, mergers, or lawsuits. But before you go off playing "Deep Throat," the Watergate source who told Woodward and Bernstein to "follow the money," make sure you are well-schooled in this game.

Reporters operate on an "on the record" "off the record" basis in order to cultivate sources whose rights they fiercely protect. If you are gaining rapport with a reporter and wish to go "off the record" or offer a statement "for background only," say so and you're almost guaranteed to be quoted anonymously or not at all. If there is a tape recorder running, ask that it be turned off.

If the Pal in your life is known for inaccuracies, or if you're dealing with ultrasensitive subject matter, bring your own tape recorder to the interview, making sure that it goes on and off in sync with his. For most interviews, such measures are unnecessary, but when in doubt, record and rest. For the purposes of most publicity campaigns, assume everything you say is on the record, and you'll be fine.

The Interrupter

The interrupter has her private hell and you can't see it. She fears that her show will drag, that you'll talk too long, and the momentum will dissipate. The fear manifests itself in excessive interruption of her guests. You make half a remark, and she's burying you with another question or her own remark. You are so riddled with questions that you are eventually unable to remember what you've already said. You just wish it would end.

SOLUTION

The Interrupter is like a novelty store finger trap where the harder you tug, the tighter the bind. The more you give in and let her change the subject every 15 seconds, the more desperate she'll be to jump around the air waves like a flea.

First, have the confidence to stick to your material even if you have to parse it out in shorter chunks. Respond briefly to each change she tries to initiate, but quickly move back to where you were. Sometimes you'll have to come right out and tell her that you'll answer that question in a few seconds, but first you have to settle the issue at hand.

There is an optimum rhythm for interrupters that you'll quickly find if you don't get rattled. Generally, she's only trying to counteract the possibility of a monotone, and, given the pedantic nature of many interviewees, one can hardly blame her. Keep your focus on your primary booking angle and you'll soon find that she'll interrupt a little less and probably won't change the subject at all until you're ready. The Interrupter likes a seesaw momentum, and if the ride is a little fast-paced, that's show biz. Keep your cool, and you'll have a good time here.

The Callers

Watch out when your host says, "Hello, you're on the air," because you don't know what sort of mutant managed to get through the screening process. The profane callers are the easiest, for they are cut off seven seconds before their nastiness can reach the transmission line. More jarring are the blunt, bottom-line types who are apt to ask you anything.

Callers generally reflect the preferences of the host. It's hard to imagine more intelligent callers than you'll find on NPR's *Talk of the Nation*, and what would *Car Talk* be without the zany interplay between the Magliozzi brothers and the guy in Champaign-Urbana who wants to know what to do about a 1986 Toyota Celica that caught on fire in the driveway? None of this is an accident. It's important to know how your host handles callers and how he or she wants you to respond to them.

SOLUTION

If you have not yet listed every negative question you can think of, do so now. Add these to the list, and develop some spare-tire responses.

"I think the idea is stupid and so are you."

"If that's what you think, sir, I'm not going to convince you otherwise. Thank you for calling."

"The Bible says that people like you will burn in hell."

(Don't discuss the Bible with a caller even if you hold a doctorate in theology. Politely inform the caller that he's entitled to his interpretation of Scripture, but you're on the program for other purposes.)

"You're a throwback to Soviet Communism."

"Thank you for sharing."

"You belong in jail."

"I don't happen to think so, ma'am."

"Would you want your children doing what you suggest?"

(I wouldn't be suggesting it if I weren't prepared to have my child do it.)

Even the most bush-league talk-show host has learned to cut people off quickly when they become abusive. When you're in doubt, look toward your interviewer. Never take bait, and always avoid sophistry. For example:

"Do you believe in evolution?"

"What's it got to do with homeless shelters, sir?"

"Just answer yes or no, do you believe in evolution?"

This type of caller has used the same syllogistic reasoning a thousand times or more, usually after a couple of belts at the local pub.

"I'm here to express my view of community-based homeless residences sir, and I'll be glad to answer any questions on that topic and only that topic."

We must stress that in most cases your host will be on the cut-off switch at the first syllable from a lunatic caller. Some of your most touching moments will come from the grass-roots help you offer listeners through the dialogue you provide on talk radio or television. And online talk shows are spreading across the landscape like tumbleweed, a lot of it superior to over-the-air broadcasting.

Be prepared for problems, but don't let apprehension of a long shot rob you of this satisfaction. The premise may be applied to the entire spectrum of problem interviewers. They'll always be around, but they're definitely in the minority.

SITE SEEING

Check out the following talk radio Web sites.

Talk of the Nation, www.npr.org.   One of the best talk shows out there.

KGO, San Francisco, www.kgoam810.com.   One of the best talk operations in radio.

WSB, Atlanta, www.wsb.com

KDKA, Pittsburgh, www.kdka.com

The originals, with many imitators:

Rush Limbaugh, www.rushonline.com.   One of the most popular (and most disliked) hosts, he certainly has an audience.

Howard Stern, www.koam.com.   There are so many imitators that you're bound to run into one of them eventually, so it's best to take a look at this site and familiarize yourself with the material. KOAM refers to Howard's modest proclamation of himself as the King of All Media.

16

Developing a Media Act

I start all media training by sitting a client down in a comfortable leather chair under the warm glow of a mica lamp. There's plenty of mineral water, coffee, Diet Coke, and herbal tea around as we have an easy conversation about the book or subject matter at hand. We're far from lights, microphones, and cameras. That will come later. For now, the client talks and I listen, jotting a few notes. What I'm looking for is the detonating core of the person, the passion that he or she feels for the subject matter. Once I find it, this client will be great on TV and radio.

I've trained over 500 clients for network television, and I've never used the term "sound bite." The words grate on my subconscious like fingernails against a blackboard. While the importance of brevity in a broadcast interview can never be overstated, a true sound bite is an editable nugget from a recorded interview, on *Dateline* for example, where producers search through hours of footage for 10 seconds of airworthy prose. Sound bites are largely a politician's tool and have lit-tle bearing on the live or live-on-tape interviews that are the grist of most publicity campaigns.

Some clients twitch in my soft leather chair. They've come in pumped and ready to bounce off walls. They've "got their sound bites down." They've worked it out with Uncle Irv who "really knows his

PR" and says you never go on television without perfectly rehearsed bites. Uncle Irv is wrong. Nothing sounds worse than the inexperienced guest trying to parrot freeze-dried responses to questions the interviewer does not want to ask.

There's always the chance that my client is the one person in two or three hundred who can reel bites off and make them sound spontaneous, so after a time, we test Uncle Irv's system in the studio. Say the client is Joshua, whose book is about a high-protein, low-fat weight loss plan and is called *The Fat Factor*. Uncle Irv has told him that he must, above all, get that title in as much as possible.

"So, Josh," I say in my most syrupy broadcast voice. "What *is* The Fat Factor?"

He clears his throat and rattles off his bites. He sounds like Jackie Gleason in the classic *Honeymooner's* sketch where Ralph and Ed Norton go on TV with a cooking device called "Chef of the Future," then disintegrate.

"Well, Bill, in my book, *The Fat Factor*, I say that losing weight is not how much fat you eat but the carbohydrates you *don't* eat."

He thinks he's provoked a follow-up question, but I sit there on our little talk show set and look at him. He begins to turn pale.

"Uh—See, if you eat good fat and not bad fat, you'll get rid of excess fat. I say that in my book. . . ."

"*The Fat Factor*, right." I ask no follow-up question. His hands begin to shake and his voice becomes a parched rasp.

"Uh—because it's n-not the fff-fat you need to think about but the fat cells. My book, *The Fat Factor* . . ."

Better he should go down the chutes here than out there. Believing that rehearsed sound bites are the essence of preparation for a broadcast interview, Josh has rehearsed short answers to questions that might never be asked, and, when the interviewer takes a divergent course—as they all do—he either flounders or uses awkward bridges to try to turn the subject back to his bites. Working that way is like sitting in a dental chair and being treated with stagecoach-era technology. We have far more effective and painless ways of getting there.

Back to the soft leather chair. Start with a very long conversation about what you want to say. Take all the time you need to answer questions. You will be asked the same questions constantly, and you will provide virtually every interviewer with the same set of answers. Your task is to make it look fresh each time out. You do this by affecting a conversational tone, leaving a lot of room for the interviewer, and giving in gracefully to the conversational flow. This is your media act, and you won't develop it overnight.

Some people think they can be funny on the air because they are funny in the office. The two environments are rarely complementary. It is one thing to be witty in a casual conversation, but it takes a lot of experience to do it at will in a broadcast environment. Jim Carrey spent 15 years in comedy clubs perfecting the rubber-faced persona that we know today. Rosie O'Donnell and Jerry Seinfeld took just about as long to make it look like they noticed something funny on the way over in a cab and decided to share it with you.

You don't have that kind of time to develop your act, but you don't need it either. You do, however, need a few practice sessions with your material in order to avoid looking uninterested in your own subject matter.

1. Repeat the list of pertinent questions in Chapter 14 into a tape recorder. For now, just read the questions. Are they all there?
2. Now repeat the answers without asking the questions themselves. Do not write out your answers but say them aloud, play them back, and say them aloud again.
3. Practice going down the list of questions and repeating them until you know them extremely well. Then answer them, a hundred times if necessary. You might think such repetition will make you stale, but the opposite is more likely to happen. If you know your stuff so well that the answers are ingrained, you'll be freer to express these responses with more variety later and depart from the wooden "sound bite" quality that a lot of newcomers take to the media.
4. If a partner is available, he or she should also ask you questions repeatedly, but this time a variation in each answer should be

demanded of you. It doesn't have to be a vastly creative departure from your previous answers—it probably shouldn't be, in fact—but the answers should now vary a bit. Tape these sessions and take the time to play them back.

5. You should now have a block of material that you can produce if an interviewer says, "Tell me about yourself," and disappears for 15 minutes. You are also at a point where you'll want to skip this nonsense, especially if you've been doing interviews already. *Don't skip it.* There are hundreds of cases in your own neighborhood where people find that they can't progress to the more competitive shows because they became overconfident, or overimpressed, with their ability to handle interviews.

Rehearse your block of material the way you would rehearse a speech. Know it the way an army recruit knows his rifle. Rehearse it with questions, then try it without them. Time yourself and see how long you can talk about your topic without any interruptions. Then have your partner interrupt you every 12 to 15 seconds, the way a broadcaster would. This does *not* mean the subject changes, only that the television format requires two people in an interview.

6. If you can start talking about our primary booking angle and progress to your secondary angles nonstop for 15 or more minutes, you're ready to continue. If not, go back and review until you know everything so well that you dream about it.

Now, throw it all away.

What?? Are you out of your mind? I've got this whole thing down so I sound conversational and you're telling me to heave it?

Absolutely. Be a Buddhist. Let it go. Now, you're ready to have fun with your material.

Have your partner take the role of a salacious morning disc jockey, a Mini-Stern, if you will. Then take the worst public radio interview you've ever heard and a comatose public radio interviewer who sounds like he's on IV Valium. Watch TV and imitate the interviewers. Be on your own version of *Larry King Live*, *Oprah!*, or *Rosie*.

Now you're ready to whittle. Get a friend involved, and ask that person to interrupt you at every available interval in the material. Be sure that there are not a lot of non sequiturs here, but a few are more than acceptable. For example:

FRIEND: "Tell me about your company, Al."

YOU: "Well, Fred, I started it about six months ago. . . ."

FRIEND: "Did you fly in from New York?"

YOU: "Yes, Fred, I did. Anyway, the company comes in response to a need I perceived in the leather goods marketplace . . ."

FRIEND: "What need? You surely can't be telling me that there's something new in leather usage!"

You will do serious damage to your prospects of being on a television show again if you cannot translate shoptalk into conversation. We have asked you to develop your material to the point at which everyone in your life, including you, is bored with it.

You are becoming tedious in a world that prosecutes tedium more vigorously than most crimes. But mastering material is the first step in developing a sound media act. Most people believe such mastery is the final step. That is why you will probably be the best guest on the talk-show couch. If you have properly rehearsed at this point, put it all away and watch a little television.

Whom do you resemble? Most famous people have a "look" that represents a segment of the population. Now is the time to be influenced by the person who represents your type. Assimilate this person's professional qualities without doing an impersonation. You can watch various types on television and see how they respond to questions and how they provide their answers. Just watch. Keep in mind the person you believe most resembles your style as you proceed with the next phases of your emerging act.

Brightening Your Material

Now that you can answer every question you'll be asked without thinking about it, it's time to seriously evaluate your conversational qualities. What have people always told you about yourself?

While we are all a chameleonic blend of personalities that reflect the many influences of our growth, we usually have a single aura of temperament that performers refer to as *attitude*. Attitude is your overall persona—droll, serious, funny, witty, taciturn, aggressive, or whatever. Transferring your everyday attitude into stage presence is beyond our scope here, but, if you think about it, you'll recognize that you do have one selling quality that puts you across. It is the strengthening of your attitude that will transform your material from so many nouns and verbs to a dazzling sales pitch, if you open yourself up and make peace with who you really are. The following is a guide to a few prevailing personality types, with a bit of advice on how to use attitude to present your material more effectively:

Serious.   People who convey a serious public attitude are forever being told to "lighten up," crack a few jokes, and have a good time. In publicity, a serious demeanor is welcome. A somber or gloomy personality is a different story, but if you are serious, go with it and be glad. There are too many would-be comics on the circuit and not enough straightforward individuals whose sense of humor is confined to nonpublic occasions. The world turns on the shoulders of serious people. Who wants to see a cabinet member doing *schtick?*

The serious personality, however, is not excused from the responsibility of avoiding boredom in a presentation. He or she is more vulnerable to it than the other types. Practice projecting the enthusiasm that brought you and your subject matter together; avoid long or technical answers; and take pride in the methodical conveyance of ideas that has probably earned you the respect of your colleagues.

Shy.   Shyness is a tough handle until one learns how to use it. Then it becomes one of the most attractive traits in the galaxy. No one seems to be able to resist a shy person who has replaced tentativeness with determination. You know what your enemies are—lack of eye contact, halting speech, and a tendency to waffle in conversation. But mastery of shyness in public is almost an everyday occurrence. There are debating champions who can pummel any opponent but don't know what to say in the intimacy of a conversation. Top 40 disc jockeys sometimes stammer when they get off the air, and many politicians simply can't operate on a one-to-one level.

Many famous people claim to be shy. I personally believe they all are. David Letterman and Steve Martin come to mind as very low-key when they're not working. Howard Stern is famously shy. Magnificent musical performers from Bette Midler and Michael Stipe of REM could be called shy. Even rock legends Janis Joplin and Jim Morrison are described by the journalists who covered them as shy. So was Elvis. They have harnessed their bashful qualities and turned them into a public asset. If you've come this far, you probably can, too. Plunge ahead.

Loud.   Some people speak with too much volume. They often come from generations of ancestors who spoke with too much volume. Loud is one of the least endearing attitudes. Even nice people who put too much diaphragm into their speech are referred to as "loudmouths." Worse, they don't always know they're loud, and, if they do know, they don't know what to do about it.

Assuming that you've been told that you're a mite loud and that you're committed to accepting it, there's some good news. Loud commands attention. You may speak with a natural authority that others have to work hard to develop, so in your efforts to tone down, be careful not to sacrifice that vocal conviction.

A permanent effort toward quieting your voice is a job for a speech therapist. For the limited, nonclinical scope of a publicity campaign, call that friend back into the room and have him or her tell you when your voice is at the approximate speaking level of the rest of the world. Then, tone it down and practice with the tape recorder. There is little else you can do.

Humorous.   There's way too much pressure to be funny. Any professional comic will tell you that the public side of a "natural" wit is useless without more stage experience than almost anyone can imagine. Maybe you can walk into a barbershop, crack a few jokes, and cause the whole place to fall headfirst into the rinsing sinks. When that happens, which is probably not often, you fantasize about playing Vegas for six figures a week. But when you go on television, you may find the humor that always got you through isn't going over.

Humor will constantly aid you in your presentation, but you should approach it with the same mixture of awe and fear that a child has when regarding a lighted match. Don't tell jokes. If you've heard a good one, your listeners probably will be able to lip-synch the punch line. Our advice is to start out with a straight approach and see if your naturally funny demeanor shines through. If so, you're en route to heaven. If not, you won't embarrass yourself.

Perky.   Perkiness is good as long as it doesn't slide into labored cuteness. If you are crisp from the moment the alarm goes off, the chances are excellent that your enthusiasm will sell your material. Your homework is to study those television guests who are just *too* adorable, *too* self-impressed, and positive to the point where you think you're going to become ill if you hear one more platitude. Learn from these people, then have a great time.

Gruff.   Gruff is like shy; when played well, it is irresistible. A little gravel in the voice, a jaded view that fools no one in its effort to conceal an underlying decency, and moments of genuine warmth will sell well for you. If your attitude is gruff, be sure to twinkle a bit lest you come off as an irascible proselytizer.

Abrasive.   Most of us can admire a little gruffness, but few would care to be regarded as abrasive. Are you regarded that way? It isn't always such a horrible thing, especially in business or law, where people don't succeed by displaying the compassion of a nondirective psychotherapist. In publicity, abrasiveness can be a real plus in a panel discussion where some opinionated mutant is dominating the conversation. For the most part, however, you're not going to sell anything until you ask those closest to you how you're coming over and make some very serious decisions on what to eliminate from your approach.

Sweet.　Sweet people are forever being consoled with the notion that honey catches more flies than vinegar. That's fine, if you want to catch flies. If your sweetness comes from a heartfelt, other-directed desire to give, everything's great. If you believe yourself to be sweet because you're afraid to be otherwise, admit it to yourself and try to enjoy the ride. You could certainly pick up a book on assertiveness training or attend a seminar, but that is up to you. The most important—indeed, the only—selling attitude in a publicity campaign is honesty.

The Alter Ego

You may be one of the lucky people who gets to play opposite your type when you go out to do publicity. If you're meek, you might become aggressive on camera, or if you're a monster in the boardroom, publicity may bring out the pussycat in you. This has to happen naturally and as the result of a genuine part of your personality peeping through for a little air. Don't try to fake it. Either it happens or it doesn't.

Now call your friend back for a few final sessions with the flash cards. Shuffle them well and put yourself through a rapid-fire session with questions, this time keeping your attitude locked in the back room of your consciousness. Don't act. Let it flow naturally and allow your friend to tell you if you're conveying your optimum demeanor. With enough practice, you will be.

SITE SEEING

As you develop your media act, watch these three shows, and investigate their Web sites, watching guests interact with three very different interviewers.

Larry King Live, www.cnn.com/CNN/Programs/larry.king.live/. This show claims to have newsbreaking, headline-making interviews—and it does. And it also is the only worldwide, live television viewer call-in program.

Rosie O'Donnell, rosieo.warnerbros.com/wb.cgi.   Rosie has celebrities, she has kids, she has a lot of fun, and she occasionally makes headlines too.

Charlie Rose, www.pbs.org/charlierose/.   One-on-one interviews and roundtable discussions with an acclaimed interviewer and broadcast journalist.

17

Radio Interviews

When we train authors for their publicity tours, we ask them to give us feedback. They all say the same thing. Television can be good and it can be bad, they say, and newspaper interviews are okay—but radio is wonderful. They reverberate with pleasant memories of callers and the intelligent conversation of their hosts— Milt Rosenberg in Chicago, David Brudnoy in Boston, Diane Rehm in Washington, Larry Mantle in Pasadena, Joan Rivers in New York.

True, morning disc jockeys can be the dregs of the western world, and some AM talkers are so far to the right that they make Newt Gingrich look like a lefty, but you will probably love your radio appearances the most. If you plan a campaign of any substance, radio stations will be as familiar to you as the front seat of your car.

In a city with three commercial television stations and one PBS affiliate, you might do a single TV appearance in either a seven-minute guest shot or a 90-second news feature. The same day should find you on the radio four or five times if you hang in and make the proper follow-up calls. You can't always get on television or into print, but anywhere on the globe, and at any hour of the day, you will be able to get on the radio. Consider it home.

About Modern Radio

Nearly a century after its theoretical basis prompted experimentation, radio remains a technical marvel. Your voice is converted into electrical energy, sent into space at the speed of light, captured by a receiver, and passed through speakers as sound.

Despite the proliferation of syndicated talk programming and regional cable networks, local radio still stakes its claim as our primary source of immediate local coverage. When the snow flies and there's going to be no school tomorrow, when a Cessna is lost in the woods near the airport, when the high school basketball team makes the play-offs, radio people are there with the story. Major-market regional stations cover a wider geography, and "local" sports might be defined in broader terms, but the theme is the same.

People take radio very personally. The small stations may be amateurish when measured against the smoothies in the Big Town, but when you appear on *Open Mike, Talk to Me, Express Your Opinion*, or whatever name they have for the local call-in show, you're apt to be facing an interviewer whose status in the community is more lustrous than any political or religious leader. People set their watches by her, name their children in her honor, keep a note pad by the radio to jot down anything she deems important, and program the station "call-in" telephone number into their kitchen and cell phones. And you can bet this local radio version of *Oprah!*" is in their online address books as well.

Small- and medium market stations are populated by two groups, the *locals* and the *floaters*. The typical floater comes into a community, gets a small apartment, and starts sending audition tapes to larger markets before he even knows where the 7-Eleven can be found. That he would aspire to the seven-figure salary of a major-market personality over the pocket change of a local station is no disgrace. If your campaign is repeated next year, you will probably find the same people in larger radio stations. Learn to keep tabs on who interviews you, write notes, and show an interest in your radio interviewers. This is not always an easy task.

Because small-market radio is the bottom rung of professional show business, it attracts a disproportionate array of egomaniacs, introverts looking for a spark of confidence, and misfits with a dark side you hope never to see. Such is the case in any creative endeavor, but in local radio the desperation somehow seems sadder. Many of the people you'll meet aren't going to make it, and they know it.

On the positive side is a delicious sense of camaraderie and a lot of people who *are* going to make it. Radio is a career start for journalists, entertainers, writers, directors, producers, and political, religious, and business leaders. They have one very important consideration in common. Jobs often end quickly in radio.

Because radio people are on the air live, the two-weeks' notice that is the birthright of civilized people everywhere is not always part of the station routine. The job often ends right after an air shift. The severance check is handed out, and the announcer leaves immediately. In major markets, unions and contracts protect against such practices, or at least make it financially difficult on management. It all sounds inordinately cruel, but radio people accept the danger as part of the exciting game they play. If you want to throw a balanced dinner party with chitchat bouncing to a variety of issues, be careful about inviting two radio people. They love what they do and can't stop talking about it.

Radio Interview Length

Aside from news feature interviews, which are usually short, radio offers the luxury of a long conversation. You're free to express yourself, sell your pitch, and perhaps answer questions from listeners.

The most dangerous element of radio interviews is that they encourage ponderousness in us. Keep your answers short and crisp while showing interest in your interviewer. Don't feel that you have to stay with a single topic just because it happens to be what you're selling.

Evaluating Your Radio Interview

"Does this stuff really sell?" is the question publicists hear all the time from their clients. There are a few thumbnail facts that might assist in your assessment of a radio station's capacity to reach listeners. You should do as many radio interviews as you can, but some are going to be much more effective than others.

AM Stations

In the 1970s, FM's superior signal made it a logical home for music, while AM began to market information and talk which it does superbly. Unless you're planning to climb a tower, the technical difference between AM and FM is of little consequence to you. Here are a few facts that tell you a little about the station you're visiting:

Frequency refers to an AM station's spot on the dial—540 to 1600 (these numbers refer to the frequency in thousands of cycles per second of the radio wave and are expressed in kilohertz, or kHz). Although there are a number of exceptions to the rule, the signals with better range are found to the left of 1200, with the smaller, more local stations operating between 1200 and 1600. To put it bluntly, the Darwinism of early twenty-first-century radio is crushing those little stations, while the stations in the middle of the dial are thriving. In general, the stations you want to be on are likely to be found in the middle of the AM spectrum. They're the biggies.

Power is as important as frequency in determining the clout of a station. The AM power range runs from a scant 100 watts to the 50,000-watt giant stations in major cities. A station in a medium market with 1,000 or 5,000 watts will do very well for you. In a major market, anything with a transmitter will serve the purpose.

We've mentioned that radio does much of its business with commuters. Prime time is 6:00 to 10:00 A.M. and 3:00 to 7:00 P.M., but radio is so prevalent in the workplace that many stations sell 10:00 to 3:00 as aggressively as commuter time. In some markets, such as Los

Angeles, where people rely heavily on automobile transportation, publicists are thrilled when they get a drive-time radio booking on a 50,000-watt station.

FM Stations

AM stands for *amplitude modulation,* and FM stands for *frequency modulation,* a mode of transmission that produces a signal far less prone than AM to interference and static. Besides music, FM is the seat of public radio, and there also is a growing sports and talk presence there as Gen X and Y (what happens after Z?) settle into adult life. Frequency and power considerations are less important to the publicity seeker than is the case on AM.

In the late 1960s, a dusty amalgam of high-power FM university stations that had been running educational and classical music tapes began a metamorphosis into a powerful network of "alternative" programming that has changed the face of FM radio. National Public Radio, which went on the air in 1970, was nearly destroyed by the market-driven policies of the first Reagan administration, which cut funding to public broadcasting by 31 percent between 1981 and 1983. NPR was $9 million in debt and so hard up for cash that it borrowed teletype paper from CBS.

During that period, a meandering, offbeat writer who seemed to have wandered by mistake into a public station in Minneapolis was making a strong dent in that market. NPR didn't have the funds to go national with Garrison Keillor's tales of life in a fictitious Minnesota lake town, so a local group put together a syndicate that became American Public Radio and, later, Public Radio International. PRI and its kin, Minnesota Public Radio, went on to lead public radio in the development of an entrepreneurial framework to coexist with government funding.

Meanwhile, NPR, to paraphrase Nietzsche, was made stronger by what didn't kill it. They won't be borrowing supplies from commercial radio any time in the near future. By the late 1990s, listener contributions reached over $100 million a year, and the NPR news staff has grown to over 200, with a weekly audience of 11 million, about the same as each of the nightly news shows on network television.

During the rough times, National Public Radio was saved by its affiliates, which are known as *member stations*. If you're addicted to public radio, you may have rubbed elbows with Bob Edwards of *Morning Edition*, Linda Wertheimer and Noah Adams of *All Things Considered*, or the Magliozzi brothers of *Car Talk*, all of whom come out in support of member station fund drives.

People always ask me how to get on *All Things Considered* or *Morning Edition*. There are several ways, which we talk about in Chapter 28, but the most important way is to become valued by your local NPR member station. Their recommendation for a national spot carries a *lot* of weight.

FM music programmers are no longer required to program long, format-busting public affairs shows on weekends. In the interest of currying favor with the always-changing FCC, however, they might do an interview anyway and use it in "short form," meaning a 30- or 60-second feature rotated to various slots throughout the broadcast day. Don't feel slighted if the interviewer spends only 15 minutes with you. The interview may be heard by more people than you ever imagined.

Ask about the station's *format*, that is, what kind of music it plays and for whom. Music stations, be they AM or FM, use a form of shorthand to define format. If someone says to you, "We used to be more AOR, then we switched over to adult contemp, but I think the PD is going with Hot Hits at the beginning of the year," he means that the radio station once played album-oriented rock, switched to adult contemporary popular music, like REM or Sheryl Crow, but may be moving in the direction of a tighter, limited play list of hit recordings.

When you hear that kind of alphabet soup, redirect your question to a station's *demographics*. It's all but impossible to make jargon from descriptions as straightforward as "adults 25 to 49."

Radio Ratings

If you visit three stations in a market and each visit leaves you with the impression that you've been to the "number one!!!" station in the city, you'll get an idea of the radio ratings game. Ratings, as compiled by Arbitron and other sources, are carefully measured, clearly reported, and loosely translated. There is but one number one in any given ratings sweep. The confusion lies with the demographics. "*We're* number one in ethnic programming. But *we* are number one overall!" (Overall would be considered the reigning champ.) Make it easy on yourself by asking how many listeners there are in the time slot or *day part* when your interview will air.

Your Morning Radio Interviews

Radio is about its mornings. An axiom in the business is that the whole day is built on what happens between 6:00 and 10:00 A.M. So, stations invest heavily in morning personalities, most of whom are cheerful and good-spirited. However, with the success of Howard Stern, the eighties ushered in the era of the "shock jock."

A lot of our clients are terrified of morning disc jockeys. They think Howard Stern and wouldn't *that* be the worst? Actually, it wouldn't. Stern, with his eternal embrace of seventh-grade pubescence and his outrageous skewering of liberal sensibility would be a week in the country compared to the Stern wannabes in places like Worcester, Buffalo, Tampa, San Antonio, and Tucson. Stern, at least, has 10 or 12 million listeners.

Morning personalities (the term *disc jockey* largely applies to the nonpersonalities who play music and keep the control room seat warm for the rest of the day) are, basically, the class clowns of today's media. They straight-out don't buy the Mr. Rogers version of America, that we are all special. The worst of them act especially irritated at multiculturalism and our changing racial climate. They'll tell you they want to have "a little fun" and may ask you about anything from flatulence to your sex life.

If you do not know, or at least *get*, this kind of radio, stay away from it. I've had clients come in for media training in the middle of a campaign shaken to the core by local shock jocks. Their publicists either never knew or never told them what they were getting into. This is not to say that all morning personalities are xenophobic, homophobic, misogynistic imbeciles, but they are there to entertain, and you need to spend time listening to what they do before you book yourself on their shows. Most of the bigger shows can be monitored online.

Morning radio extends far beyond the "Morning Zoo" formats of music stations where the jocks hang out. Every NPR station has its own local edition of *Morning Edition* news, and talk stations, oldies, and sports formats begin their day with their strongest talent. You'll do fine on morning radio, but it's wise to ask if the station can be heard online.

A morning drive "radio tour" is, basically, a TV satellite tour without the camera (see Chapter 18) and often without the satellite. You walk into a studio, sit down at a microphone, and talk to a different personality every 5 or 10 minutes and plug away. You can set these up yourself, but many publicists bring in specialists such as New York's Planned Television Arts, a division of Ruder Finn.

Over the past 10 years, PTA publicists have learned to match morning radio personalities with the guests who will best fit their formats. They have brought former presidents, movie and television stars, sports figures, and celebrity authors to morning radio. They know when to book a *Morning Edition* and when to book a "Morning Zoo." PTA has its own studios rigged with digital telephone lines, which allows host and guest to sound like they're in the same room.

So, can *you* do this at home? In some form, yes. It's important for you to get on as many morning shows by telephone as you possibly can, especially if you have something a little offbeat. But the big stations are spoiled. A major market morning personality is offered rock stars, ex-presidents, best-selling authors, and sports superstars, basically the same guests as a network morning show.

If you get through and they say yes, the producer may ask you the same questions they'd ask any publicist.

"You anywhere near an ISDN line?"

Say what?

"You know, a Zephyr."

Huh?

"A digital box, so you can sound like you're in the same room."

Just so you know, ISDN stands for Integrated Systems Digital Network, and it's a little box that most public radio stations and professional recording studios have on their phone lines. A "Zephyr" is a brand name, like a Corvette. Like the "Switch 56" that preceded it and all the boxes that follow, the Zephyr renders the noisy phone line as obsolete as a rotary phone.

If you're talking about one interview on one day, your answer is that you're working from home and, gosh, you don't happen to have a digital box on the phone you picked up on sale at Radio Shack.

But say you want to reach five million or more upscale commuters in a single morning, and, a few weeks later, do it again, then hit the same markets again as a guest on the afternoon shows. After all, people on the return commute are probably in a better mood than those facing a day of work. If you're going to do it right—10 or 15 stations in a single morning, rather than a scattershot amalgam of phoners, you should rent an audio recording studio with ISDN facilities for half a day. We've found the best deals with local NPR member stations, which offer a much better rate than professional recording studios.

Beyond the big markets, there are hundreds of smaller markets and many hosts who will want to hear what you have to say. Chapter 30 will help you find them. We've included an actual morning drive radio schedule. You can do the same thing in the afternoon and visit radio talk shows on the big city stations just about every night of your life.

Radio is your best media pal and should be regarded with the same lifelong affection that we reserve for a few special friends. It will always be there for you.

SITE SEEING

Listen to these stations and hear how the interview techniques differ.

Talk Radio!

WBZ, Boston, www.wbz.com.   One of the premier news and talk
stations.

KOA, Denver, www.850koa.com.   A longtime powerhouse that dom-
inates the Denver market.

KNX, Los Angeles, www.knx1070.com.   One of the most influential
stations on the West Coast.

Public Radio:

WNYC, New York, www.wnyc.org
KCRW, Santa Monica, www.kcrw.org

Jocks:

Howard Stern, www.koam.com
Don Imus, www.everythingimus.com

18

Television Interviews

The word *television* is no longer adequate to describe the pyrotechnics of modern video. Your television screen is morphing into an Internet portal that enables you to shop, bank, study, invest in the market, protect your home, make an airline reservation, view an athletic event, see a movie in 3-D without glasses, conduct a meeting with someone half the world away, send mail, and for all we know, order a test-tube baby. Preparing for television is one of life's necessities because, like it or not, we're all going on the tube.

Ironically, television's evolution into narrowly targeted audiences brings it closer in mission to the radio it superseded over 50 years ago. With satellite television's capacity to receive as many viewing sources as a free market economy will allow, we now have a video spectrum so complex that our viewing guides could become as thick as our telephone directories.

Beneath the dozens of modes of video transmission flow channels, subchannels, subsubchannels, networks, cable networks, subnetworks, subsubnetworks, and programming sources into infinity. If you ever harbored any idea about escaping to a Pacific island to avoid the complexities of civilization, now's the time to buy your ticket. Otherwise, prepare to go on television.

In the control room, you'll find a director who wears headgear a la Madonna in concert and faces a wall of monitors. His or her job is to keep the production under control by telling everyone what to do. The rest of the crew, you'll notice, also wears headsets. Also in the control room are an associate director, an audio operator to make sure the microphone on your lapel doesn't distort your voice, a technical director to keep everything (especially video integrity of the picture) humming smoothly, a graphics operator to summon a show's titles and logos, and any number of videotape operators. A local production might have a single person performing these functions; a network telecast will have more than those just described.

On the studio floor are camera operators, a floor director, one or more electronics technicians, lighting specialists, a makeup artist, segment producers, associate producers, interns and "go-fers" (who go-fer coffee and paper clips), station personnel, and other functionaries who can make your first on-camera interview as terrifying as hanging over the side of the Grand Canyon by a piece of unwaxed dental floss. Be prepared to see these people, and for the first few television experiences remind yourself that they'll be there. Eventually they'll cease to be scary.

The crew will be indifferent to you, and who can blame them? They do this every day. In a major market, even the sorriest talk show gets celebrities who prowl the publicity circuit. You are today's fresh pastry, interesting but not especially unusual. Before air time be prepared for private little jokes that might include you without your awareness as the camera operator focuses on one of your freckles. They love it when a man's fly is unzipped. They have to zoom in and out to focus before going on the air, so why not do an extreme closeup of a half-mast zipper? Don't worry, you won't go on that way. Some devastatingly attractive 22-year-old woman from the production staff will whisper in your ear and make you wish you had drowned as a child. Do yourself a favor and avoid all this. Check yourself out thoroughly before you get to the set.

For the most part, the crew just comes to work and performs in a calm, professional manner. It would be a bad idea to judge their reaction, or lack of it, to your interview. Occasionally, a technician will inform you that you were fascinating, or that he was moved to tears. Not to be cynical, but this one is moved to tears three or four times weekly. It should also come as no surprise if your interviewer has little to say to you off-camera. He or she may be apprehensive about chitchat for fear of diluting energy, a very real superstition based on hard experience. A staffer may ask for your visuals and, if you don't have any, groan, "Oh God! Talking heads!" or some other flattering remark. You will note then, if you had not done so before, that sensitivity is not a requisite for a job in broadcasting.

A television environment has more ritual than a Space Shuttle launch. Hand signals fly. Cue cards and teleprompters appear as monitors are wheeled in. You might hear someone say, "Quiet on the set," as very hot lights come on and start to bake you. No one has told you where to look, and you wonder in a panic if you're supposed to direct your attention toward the camera or your interviewer.

Don't worry about anything but your now-rehearsed act. Sit up straight but don't be rigid, and look only toward your interviewer. Stand by to be interrupted, for television differs dramatically from radio in the pace and momentum of its interviews. Your host's job depends on providing a very quick pace. Ten- to 30-second responses to questions are the norm here.

Visuals

It's perfectly all right if you don't have a set of supplementary visual aids during a television interview. If you do, however, they'll probably be an asset. Is there anything you can physically carry to a television interview that will assist in your interview presentation? If not, is there anything you can put on videotape? If your company has Betacam video equipment, you may be able to shoot a short demonstration tape of your product (producers refer to this tape as "B-Roll"). Otherwise, check the phone book under *video* and you'll be able to find an inexpensive video facility that can shoot a tape for you. If you bring in a demo tape on home video, they'll just shake their heads at you; the quality won't cut it.

Photographs should be mounted on a background of thin but firm blue or black cardboard that is easily scanned in the control room switching system. Some small market stations still accept 35mm slides, once the standard in television, but a digital disc is more the norm today.

To save a frantic moment before the show, bring your business card or an index card listing your company or product, phone number, Web site, and e-mail number, for entry into the Chyron computer graphic. This may not be necessary, but if a member of the crew asks for it, just hand over the card and be assured that your pitch is being flashed beneath your head as you speak.

Whatever you choose to use to visually supplement your appearance, always have them prepared well in advance. It's helpful to have quality B-Roll or other visuals ready to be sent by messenger during your pitching stage. It's only to your advantage to be able to offer a producer a visually stimulating presentation if he or she wishes to preview it before making a decision about you; it makes the job easier and could make the difference between a booking and a "maybe next time."

The Remote Interview

A common publicity experience is the remote interview: a reporter and crew arrive at your home or office and shoot for an interval that ranges between 30 minutes and several hours.

Give them something to see. If your office is less appealing than an outdoor garden, take the crew outside, weather permitting. If there are especially interesting visuals that can be intercut with your conversation, be sure to point them out. Your product or company logo may be conveniently placed among books and trophys on the shelf behind you, but be flexible if the crew insinuates that it looks like overly blatant salesmanship. If you do choose to be interviewed at your desk, keep in mind that a computer screen creates a distracting vertical static on camera, so position yourself—or your monitor—away from the lens. The crew might not care, but you will when the jumping lines of the monitor draw the viewer's eye away from your pitch.

Try not to position yourself directly in front of a window without draperies; backlighting is great for Frosted Flakes commercials, but not for your pitch. No matter what location you choose, remember that the crew is there to break up the tedium of the studio. Help them out.

Be careful what you say in a remote interview. All of your great pearls of wisdom will be compressed into a short feature or inserted into a story with a broader scope. The responses that you feel give the opportunity for "great copy" may come back to haunt you when the editing is done.

Feed the crew. Have coffee and pastry available. The interviewer has to avoid fattening indulgences, but the lighting and camera people sometimes endure hours of jumping in and out of a van. They'll make you look good if they're happy with you.

If you're running a company that demands your time and the crew would like to take four or five hours away from the day, you need not feel compelled to accommodate such a request. Be polite but excuse yourself.

Finally, expect the unexpected. If the crew wants to get additional footage, they may ask what's behind "door number two." If there is something in your home or office that you wouldn't want the general public to see, remove it from the premises. It's not unusual to get footage of a subject at work shuffling papers or talking to staffers. Make sure your papers are already well shuffled and that your staffers look presentable the day of the interview.

The Television Satellite Interview

From Kosovo to Columbine, we've become so familiar with TV satellite interviews that we give little thought to their implementation— until it's our turn to be on live. The format is easier than it was in the bad old days of the 1980s when they'd shackle you to an earpiece called an IBF that seemed to weigh about fourteen pounds. It was always a bit of a guilty pleasure to watch Henry Kissinger on *Nightline* sink into disorientation as a small piece of plastic snatched something from him that neither Mao Zedong nor Watergate ever got—his composure.

"I cannot hear you, Ted. Ted, can you hear me? Are ve on, Ted?"

Actually, he couldn't *see* Ted Koppel either, because you can't watch a monitor on a live television remote without getting vertigo. There's a gap between what you hear on the IBF and what you see on the monitor, so your interviewer appears to be moving his mouth out of synch like Chevy Chase in an old "Weekend Update" sketch. So, the production assistant may tell you to think of the interview as a telephone call, and to look directly into the camera and answer the questions.

Being on CNN live is fun. You're probably on in Beijing and Lisbon, London and Moscow. Your old high school rival may have taken the head cheerleader to the prom, but you're the only face on CNN right now. But you don't feel very big. You feel diminutive because you're on this stool so high your feet can't even touch the ground, with a fake painting of a skyline behind you and an interviewer you can't see. And though the IBF—short for *intermediate broadcast frequency*—no longer flaps your right ear forward into an elephantine pantomime, the sound still hasn't improved much.

Sometimes you'll take live calls, which today are significantly improved over the early nineties, when CNN guests were bombarded with calls from Howard Stern fans who would offer an earnest question when queried by the call screener, then ask the guest what he or she thought of Stern when they went live. (I fielded one of those on a segment about corporate business presentations.) Conventional wisdom in the early days of C-Span was that you'd get a question on abortion even if you were there to push your cookbook. I trained an Audubon Society spokesman for a C-Span segment on migrating hawks and—sure enough.

Today, we have Caller ID and very tight network security. You want to play pranks with CNN, they'll call back and tell your mother. Or, your spouse. Or, if you keep it up, maybe you'll get a visit from a process server or the police.

In the 1980s, the TV satellite tour emerged as a powerful, if costly, publicity tool. If you're pushing a product with major corporate backing, sooner or later you'll probably do one. More likely, the technology will enable you to pitch a major television station even if you're not headed for the city where it's located. Most of them have reciprocal arrangements with local studios. If they want you badly enough, they'll spring for a satellite remote.

The format rarely varies. You sit in a small room on a chair, look into the camera, and talk for several hours to a succession of local news anchors that you can't see. You'll emerge with the disorientation of a cat that got caught inside a vacuum cleaner, but your message will be out there.

In the heyday of *Nightline*'s use of the form, Ted Koppel was known to watch his guest flinch and twitch as he or she watched the program's opening piece by an ABC news correspondent. Whatever seemed to rankle the guest served as a cue for his opening question. Even Washington-based guests were not spared. They watched the correspondent piece from an adjoining studio and, after the first break, you'd hear something like this:

"Joining us from our Washington studios is Reagan administration press secretary Larry Speakes. Larry, does the president share Oliver North's view that selling arms to the Contras was 'neat'?"

It made, as they say in the trade, for *great* television.

In the late nineties, Koppel varied his routine, often going into prisons or to a Baltic battlefield, leaving Tim Russert of *Meet the Press* to carry on the tradition superbly as television's Master Satellite Picador. Watch and learn. Your *News at Sunrise* anchor isn't likely to be as compelling, but you have to make it all look just as real. How do you do that?

It's a knack, like exercising on the Nordic Track or driving with a manual clutch for the first time. Here are a few tips:

1. Look directly into the camera and carry on a conversation. It's the only television experience where you do so. Expect to be interrupted every 10 or 12 seconds, as you would be in a live

studio interview. Look thoughtful, never defensive, even if your interviewer asks questions you don't like. If your nose itches, don't scratch it.

2. Remembering your interviewer's first name is more vital than usual in this rather impersonal format. There's usually a schedule in front of you and a break between interviews. Companies that set up these sessions assign a producer to sit off camera. Ask that person to remind you of the host's name. They set up the same interviews every day, sometimes two or three times a day.

3. Be courteous and don't ramble. Once you have the floor, it's more difficult for your interviewer to interrupt you than other broadcast formats.

4. As with all television interviews, let your host do the plugging, which she's likely to do at the beginning or end of your interview.

5. If the damned IBF falls out of your ear, politely tell your host that you've lost the signal and permit the producer to scoop it up for you. Don't duck out of camera range like a soldier being shot at.

Kiss Me Again

Constantly put your repertoire of question responses through the strainer so that you're prepared for the cardinal rule of television conversation, brevity. Any question that can't be answered within the medium's 10- to 30-second attention span hasn't been properly reworked. If you have many thoughts and subparagraphs to your material (and you should have enough, remember, to talk for 15 minutes without interruption), you can always keep coming back toward your main point.

Television is far more focused on *who you are* than on *what you have to say*. If you are effective, long after your text is forgotten your image will be remembered. Don't worry if you didn't get to say enough. In publicity, there's always tomorrow.

SITE SEEING

www.tvindustry.com.   Daily news, and feature articles on the art, technology, and business of television.

National Association of Television Programming Executives, www.natpe.org   Runs the kick-off event of the TV industry as the top suits and stars of the business show up to hang out with local owners and programmers. These discussion groups will show you how commercial television really works.

World Now, www.worldnow.com.   Takes broadcasters beyond their deadly early sites that showed grinning pictures of on-air personalities and love letters from the audience. It's a good site to see what's going on.

19

Print Interviews

Newspapers and magazines aren't going anywhere. They shrink, merge, struggle, and fuse with electronic technologies in the conglomerates, but we still like to read newspapers and magazines. Call them dinosaurs, say they're losing their clout, but do not write their obituaries. The Internet takes them online and expands their coverage, but print remains a credible news source and probably the most effective media outlet available to you.

When you and your picture appear in the newspaper, or in a regional magazine, people remember it for a long time. They clip it, file it, take it out years later and remind you of what you said. In print, you have credibility that carries its own mystique. Print is probably also the only medium that will come close to covering your full story.

The print interview is unique in its interpretive nature. Someone will be writing about you, describing your office or den, talking about your children, and quoting you. You'll say a lot and be quoted a little. Be sure that you speak to a reporter in language that accurately reflects the image you want to put across.

Say: "I think the Net has too many obsolete modems."

Don't say: "A lot of morons are glutting the market with their second-rate modems."

If you were the writer of a modem article, which quote would you choose? What choice would you have? If an executive calls his competitors morons, you're certainly not going to go for the tamer quote. You might even want to encourage this spiciness by asking your subject if he would venture to name any of those morons.

"Let me go on the record as saying that there hasn't been an IQ of over 75 at Webscape Modems since the seventies."

Now if you were the reporter, your heart would be pounding through your shirt. You would certainly not wish the subject of your interview to restrict the flow of his words. It is not a reporter's job to do that. You might even press forward.

"I gather then that you are saying that the president of Webscape lacks intelligence?"

"I'm saying that the president of Webscape Modems is a moron."

There is only one moron in this transaction. If the whole hypothetical case sounds far-fetched, and if you believe that a person smart enough to take a company from an upstart to an IPO is too savvy to make such remarks, you are mistaken. People who are otherwise brilliant make phenomenal blunders with reporters, especially in print, where there's no technology to keep us in check. In a situation such as this, a good reporter would encourage a sense of bravado. The headline: Modem Prez Calls Competitors "Morons."

"But I thought it was off the record! I'm ruined!" says the ruined modem president, who will be outside playing the guitar for pocket change before the end of the week. Once you make a negative public impression, you're stuck with it—regardless of update stories or retractions. You don't have to guard every word, but bear in mind that a reporter does not owe you any explanation for the tone of his article. Treat a reporter as you would treat a live microphone.

John Rocker's 38 saves in 1999 as a relief pitcher for the Atlanta Braves couldn't save him from the permanent damage he did to his career when he told a *Sports Illustrated* writer how much he hated New York. Perhaps forgetting that ballplayers don't have to take mass transit, he described New York fans as "degenerates" and a subway trip to Shea Stadium as "some queer with AIDS right next to some dude who just got out of jail for the fourth time, right next to some 20-year-old mom with four kids."

But despite vituperative rants with New York fans, and a seeming awe that "foreigners" could walk the streets of the Apple unescorted, Rocker's problems accelerated when he described a black teammate as a "fat monkey." Maybe he forgot that he played for Atlanta, home to Martin Luther King and a city where African-Americans are not viewed as "minorities." The Atlanta City Council immediately passed a resolution calling on the Braves to dismiss Rocker. Baseball commissioner Bud Selig demanded that the pitcher submit to psychological testing.

Rocker's case is more flamboyant and openly ignorant than others, but recent history is filled with career-busting blunders. Jesse Jackson referred to Jews as "hymies" and New York as "hymietown." Former agriculture secretary Earl Butz left office after referring to African-Americans as wanting only loose shoes and a warm place to go to the bathroom. The list is a long one.

How, you might ask, can this happen? Was John Rocker really *that* hateful or stupid? Only he knows. He was a good student and his living arrangements during spring training did not bespeak the racism and xenophobia of his words. So what happened? He did not treat a reporter like a live mike. A 25-year-old pitcher with a 95-mile-an-hour fastball is likely to play baseball, but you won't find him doing a lot of the lucrative commercial endorsements that can exceed a player's salary.

Despite a public apology and 15 more years of unquestioned dedication to the civil rights issues that have defined his life, Jesse Jackson was never a serious player in presidential politics after his remarks regarding Jews in New York. In each case, the subject *thought* he wouldn't be quoted. Jackson was in a room with only black people, one of whom was a reporter for *The Washington Post*. Rocker invited the *Sports Illustrated* writer on a hunting trip, and more than likely believed he was not on the record when he misspoke.

Earl Butz doomed himself on an airplane when Pat Boone asked him why the party of Lincoln was not doing more to recruit African-American voters. Sitting in the group was former White House special counsel John Dean, who had written a best-selling account of his Watergate experiences and was working as a journalist. Butz surely didn't think he was speaking in public.

Do the right thing. This is not the 1940s, where trading ethnic barbs and slurring whole groups of citizens was tolerated. Forget what Howard said on the radio this morning. You're not him. Shock jocks are multimillionaires, most of whom, including Stern and Imus, do not make racist remarks in their private lives. Some, like Washington's "Grease Man" have been fired for racial slurs. You would be too. A reporter is there to report, always.

The positive side of the equation comes with the length of the feature. In print, you can express yourself without the constant interruptions of radio and television. And, as long as you don't make prejudicial remarks, there is no reason to assume that the reporter is out to get you. There is a bundle of nice news published every day, and you're probably going to be part of it.

A good journalist will make you want to talk about interesting things, and you must be sure that those things are in your best interest. Know your act and glide from one topic to the other as you would in any environment. If you meet a reporter for "a drink," make sure it's nonalcoholic.

The Internet has given every sizeable newspaper and magazine an international forum. Your piece may linger for weeks in the publication's online edition. Or, you may be interviewed by one of the Webzines whose primary focus is online readership.

If something is "off the record," be sure that you personally clarify what that means—no reference will be made to this comment in this piece or any other. And make sure the tape recorder goes off. If you don't trust the reporter, don't say anything off the record. It's that simple. When we train for print interviews, we counsel our clients to assume the entire interview is on the record.

If you are dealing with extraordinarily sensitive material, some of which is on and some of which is off the record, tape the interview yourself. You're under no obligation to confess if your interviewer fails to probe. Sometimes they don't even want to. A feature writer for the "Lifestyle" section probably isn't looking to roast you on your own backyard grill.

There is also the possibility of inaccuracy. Part of that is the human nature of interpretation, and part is that issues are not always as ice-water clear as you intended them to be in your discussion. If something is important, repeat it, pause for emphasis, and approach the conversation with the showmanship you use in television.

Know your good side if a photographer accompanies the reporter. Sometimes the pictures will be taken at a later date, either at the newspaper itself where the lighting is right or at your most photogenic location.

Visuals are as important in print as they are in television. A photograph dramatically increases the value of a feature.

If your interviewer is a columnist, be familiar with his or her work well in advance of the interview. A simple online search will yield a library of his or her most recent columns. If the column is gossipy, ask if you can submit items at a later date. Be sure to get the columnist's private fax, e-mail, and direct phone line. These numbers are invaluable in a pinch and are often unavailable to just anybody. You will be amazed at the power of this type of relationship.

It may take a while for the publication to run your piece. Be polite when inquiring whether the article has been scheduled, and don't be a nuisance. If it doesn't run at all (and that happens periodically), don't blame yourself. Sometimes editors rule out features because they resemble recent stories, or because someone just didn't like the flow of the writing.

When the article does appear, the whole process will have been worth it. In addition to print's bestowing credibility, nothing generates more publicity than a good clipping. At the very least, your family will be impressed.

SITE SEEING

Time magazine, www.time.com.   Search the *Time* archives and learn from some infamous interview blunders.

The New York Times, www.nytimes.com.   This is a great place to check out interviews with world leaders, artists, entertainers, athletes, and business people. See how these folks handle themselves and make news "that's fit to print."

Pasadena Weekly, www.pasadenaweekly.com.   For a great example of an alternative weekly paper, check out this site and find out what citizens of the Rose City are interested in reading about.

20

Controlling the Interview

Watch Sunday morning television as John McLaughlin skewers one of his group of journalists and columnists with the Socratic aplomb of the Jesuit educator he once was.

"Will the president recover from this political Hiroshima that places his historic prestige somewhere between Warren Harding and Millard Fillmore . . . I ask you, Eleanor Clift . . ."

Now change the channel and watch Sam Donaldson pin a politician to an issue like a butterfly to a cork board. Then on NBC check out Tim Russert as he goes head-to-head with the British prime minister with a clear, straightforward question that leaves no room for ambiguity.

All will answer, but they won't answer the questions they are asked:

"John, I think you have this president confused with your old boss, Richard Nixon. The *real* issue is whether moderate Republicans can rally the right wing behind them, because if they can't . . ."

"Polls come and go, George, but the *real* race for the presidency is won, not in New Hampshire but on Super Tuesday where the senator finds his true momentum."

"Tim, as we've often discussed, *we* can't do anything until the Palestinians give us assurances which are simply not forthcoming. Since 1973 . . ."

Notice that the interviewer warily presses on, often repeating the question, and the subject of the interview continues to push his own agenda, spinning his story into enthusiastic sound bites in a dance where everyone knows the steps. This is the often misunderstood but vital process known as *bridging* the interview. I call it running an "L" pattern. You acknowledge the question thoughtfully (the base of the "L") then use an emphasis to go down your own path. You can always use your voice to change the course of an interview.

"Yes or no, Mr. Oppenheim, should tryptophane be a prescription medication?"

"The issue to me, Bill, is not whether it's a *prescription* medication, but whether we have more *regulation* of tryptophane—which we badly need. Here's why . . ."

Your interviewers have an obligation to keep from turning your conversation into yet another commercial on an oversold show. Some will plug your pitch harder than others. It's up to you to strike a balance between where you want the interview to go and where the interviewer wants to take it.

Interviewers are happiest when their programs are going well. If you shine most brightly when discussing the topics most conducive to your plug and place less emphasis in areas of conversation that interest you less, you'll have a lot more input into the course of the interview. Let us illustrate with a hypothetical case.

After finding that your exercise and diet program works, you put together a small book that the major publishers decline. They do so on the basis of two criteria: They have large inventories of their own yet-to-be-published books that are similar to yours in format, and they are candid enough to tell you that books of this nature sell best when they are written either by a medical doctor or by a well-known personality. You are neither.

Undaunted, you use publishing software to produce your own booklet, and hit the road for its publicity. Let's look in on one of your interviews:

"I'm Les Martel with Cindy Barbour, author of a new book called *Be Thin Next Month*, a 30-day diet and exercise program that she says will give any overweight person a fresh start in the short space of a month. Welcome to *Good Morning Charlestown*. Why did you decide to write this book?"

Naturally, you've anticipated this question and have prepared an answer that gives you the opportunity to take the reins.

"Well, Les, the book comes as a result of my own experience when I took off 20 pounds in 30 days and kept it off. You see, there are thousands of diets and exercise programs, but very few work because they lack one basic element . . ."

(Does Les really have a big choice about what he can ask after your pause?)

"What's that?"

"A personal contract with one's self, Les. I've found plenty of diet and exercise program books, and they're all effective enough, but I've never found one with a personal contract. That's where my book begins. In fact, I have what I think is a unique offer to readers."

"Tell me about it."

"I offer a box of their favorite chocolates plus a full refund if they choose not to advance beyond page 3 of *Be Thin Next Month*. I consider page 3 to be the most critical page because the plan can't proceed without it."

"Let me read aloud from page 3 of *Be Thin Next Month*, Cindy."

Many people fall into the trap of believing they're selling their product by continuous repetition of its name:

"Well, Les, in my book, *Be Thin Next Month* . . ."

"In *Be Thin Next Month*, I say . . ."

"Before I wrote *Be Thin Next Month* . . ."

A limited amount of such hype is permissible, but if the guest overdoes it, Les has options, too:

"Frankly, Cindy, I wish you wouldn't mention the title so much, because I'm not sure of its validity. You're not a doctor, and you're putting out a diet." Or, "Cindy, I want to thank you but we're out of time."

Your host can always run out of time and extend the next interview segment. If it's a live interview where there are no other guests, there's always the phone. Anyone who interviews daily knows how to get tough. The sweet ones enjoy the change, and the tough talkers simply return to a natural conversational tone. Either way, you're in for a bad time if you oversell. Suppose, though, that you've taken the time to come all the way to a studio and there has been no plug. Then it's up to you to slip one in:

"That's all the time we have, Cindy. Thanks for showing us those great exercises."

"My pleasure, Les. I'd like to remind people that all the exercises can be found in my new book, *Be Thin Next Month*, on special this month at Pen & Ink bookstores in the greater Charlestown area."

In most cases, the plugs will come at the beginning and end of a broadcast interview with titles appearing under your name as you speak to the televison audience. That's why you have been advised to carry a printed index card to any TV appearance.

Coping with the Hard Questions

Suppose that the two questions you dread most come up anyway (If they're obvious to you, they're probably equally apparent to your interviewer):

"Now with all due respect, Cindy, you're not a doctor, and I must confess to a philosophical objection to laypeople with diet books. I have to tell our viewers to beware of *Be Thin Next Month*. I hope you can understand why." And, "I understand that seven major publishers have turned this book down. So, I must ask you, why should we trust it?"

The press always gets an honest answer, or extracts a severe penalty from those who lie. The first step in controlling an interview is to prepare your case, its selling points, and its legitimacy before going under the lights. There are a number of ways to do that in the example of the diet book. Cindy could have had a physician consult on the book and write the foreword, ask the family doctor to endorse it, or solicit the advice and endorsement of a legitimate professional society.

"I agree, Les, and that's why the foreword of the book was written by Dr. Perry Foster, who is on the staff of St. Luke's hospital here in Charlestown."

(If she takes a brief pause here, she ends this line of questioning and moves quickly to her next thought.)

"Which reminds me, Les . . . when we were going through the exercise portion of the book, I asked Dr. Foster about the efficiency of sit-ups, and he said . . ."

Or, suppose there was no Dr. Foster in the preparation of her book. She realizes she should have thought of a medical endorsement, but now it's too late.

"While it's true that I don't have a medical degree, Les, I provide 40 Web sites in the book where doctors who spoke to me have endorsed either our plan or similar programs. I'm confident that any M.D. in practice would not take issue with the menus, which were prepared in accordance with published standards of the American Dietary Association, or the exercises, which have been used for years. In fact, I advise all my readers to see a doctor before undertaking any diet or exercise program."

Here, the author is falling back on a second line of legitimacy. When you check your own pitch, you'll always be able to find something that makes sense, or you wouldn't have come on the show in the first place. The key is to know ahead of time what's going to occur, and if you are surprised, to take a beat and not panic.

As for the question of Cindy's book having been rejected by major publishers, the truth wouldn't be a bad idea:

"Seven publishers turning down a book is a rather common experience for even the most seasoned authors. I was not discouraged by the publishers but was told that they had plenty of diet books, so I decided to form my own publishing company. I did take off 20 pounds in 30 days. Dozens of people I know have had similar successes, and I know my plan works."

The key principle of controlling an interview is emphasis. Be direct, never evasive, and always introduce the next topic yourself if the conversation is in an area where you are not comfortable.

Conversational Bridges

Since controlling an interview is a matter of emphasizing areas of conversation, it's a good idea to develop and practice the conversational bridges that make change possible. Here are a few suggestions:

"You mentioned rainfall before, and it reminds me . . ."

(The "you mentioned" transition is always good once per interview because it unifies your thought with something the host said earlier.)

"That reminds me . . ."

"Have you ever found yourself in this situation, Les? You're walking down the street and suddenly . . ."

One thing you should know about . . ."

(You can initiate a new topic—anything. There's no need to wait for an invitation.) However, always let the interviewer do the plug. But if that doesn't happen:

"At MegaModem, we believe . . ."

"The first time I saw one of those Blueline DSL five hundreds, I thought it was a shovel."

"I bet you didn't know that this widget has more than 300 uses."

You will never be—and shouldn't be—in absolute control of your interview. With directness, a positive approach, the establishment of legitimacy, and a determination to take charge without being pushy, you *will* be more comfortable and more productive in your new role as interviewee.

SITE SEEING

Meet the Press, www.msnbc.com.   Politicians and world leaders go head-to-head with top print and broadcast journalists.

The McLaughlin Group, www.mclaughlin.com.   Lets you weigh in on the weekly commentary show.

The Capitol Gang, www.cnn.com.   Check out what's happening on the Hill and in the studio.

21

Adverse Publicity

It usually starts with a single call, perhaps when you're at home and not insulated by the protective machinery of an office staff. The reporter is friendly but direct. There is a document with your signature linking you to some dreadful group, event, fraud, or other criminal activity. Sometimes it's about someone you love, or a close associate. So begins a time when the press becomes more terrifying than your worst nightmare.

Adverse publicity requires a constant vigilance, a stamina beyond your finest athletic accomplishments. Life as you know it ends for the duration of the crisis; every hour of every day passes as painfully as the slow throb of an infected tooth. Reporters may camp in your neighborhood, interrupt you at a restaurant, interview coworkers and employees, and relentlessly pursue the truth you would rather not tell them. You may find yourself the innocent victim of an investigation that destroys your career.

Those who have endured the hot end of investigative journalism remain affected by the experience for the rest of their lives. One wrong move and you're imprinted in an unfavorable manner.

What would you have told Bill Clinton to do about the emerging Monica Lewinsky scandal in January of 1998? Could you have guessed that his decisions would get him impeached in less than a year? Probably not. Like Watergate, the scandal began as a dark but small event of human frailty that was expected to go away, but instead grew into a history-turning event.

If you were a media consultant and got a call from John and Patsy Ramsey on December 26, 1996, reporting that their little girl had been murdered in their home, they didn't do it, and they were becoming prime suspects, would you have known what advice to give them?

Of course, I hear you saying. You'd tell them to cooperate with the police and get a good criminal attorney. Let the system do its work. And if you've ever been around cops, you'd probably tell yourself they're guilty as sin.

Okay, but what if they had nothing to do with their little girl's murder? Hey, Bill, you say, I may have been born at night, but not *last* night. Everyone knows that murders of this kind are committed by family; people don't just come in off the street and kill little girls.

Actually, they do. The 1993 tragedy of little Polly Klass of Petaluma, California, is one public case of a child abducted and murdered by a paroled sex offender. She was a middle-class child stolen from a "good" neighborhood, and therefore the tragedy generated a lot of media. You don't read about a lot of the cases because they happen in neighborhoods where life is thought to be cheap. But it happens more than you think.

I have no involvement with the Ramseys and no opinion on whether they killed or facilitated the killing of JonBenet. And even though I have long experience in helping people deal with the white heat of negative publicity, in the midnight of my soul, I would not have had a clue as to what I would have told them had they called me on December 26, 1996. And if Bill Clinton called me up and asked me what to do about the Monica scandal, I wouldn't have known what to tell him, either.

Neither would you. When the media volcano erupts, no one knows how far the lava's going to go and who it will bury. Clinton and Nixon were masters at media power plays. They had gotten themselves into, and out of, some very tight spots by the art of the grand television posture. Negative publicity was nothing new, but it had never caught up to them in any seriously damaging way until one day things got out of hand.

It never caught up to Ronald Reagan, although some historians now believe he knew more about Iran-Contra than he ever let on, and, had we known, his charm might not have carried the day. As it was, there was serious talk of impeachment hearings. We can come up with a million things the Ramseys should have done—release new family video and initiate litigation if necessary to stem the spread of that hideous beauty pageant footage, issue a statement to the press, look bereft, cooperate better with the police. Any idiot can look back and know that. But while it's happening, none of us know very much.

If the investigation had not been botched, we'd know more about the culpability of the Ramseys. But what we knew for three years after the murder is that they *looked* guilty to many of us and therefore they were. That's just not good enough, but welcome to the court of public opinion, where you can be found not guilty by the justice system and spend the rest of your life being jeered, spat upon, and ridiculed as you carry the weight and the taint of bad publicity.

In his book, *Public Relations on the Net*, California-based consultant Shel Holtz delineates two principal forms of the madness. There's the *meteor crisis*, where you're bombarded out of the blue with a disaster you never expected, such as a plant explosion, and a *predatory crisis*, where your problem is the deliberate work of an adversarial force such as a business or political competitor. How you conduct yourself in the unknowable early hours of a crisis will determine everything that happens later.

Most of us will never face a Nixonian or Clintonesque level of taint, but we could face a lawsuit, an arrest, or an indictment, all of which can create a portal for predatory publicity even though none of these legal actions imply anything resembling *truth*. If a DA wants to indict you on scant circumstantial evidence, the Ramsey case notwithstanding, she probably can get a grand jury to do it.

If a disgruntled former employee or lover wants to sue you, all he has to do is file. And, depending on where you live, the police have a very wide berth to cuff you in front of your neighbors and hold you in custody for two or three days. You can sue for false arrest—but don't expect Judge Judy to glower at the arresting officer and tell him he's done you wrong. Most judges lean in the direction of police support, especially if the arresting officers have a clean record and no apparent prejudice toward the accused.

Once these things happen, the press has a large window through which to drag you into the court of public opinion. Be ready.

Lesson number one is watch what you say, or, as many lawyers advise, say nothing at all. There is no escape from the press, but there are ways in which you can survive the experience to your best advantage. We offer hypothetical cases for both the wrongly accused and the legally culpable, beginning with the former.

When You Are Completely Innocent, This Is an Outrage

This scenario makes law enforcement people snicker because it runs contrary to their experience. In their lives, a totally innocent person in the system is as rare as a snowball in Costa Rica. However, if you press them, they'll tell you they've been known to file charges more on hunch than concrete evidence, and they've been wrong. Checks and balances, they say, are a good thing, for, while a hunch can be a very productive impulse, it can also be very wrong. You have a judge to throw it out of court.

But once the same case goes before the house without walls we sometimes call the court of public opinion, perception has a way of becoming reality. Ask Richard Jewell, the security guard accused around the world of planting a bomb in Atlanta at the 1996 Summer Olympics.

To seasoned cops and FBI agents, Jewell's media-fanned heroism in the aftermath of the bombing fit a suspicious pattern of the "hero" creating his own valor. Arson investigators know the scenario well. A neighbor sets a fire to emerge heroic as the rescuer. If Jewell had not been interviewed and hailed as a hero, he probably never would have been publicly hung out as a "suspect."

But he soon found himself in a Hitchcockian nightmare of being falsely accused and found guilty in the court of public opinion—a kangaroo court in this instance because Jewell didn't do anything but try to help people after the bombing. He got excellent legal help, and we began to buy his sincerity as he went on the air with Larry King and others explaining his nightmare in an open, nondefensive manner. But for a time, many of us nodded knowingly when Jewell was nabbed and processed as the perpetrator. Of course, we said, the guy needed to be a hero to revive a flagging career in law enforcement.

It's terrifying to think that any of us could be Richard Jewell, fed to the press on a "perp walk" where you, as a "suspect" are paraded past a row of cameras and microphones with reporters shouting your name. This nightmare can be played out with no indictment or resolution before the courts. All you need to be is a "suspect." It can happen to anyone. So, what do you do if you're completely innocent?

A very human response is to go public immediately and nip the problem in the bud. If the reporter has called you, however, it is likely that erroneous circumstantial evidence has implicated you enough to warrant a thorough examination before rendering any statement. It is also possible that a party whose identity is unknown to you at this time is attempting to deflect culpability by accusing you.

The reporter may use pressure. There's a deadline, so-and-so says you authorized the misappropriation of funds, and if you refuse comment, he'll have no choice but to print that. It won't look very good for you. There's nothing wrong (even though you may be made to feel otherwise) with a simple assertion of your innocence and a refusal to comment further until you have had the opportunity to examine the evidence. Leave it at that and get an attorney.

Your lawyer should be a fighter who isn't afraid to stand firm with reporters. Some see any publicity as a bonanza to be used in a later race for public office or a permanent slot as a TV commentator. Beware of this type, although many competent attorneys seek election and appear regularly on TV. Once you choose an attorney, you'll have to make a few fast decisions.

THE WRITTEN STATEMENT

In recent years, even television reporters have come to accept a firm written statement as a pro forma course that people with legal difficulties take. If you're directly accused of wrongdoing, you may want to draft a statement that will ward off such damaging comments as:

"Neither Mr. Sherwood nor his attorney, Robert Cohen, returned numerous calls made to their offices on Tuesday."

Or,

"While Sherwood has refused to comment, sources inside North American Microchip report that the executive has not been seen since reports of his alleged misconduct surfaced last Monday."

You may prefer instead to issue a formal comment such as:

"My attorney, Mr. Cohen, and I have conferred with the District Attorney's office and disclosed as much information as we have available. I am confident that this matter will be resolved through proper legal channels. I wish to state unequivocally that I have done nothing illegal or unethical with regard to this matter."

Now there's something to print or broadcast. It says little, but it says *something*. When the questions accelerate, you might add the following verbal remark:

"I have been advised by my attorney that any further comment would be inappropriate at this time."

THE FIRM DISCLAIMER

In some cases, a direct response to specific allegations is the best course. Make sure that your attorney reviews your case with you and participates in your decision. Then be prepared to stand calm during some very tough questioning. Start with a prepared statement that you'll immediately make available in the form of a written release. Be as specific as circumstances and your lawyer's advice permit.

Never lie. Once you get caught in any kind of misstatement, you're going to be in a vulnerable position for the duration of the crisis. Once you firmly deny your story, make yourself available to as many interviewers as you can handle, but don't misrepresent anything. And remember that a half-truth is the biggest lie of all.

Bill Clinton had become a life master at mincing words before the Lewinsky scandal, when he said he had never "had sex with that woman." By a literal interpretation of his words, he hadn't consummated the relationship, but he certainly did have sex with her and the misstatement damaged his credibility beyond repair. The public judged it a lie, and his political enemies were able to carry the issue all the way to impeachment. So, if William Jefferson Clinton couldn't fan a half-truth into redemption, don't be naive enough to believe you can.

THE LIVE SATELLITE CONFERENCE

Many of the big PR firms advise their corporate clients to speak to a select group of journalists by phone and satellite early in a crisis. They grill them mercilessly in mock interviews. I've been known to do it myself. This is a strong course if you're in a business where you know a small group of reporters who cover your company as part of their beats and you want to speak exclusively to them before going into silence. The satellite format has a number of advantages and disadvantages that we address in Chapter 26.

One advantage here is that you went before the press, made your statement, appeared willing to answer questions, and got your message out. No one expects you to be able to comment on pending litigation and they're likely to understand if you don't answer the tough questions they are required to ask. But you *faced* them. The footage is then released to any broadcast outlet that wants it and it is treated as news.

THE VIDEOTAPED SATELLITE RESPONSE

I personally hate this course, but there are times when it's useful to record a video statement and distribute it by satellite to the nation's television and radio stations. It gives them a picture. However, local anchors and reporters go way out of their way to issue a disclaimer that the following footage is released by the company on satellite and should not be considered "news." Their disdain for the canned response to which they can ask no questions is seen in their body language and intonation. But, it is a picture and it gets a message out.

THE TOTAL SILENCE

If you refuse to say anything at all—nothing—you can never be misquoted or quoted out of context. If you choose this difficult course, we recommend that you say nothing at all instead of the terse "No comment" that comes across as evasive. Total silence, as is the case with other courses, should be undertaken only on advice of at least one attorney.

THE SINGLE INTERVIEW

Sometimes you trust a reporter and want to share your story with him or her. This path is flooded with the danger of mistreatment and relentless hounding by competing publications or stations. But if it's a comprehensive account, thoroughly documented, and verified in every way possible, it can also send the pack to their next story.

In the William Kennedy Smith trial of the early nineties, his accuser, Patricia Bowman, took this course with Diane Sawyer, thus enhancing her credibility. She could have made some serious money if she'd gone with a tabloid show.

Juanita Broaderick, the Arkansas nursing home owner who accused President Clinton of raping her in 1978 when he was Arkansas attorney general, told her story exclusively to Lisa Myers of NBC News, then faded back into obscurity. She, too, could have made a lot of money by signing a tabloid TV and press contract, but by going with NBC she conveyed a credibility she would not have had otherwise.

However, it must be said that both women were known to be financially secure, so their courses might be considered a luxury.

Jennifer Flowers went public about her affair with Clinton in the *Star* for money and was far easier to discredit as a money-grubbing floozy during the 1992 presidential campaign. But the public never forgot her, and years later, free of the restraints of exclusivity contracts, both she and her story seemed far less sordid.

Going to the Spin Mattresses

At the outset of the O.J. Simpson trial, I interviewed Alan Dershowitz for cable television. He had just lost an appeal for Mike Tyson that he felt could have been successfully handled by any third-year law student. But his formidable legal skills couldn't get Tyson out just then because public sentiment was running rather high against such an outcome. I asked this master of the appellate spin what role media wars played in his legal strategies. His answer surprised me.

Dershowitz said that day in and out, he preferred a quieter, legalistic approach to most of his cases, but if the prosecution starts a leak war, the gloves come off. Like his fellow Bostonian on OJ's defense team, F. Lee Bailey, Dershowitz is no shrinking violet when it comes to going on TV, but strategic leaks by the government are usually the impetus for his celebrated battles in front of the cameras.

Whoever fires the first shot is immaterial. When adverse publicity begins, you're sure to get a call from a reporter—a nonpublished number is rarely an obstacle—asking you to comment immediately on an "exclusive" comment she just got from someone about you. If you refuse to talk, she'll have to run with the damning charge and report that she reached you and you stood mute—and, hey, that's not good. It's going to make you look bad. I think it would work better for both of us if you talked to me. I only have 10 minutes before my deadline.

Get off the phone immediately and call your lawyer. You're in a spin war. Mobsters used to call holing up for major family combat, *going to the mattresses*. According to *The Sopranos*, such shootouts went out with Buick Roadsters, but the concept is a fit when it comes to spin. Someone's going to say bad things about you to the press and use your chosen course of silence against you. It may be a flat-out lie.

The answer to this no-win situation varies, but you need to plan for spin from your very first legal conference. A smart lawyer will probably tell you to stick with whatever strategy you decide — talking to a single media source, remaining silent, or holding a press conference at the outset.

The best investigative reporters are very straight. They don't lie, and woe to you if you aren't straight with them. But some reporters have been known to — let's just say refract the truth when they want a good quote. No problem, you think. You just won't pick up the phone. Thank God for answering machines and voice mail. Wrong, mon ami. They do this every day.

"Call me at 555-2345. The cops found the women . . ."

Click in mid-sentence . . . *What Women?* There are no women to be *found* here. I'd better straighten this out. You call and eternally regret the choice.

Or,

"I'll be here for an hour, then I have to file. We really need to straighten out this molestation issue — Oh, did they tell you yet about the indictment?"

What?

Pick your course, stay with it and plan, plan, plan for the spin wars. And make sure your lawyer is as good as Dershowitz. Mortgage the house if you must.

REMAIN COMPOSED

Never appear to be rattled or defensive. Crisis communication is about symbols. Remember Saddam Hussein with the little boy, bodies littered at Bopal, dead seagulls and oil-soaked seals after the *Exxon-Valdez* oil spill. About the last thing the Clinton administration wanted to see was a photograph of a camouflaged raider who looked like he just jumped out of a Tom Clancy novel with his gun pointed toward a terrified Elian Gonzalez hiding in a closet.

You never saw Ken Starr shielding his face or covering a camera lens, but you never saw him reveal anything either. Off camera, the man probably did so much leaking, he made the *Exxon-Valdez* look seaworthy. What will we remember about him forever? More than likely, his calm as he passed by the cameras daily with his morning container of Starbuck's coffee.

One piece of eloquence I'll always remember is something Starr didn't say. When asked by a friendly Congressional questioner if he liked being the last Independent Counsel, he cryptically referred to a popular country tune and left us to fill in the title, "Take This Job And Shove It." Besides providing a laugh from a most unlikely source, Ken was doing a little spin dance. Me, a zealot? Whatever gave you that idea?

UPDATE YOUR WEB SITE

False rumors on the Internet can do you in faster than the bite of an asp. Several years ago, a posting to several Usenet news groups claimed that fashion designer Tommy Hilfiger had been kicked off *Oprah!* for making racial slurs. The fact that it never happened did not prevent angry members from copying the slur, cross-posting it to other groups, and e-mailing the lie across the globe. The rumor immediately became accepted as fact, and the company spent months playing catch-up. You can probably still find angry calls to boycott the company online.

The Web is rife with "rogue" sites that traffic in innuendo and rumor as soon as a crisis occurs. An untrue message that takes on the momentum of truth online is called a *meme*. This, you do not need.

Because the public and the press can gain access to the same information at the same time, you'll need to constantly monitor what they're saying about you online. There are many services that can do this for you, or you can do it yourself, but you'll need a strategy for dealing with rumor promptly. Most specialists who deal with Internet media crises urge a patient, measured response, referring readers back to your home site. Some go so far as to suggest a link to the erroneous information as an acknowledgment that you know about the attack sites and refute the information. But whatever you do, never obfuscate online.

When TWA flight 800 crashed off the coast of Long Island, the airline virtually shut down its site, leaving reporters and the public with a blank home page that remained unchanged for much of the summer of 1996. It is imperative that your information be dated and updated constantly.

The Lewinsky scandal was probably the first history-making news to be broken on the Internet, when columnist Matt Drudge released the explosive story days ahead of *Newsweek*, forever altering the way we receive major news. Live coverage of the release of the Starr report was broadcast as it came off the Web. This genie is not going back inside the bottle. The time for an Internet strategy is long before the fire starts. Barring that, it's probably the first thing you should think about.

NEVER TALK TO THE PRESS IF YOUR HEAD ISN'T CLEAR

Until the late 1970s, booze and press went together. If you threw a press conference, you put out some hard liquor, even at 11:00 in the morning. If you were being interviewed, you frequently met the reporter "for a drink," which meant alcoholic beverages. Today, such meetings have gone the way of avocado refrigerators and Polaroid Swinger cameras—and not a minute too soon. Many uninitiated interviewees found themselves stuck in bars like flies on sticky paper as the reporter, seemingly unaffected by the alcohol that anesthetized the interview subject, bore in on one tough question after another.

Today, you're more apt to find yourself in the same trap if you're ill or on painkillers or other prescription medication that affects your consciousness. Yes, you may feel a five-minute call will set the record straight. If you want some perspective on how gracious you're going to be if a reporter starts hammering you with pointed questions, think of the time your four-year-old put a loud toy in your ear just as a decongestant kicked in, or the time the cat bit your toe when you were hung over. It's acceptable to excuse yourself and get off the phone.

When You're Guilty as Charged (Sort of)

If you dumped arsenic into a water supply, my fondest wish is that *Dateline* does a hidden camera investigation and nails you. However, such monstrous human events are rarely the work of a villain who twirls his mustache and says "Heh, heh, heh, power will be mine, now." You're probably just the person in the middle protecting your job and your boss, who is now retired with several mil in St. Martin while the press is stomping your face with cleats.

Let's say that you did what they're saying, but there are all kinds of extenuating circumstances that they're simply not getting. You have all of the options of the innocent with the addition of more vulnerability during the earliest stages of the crisis. You can say things that you'll later regret but won't be able to take back. You also have the joint dilemma of coconspirators, if there are any, talking to the press while your own attorney advises you to keep silent.

For the duration of the crisis, you're a marked person. If there's an indictment brewing, people below you will cut a deal to burn you and you'll be asked to make a deal to burn someone higher on the food chain. The person who can bring the highest-rank, most publicly culpable figure into court wins. If that happens to be you, you have some very big problems.

Admit your involvement to yourself and build a worst-case scenario, enumerating with your lawyer all of the facts that could come out in the investigation. Reporters make friends quickly, and they're not going to be shy about using whatever tactic is necessary to get their story.

If you can develop the presence to regard the press with the professional wariness of an adversarial relationship, you're less likely to lose control. Don't try to win them over and don't try to scare them away.

Stay in control. Whether you want to let your lawyer do all your talking for you is something to work out early in the crisis. Typically, they want to and typically they're not very good at it. Some very fine criminal defense attorneys get before reporters and implode. They rant, posture, and volley sound bites that they think are clever or appropriate but make you look guilty. This is not to say you should go on the air to reveal your legal strategy or your attorney's interpretation of the law. But sometimes the client is better than the lawyer at asserting innocence.

The "don't lie" rule applies more rigorously than ever when you have the vulnerability of legal exposure. But you're under no obligation to confess either, for you are innocent until a court of law says otherwise. Don't try to fan the publicity flames, hoping that the negative exposure will get your case thrown out of court. That rarely works.

Be strong and professional. Don't be goaded because a mob accosts you with lights, microphones, and cameras. Don't throw your coat over your head like some street mugger caught snatching a purse. As difficult as this may be, act as though they're not there.

"The best defense is a good offense," you may say as you start coming on strong. Sometimes that works, but it works a lot better for the innocent. If there's solid evidence adding up, you're going to look awfully silly for having roared.

Whether or not you are culpable, develop a post adjudication strategy. If you're accused unfairly of making inappropriate racial comments or mismanaging funds and can't say anything during the mainstream of the crisis, plan to write an article or at least an editorial response once you've had your day in court. Then, use the article to get yourself on television to show the public who you are.

Don't give up. Your story is as perishable as grapefruit in a supermarket. Eventually the clamor will die down and people's memories will dim. They're likely to remember more about your presence than the facts in the case itself. If you remain publicly sincere and courageous, you will be remembered that way by many. If you twitch, wail, hide, or clam up, the damage will linger. Eventually, though, you will become a stale piece of news. And that's the best news of all.

SITE SEEING

Crisis Management Public Relations:

Hill & Knowlton, www.hillandknowlton.com.   When it comes to media crisis management, these folks are like a huge criminal law firm. They might or might not be the best for the crisis, but they're likely to be a first stop for any corporation, government, or high-ticket individual with a media problem. They have a special "Reputation Protection System" or RPS, with its own site. www.promptrps.com.   A little stuffy and self-congratulatory, maybe, but, hey, they don't duck when the fire starts.

Kathleen Sindell, www.kathleensindell.com.   A Washington-based consultant specializing in crisis management.

Reputation Management Associates, www.mediarelations.com. These professionals specialize in corporate crises.

22

The Tour Circuit

It's 3:00 A.M., and you wake up in a panic. You don't know where you are, and, for an instant, you're not even sure who you are. The surroundings of the room tell you nothing except that you're in a hotel and it's indistinguishable from where you have spent the last 10 nights. Then it becomes clear. You're on tour in Columbus. Or is it Cincinnati? Right, Cincinnati. Columbus was yesterday. Wasn't it?

Media tours are the twenty-first-century version of the vaudeville and lecture expeditions of the pretelevision era, and, in many ways, they've returned to those roots. In the 1970s and 1980s, tours were all about radio, television, and press interviews. Today, they are an amalgam of online chats and other Internet publicity, live conversations with morning radio personalities, television satellite interviews, and personal appearances at banquets, retail outlets, universities, and professional associations. But tours are still mostly about media appearances.

If the subject is timely, a tour is an efficient and economical promotional mechanism that enables anyone to saturate the nation through local media exposure. If a tour doesn't move what you're selling, nothing will.

Before attempting the rigors of touring, there are a number of items to keep in mind:

Do you have the budget?   A tour may be efficient, but the costs are not measured in coins. Air travel generally occurs during peak flying hours, hotels in major cities top $200 a day for even modest accommodations, and the long-distance calls add up.

Is there enough time?   The biggest mistake novice tour publicists make is not allowing for the lead time required by most television shows. Your material should be in the producer's hands four to six weeks prior to your arrival in a city. You'll need to factor in the number of missed telephone connections with production people, and the amount of time you'll spend on hold before getting a booking. A healthy five- to ten-city tour often has 50 to 75 bookings that come as the result of hundreds of calls.

Is there enough product distribution to warrant the time and expense?   There's no point in going anywhere if a city's market for your pitch is not clearly anticipated and well stocked.

Do you have enough in the budget for the proper reference materials and perhaps even a professional consultation?   A common experience at PR firms begins with someone walking in the front door with a great idea. He'll book the smaller cities, and all the firm has to do is take care of New York, Chicago, Los Angeles, and the national shows. The "client" is then shocked to learn either that his money is declined or that there is virtually no difference in price between this "no-brainer" assignment and a full-blown campaign.

More information on national media appears in Chapter 28. In the case of large markets such as New York, Chicago, and Los Angeles, no one has an easy time booking cities where producers routinely choose between Nelson Mandela, Matt Damon, and Harry from Caller One. As in any business, PR firms charge according to the expenditure of time and personnel. Knowing something about these realities should help you prepare to deal with a professional publicity firm. Perhaps you'll find that a professional consultation is well within your budget after all.

You may want to hire either a freelance publicist or a capable person to make the phone calls. And, you'll need a good cell phone and a service that doesn't lose too many calls. In tour publicity, it is not possible to be away from the calls once booking begins.

All of the booking rules in Chapter 12 apply to the making of a tour, with the added factor of momentum. Once you set cities and dates, you are locked into a mail/overnight express/phone/scheduling pattern that will topple the tour in domino fashion if the pace falters. You will experience intense aggravation. You don't have to accept the tour's challenges to your mental health—insults, changes in schedule, last-minute cancellations, hotel hassles, airline blunders, indifference, and rudeness—as permanent in your life, but for the six or eight weeks of your tour involvement, you would do well to brace for frustration.

Pretour Planning

First, choose your cities. You need to learn something about the demographic content of each city you visit, along with getting a thumbnail notion of its local media picture. If you're selling snowmobiles, you wouldn't go to San Diego. That one is obvious. But if you're using a rodeo to sell alcoholic beverages, or an athletic event to sell cigarettes, there are areas of the country where you will be unwelcome. Having chosen your cities, sit down with an atlas and line them up geographically:

Boston
New York
Philadelphia
Pittsburgh
Cleveland
Minneapolis/St. Paul
Denver
Los Angeles
San Francisco
Portland

Take your cities to a travel agent and try to work out the most economical package available. Price wars notwithstanding, you probably won't benefit from any supersaver rates on the short hauls of a promotional tour. Generally, you don't need more than one day in each city.

Keeping Track of Your Information

There is a lot of information to keep on hand during the several weeks you'll need to book a tour. Whether you use the latest electronic notebook from Dell or an old-fashioned legal pad with one page for each city, you'll need to separate your documents by city and judiciously make notes as bookings come in.

New York, Tuesday, 10/24/02.

Hotel: The Marriott, Marquis, 45th & Seventh 212-555-4321

5:30 AM—MSNBC, *News at Sunrise*, Jeff Fargo, Segment Producer—212/321-2104, Left Voicemail message, 8/19, call again after Labor Day

7:30 AM (Live at 8) *New York Live*, New York Cable—Christy Ross, producer, e-mail *Cross@NYC.Com*; booked by e-mail, 8/22. Call to confirm 10/23 212-861-970

9:45 AM (Live at 10) *The Ron Mazell Show*, WOR Radio, 1440 Broadway, Corner of 40th and Broadway, Eleventh Floor, Studio B. Contact: Jaylene Dennis, 212-552-3486 Booked 8/24/call to confirm 10/22

(Take PATH Train at 23rd Street and Sixth Avenue to Hoboken—10 Min, take cab)

11:45 AM (*Live at Noon*), Noon News, Cable 12, 316 Hudson Street, Hoboken, NJ

Patrice Maynard is the segment producer—booked 8/31, call 10/21, between 9 and 10 to confirm 201-448-1212, Ext 48. Confirmed by *e-mail—Pmaynard@cable12.org* 10/31.

Take PATH Back to Manhattan

3:00—Press Interview, *The New York Alternative*—11 Riverside Drive, Suite 2102, Reporter: Jim Sinclair, confirmed by e-mail with assignment editor Julie Ross, 212-555-3407 *jross@mindnet .com* reconfirm, 10/22

Unless you have already proved yourself to be extraordinarily strong in enduring interviews, it is recommended that you spend no more than two weeks on the road during your first tour. If you wish to continue, book another leg.

Now that your notation documents, however you choose to organize them, are lined up in geographic order, assign dates to each city. Remember, one date to each city, and don't book any cities for Saturdays or Sundays unless you have a special event planned that will warrant weekend publicity.

Scan your reference material and take careful notes on what you consider the best shows in each city. Don't write them on a grid but make pencil markings within the reference text itself. Sunday morning radio interviews and public-access cable shows are wonderful for media training, but you're in a new league when you start touring. You want the best shows you can find.

Open any PR reference text (see Chapter 30) and look for television and radio programs that are on the air every day. Live shows are usually better than taped programs, but there are no ironclad rules. The references usually tell you where the 50,000-watt all-talk AM stations are, and you'll soon learn to pinpoint the morning talk shows that have the most consistently surveyed audiences. The references also give estimated audience figures. Make a list of your preferred bookings for each city. For example:

Toledo

AM Toledo, WTOL-TV: Betty Simon (318) 222-3300, *BettyS@wtol* .com

The Denise Brisson Show, WDBS Radio: Peg Bailey (318) 490-1230, fax, 490-1232; *e-mail—pbailey@mou.com;*

The Jerry Clarke Show, WRBJ Radio: Jerry Clarke (318) 791-4545, takes calls on cell phone mornings before 10—(318) 997-8877; e-mail, jclarke@wrbj.com

The Toledo Express:
Lifestyle: Gary Girard (318) 344-4676, e-mail *girard@tol.com*
Around Toledo: Patty McMahon (318) 344-4658 patty@tol.com
About Women: Marcel Dumont (318) 344-4692 dumont@tol.com
Business: Bob Madden (318) 344-4625 bobby@tol.com

Toledo Today, WDEV-TV: Kenny Foster (318) 791-8500 Kenny@ch12.com

Impact, WJMR Radio: Chris Katz (318) 791-3300 *Katzl@jmr.com*

Perspective, Toledo Cable: Carolyn Rosser (318) 344-2102 *Clyn@atb.com*

Dr. Jerome's Diary, WDPP Radio: Dr. Jerome Parnell (318) 344-2121 jerry14@newsrad.com

Toledo magazine: Terry Daniel (318) 222-4444, *tdaniel@tolnet* .com

Now you'll need to make a preliminary set of calls, faxes, or e-mails to meet the contacts and let them know that you're sending material on your topic and would they be interested? Not everyone does it this way. Some professionals never make a call without sending material, and others never send material until they've heard the word "Yes." Since you don't know the contacts, a preliminary round of calls is highly recommended. Now get set for the first round of booking blues.

"I'll have to get back to you."
"I'm really busy right now."
"Send me an e-mail. I'll get back to you if I'm interested."
"Why are you calling me? I never take calls. Send me an e-mail."
"I never check *that* e-mail. Try voice-mailing my cell phone."
"We're going on the air in two minutes."
"Too bad I didn't hear from you last week. We just did that topic last Thursday."
"We never do that topic."
"It sounds bo-ring."
"Call me Friday."
"Send the materials and I'll look."

Don't count on the person who says, "Yes, that sounds really interesting," to even remember your call next week, let alone be interested. But keep plugging, stopping only for meals, and a pattern will start to emerge for each city. Sometimes you'll have to use Express Mail or a comparable overnight mail service. You won't like it, but time is everything once your cities and dates are set. Do not dwell on a single city as you book. If a major television program or newspaper fails to materialize in any city, skip it and rearrange. You don't want to endure the expense for a few taped radio interviews. Once these preliminary calls have established who in each city is or is not interested, do your mailings and make the follow-up calls. The following guidelines should help to assess your booking priorities for various types of interviews:

Morning television talk shows. Book three to four weeks ahead of your arrival.

Live radio shows that appear on the air every day. Book three to four weeks ahead of time.

Taped television interview programs. Book about four weeks ahead of your scheduled arrival date.

Television news features. Book extremely close deadline, sometimes on the day of your arrival itself.

Newspaper press interviews. These all-important bookings sometimes can be booked a month ahead of time, and sometimes at the last minute.

Taped radio interviews. Book about four weeks ahead of your arrival—but they can often be used to fill out a schedule near the last minute.

Local origination cable shows. Book usually about three weeks ahead of time, sometimes at the last minute. Make certain that they've been on the air for a while before booking them. Sometimes these bookings are a total waste of time on tour.

Telephone Interviews

A tour is not a vacation, and there's no reason to take the afternoon or the evening off. There are hundreds of radio stations and small newspapers dying to speak with you on the telephone. If you're not going to a particular city but want exposure, check your references for stations or publications that offer telephone interviews.

Confirming Notes

Notes of confirmation are especially important when you're on the road. Be as specific as possible:

Mr. Peter Pellenz
Night Talk
WOR Radio
1440 Broadway
New York, NY 10018

Dear Mr. Pellenz:

It's a pleasure to confirm the appearance of Mr. Steve Dworkin on WOR's Night Talk. Steve will arrive at the WOR studios at 11:45 A.M. on Monday, June 22, for a live interview at noon on the 24th floor of 1440 Broadway.

Please call me at 212-345-6758 or email me at JR@csound.com if there are any further questions or information that might be helpful. I understand Steve will be through at 1:00 P.M., but that you might want to keep him for an extra half-hour for promotional announcements. Thanks so much for your interest. I know it will be a great interview.

Best,
John Rockwell

You may want to use only a preprinted postcard instead:

Confirmation of Interview
GUEST: *Steve Dworkin*
DATE: *Monday, June 22*
AT: *WOR, 1440 Broadway, 11:45 A.M.*
UNTIL: *1:00 P.M. with possible taping until 1:30*
FOR FURTHER INFO CONTACT: *John Rockwell 212-345-6758 or JR@csound.com*

I'm bigger on "snail mail" than e-mail for confirmations, but any variation on the theme is appropriate. If possible, keep copies of all confirmations with you on the road. You'll have many experiences when you'll be glad you did. You'll also want copies of the travel agencies' hotel confirmations lest you find yourself sleeping on a park bench because there's a convention in town and somehow the computer failed to register your impending arrival.

Personal Appearances

Personal appearances can be the most satisfying piece of the tour—
or an embarrassing fizzle—so it's very important to know how many
people are actually expected. Personally, I'll show up anywhere
there's a pot of coffee and a gap in a schedule, but if I'm setting up
an itinerary for a busy or famous client, I want a very compelling
reason to use up an hour or more of that person's time. If the meeting planner says, "Well, you just never know how many people are
going to show up," I'll take a pass. However, if she says, "You never
know, of course, but we had 20 people for the author of *Software on
Parade* and over 500 people when Michael Dell came by, I feel
assured my client will be in professional hands, so I'll book it."

In planning your own tour, check with the Chamber of Commerce
and other local organizations for the business breakfasts and association meetings that are always looking for speakers. And once you have
made this contact, the subject of the honorarium may come up. If
they have one, take it, of course, but my view is that you contacted
them and you're there to collect business cards and pitch something,
not sell your services as a speaker. Ease off on heavy negotiations.

Chances are, you'll meet someone who *has* a real budget and will
bring you back in the style to which you would like to be accustomed, say, business or first class and an honorarium very much to
your liking.

That will not happen in library groups and other nonprofit organizations, but the experience can be very rewarding, and these
groups are superior to business associations at getting you what you
really came for, attention in the local press.

Printing Up the Schedule

Once you leave home, your schedule will become something akin
to a life jacket. Careful input of the schedule information is an
imperative that is often overlooked by even the largest public relations agencies. Everything you need for a day of publicity should be

printed out on a *single page* and in order. See illustration of printed tour schedule.

On the Road

While you're away, someone at the office should have a copy of your schedule. That person should also reconfirm interviews and flights the day before your arrival in a city. If there is no one to do this for you, make time to do it yourself. Sit down with your cell phone and the schedule and *reconfirm everything!* The history of touring is littered with the bruised egos of people who endured the humiliating experience of having interviews canceled, showing up at the wrong place, or other horrors that can be avoided simply by calling a day ahead of time.

Following Up

The same follow-up notes that you use in local publicity should be done when you come home from a tour. They always pay long-term dividends, even when you swear you'll never see your interview contacts again.

When you come home, you'll want to sleep for a month. You will have exhausted yourself and made mistakes. Some of the errors will make you want to cringe—you made a joke about bleached hair to a hostess with bleached hair, you showed up at the wrong time for a radio interview, or you rambled on about obesity when there was an overweight person on the talk-show panel. You may feel an uneasiness about what you actually accomplished. But you will know a secret. You will know how to do a tour, and, once you shower away the jet lag, you may even want to try it again.

SITE SEEING

Council of Public Relations, www.prfirms.com.   If you decide to bring in a tour pro, do some research at this site first. Their "Find a Firm" database allows you to locate a firm in your area to guide you through the rigors of a tour.

Weekend Today in New York, www.newschannel4.com.   Check out this broadcast of the NBC flagship station for a great example of the kind of morning shows you'll encounter on the road.

AAA, www.aaa.com.   You'll need a warm bed and a wake-up call. Unless you don't plan on sleeping, check out accommodation ratings across the continent.

23

Event Publicity

*E*vent publicity is the gathering of exposure for a specific occurrence at a specific time. Whether your event is a yard sale or a rock concert, you will be called upon to work under deadline pressure with an ad hoc group of people who are often meeting for the first time.

Pledge drives for operations, marathons, sales of all kinds, and other mundane events receive a great deal of publicity when they are pegged to human need. Such effort is but a single facet of event publicity.

Usually events are publicized for more optimistic reasons. Sometimes, your church needs a roof, or the town seeks a traffic light at a dangerous intersection. Perhaps you wish to rally people around a political issue that you consider to be vital. Regardless of the cause's importance, there are certain do's and don'ts involved. There are also risks. The following pointers should help:

1. Pick a type of event that no one else is doing. If there have already been three walkathons this spring, you'll have a difficult time garnering exposure.
2. Choose the location as carefully as you would choose your own neighborhood. Can people get there? Will they want to go there?

3. Get a Web site, or at least a page, with a workable domain name dedicated solely to the event. Take your most reliable volunteer and assign that person to updating information, checking the site several times a day, and following up on any postings or queries. This is a one-shot site, so don't spend a fortune on design or graphics. It should be pleasant to the eye and professional, but it doesn't have to be the Site of the Year. Remember Rule #1 of any publicity site—that it provides a clear way to reach a knowledgeable person.

4. Everything takes longer than you think. Be generous in allocating time on the project. If the clock runs out, you could end up with no coverage.

5. Have a "Who, What, Where" sheet prepared at least a week in advance. This usually involves the cell phone numbers of the key people in attendance. Fax or e-mail it to the Day Book, photo, and assignment desks at the same time.

6. Make sure that there's sufficient space, sanitary and parking facilities, and a power source for the press. Bear in mind that TV vans need to be in a clearing to raise their satellite masts.

7. Pick a day when you're reasonably certain that a competing event will not occur. Parades, carnivals, and other public gatherings must obtain permission from the municipality. Check with your town or city government.

8. The more commercial the event, the more innovative it must be to warrant coverage. The press may be generous with worthy causes, but spectacles staged to sell soap have to offer a promise of novelty.

9. Start way ahead of time in getting the required permissions from the appropriate community authorities. You might be in a hurry, but they never are.

10. Small towns work better than large cities. It's not impossible to get coverage in a city. People do it every day. But television crews are skeletal on weekends, when most events occur, and your coverage potential will depend on the value of hard news made that day.

11. Advance publicity is often more important than coverage of the event itself. Again, start early and get your campaign site plugged in as many places as possible, being sure to cover the hidden corners of media—event listings in weekly and non-English papers, radio station community bulletin boards, your local cable channel, your community Web site.

12. Collect the business cards of anyone who shows up, especially the photographers, many of whom are freelance. They're a very useful addition to your press database.

13. There is nothing quite as wonderful as a stunt that works, but stunts have a way of backfiring. You may find yourself hiding from the press instead of cultivating it if something goes wrong.

14. The more dangerous the stunt, the more likely it is to get coverage. Need we remind you that you're going to get sued if someone gets hurt?

15. Children, especially little ones, are always a big draw. They're also the most vulnerable to motion sickness and all kinds of danger, and they make a *lot* of noise.

The event follows a different pattern from booking guest shots. First, assess what you want to publicize and whether it ties in with any established date. There really *is* an Arbor Day. There is also a national Meat Week.

Wire and syndicated news services keep a "Day Book" of upcoming events, which they transmit early each morning to all subscribing broadcast stations, newspapers, and magazines. No matter where you live, you're not very far from a regional office of the Associated Press. Call them and ask that your event be designated in the Day Book. Also call your local cable news channel.

Local television and cable stations often have news features with names like the "New York Minute," or the "Miami Beat," which are basically press releases on the air. If they can't send a crew, they may well accept footage and copy from you, provided it's professionally shot. Ask what their specifications are.

In addition to your release, there is a feature called "Community

Calendar," "Town Crier," or some other similar name that is common to most radio or television stations. While the FCC has relaxed its hold on station programming, they still are licensed to serve the community, so they give time away. To you. You can get extraordinarily valuable advance coverage if you plan ahead, and most public service directors welcome an e-mail contact:

> To: Steve Auger, Action 4 News
> From: Jesse Cawley, Women's Auxiliary, American Legion Post 79
>
> Steve,
> As promised, here's our announcement for Community Calendar. Thanks for thinking of us:. "The women's auxiliary of American Legion Post 79 will sponsor a children's auction on Saturday, June 23, at the Bow Grange Hall from 10:00 A.M. to 6:00 P.M. Proceeds will benefit the Post 70 Scholarship Fund."

Then, stay on the phone as often as possible as the event draws near. Will the television station send a crew? Will the newspaper send a photographer? Keep on top of it until the very morning of the event.

Try to enlist the aid of local luminaries whose presence will help draw attention to the event. They can always be put to work cutting ribbons, opening the festivities, receiving awards for their community service, firing the starting gun of the race, or whatever. Part of the mayor's job is to put up with participation in worthy public events. Yours might as well be one of them. If there are voters present, most politicians will consider the event worthy. Local television people and disc jockeys can also sometimes be coaxed into helping with these tasks. In a sense, they're looking for votes, too.

Avoid planning an event that's too complicated. Costumed re-enactments of local historical occurrences are a good draw, but if they become too complex, you're apt to find yourself hosting a party that no one wants to attend.

There are many surprises in event publicity, the biggest of which is that sometimes the event is not publicized at all. When in doubt, see a public relations consultant. You may find the fee a bargain. If you're planning a stunt of any kind, see an attorney, a public relations consultant, and your Aunt Madeline who has great intuitive powers.

If you follow the guidelines, you'll get through it. The following suggestions can either be adapted in concept for your own event or may spawn other ideas. Remember—even if you're a registered non-profit corporation, there are local and state laws governing fund-raising and public events.

Live Auction Sales

People love the atmosphere of competitive bidding. Auctioneers usually work on a commission basis, and they work very fast. The combination of local dignitaries trying their skills as guest auction-eers and the jackhammer mouth of a professional works extremely well. Check local laws. Not everything can be auctioned off.

Virtual Auctions

EBay has revolutionized the way we sell things and they're local-ized, as are other Web sites. So, it's great fun to display the col-lectible object at the event, but take bids on it from all over the world. *Today* show host Katie Couric, who lost her husband Jay to colon cancer, auctioned off the green room log, signed by every guest to appear on *Today* in 1999, on eBay. She not only raised tens of thousands of dollars for the cause, but she gave scores of priceless plugs as she promoted the auction on NBC.

Talent Shows

The press loves anything that utilizes the talents of the very young or the very old. However, as suggested earlier, these are the most fragile members of society, so be especially careful. Talent shows, contests, quizzes, and other mildly competitive events are a lot of fun.

Getting Physical

There seem to be two types of people in America—those who are fit and those who claim they'll one day stop procrastinating fitness. Either way, arm wrestling, running competitions, softball games, or anything that brings out the athletic fantasies in us will probably work if it hasn't been overdone in your community.

Used-Merchandise Sales

People probably want to bargain more than they actually need so-called deals at used-merchandise sales. They don't draw much publicity unless there's an extraordinary angle, but not all events require much more than a brief announcement in the newspaper and on local stations.

Costumed Events

People love to dress up. The more people you persuade to dress in costumes, the more likely your possibility of coverage. Again, try and peg your costumed event to a particular day or point in history.

Animal Events

If you've ever had your picture taken cuddling a lion or leopard cub, you were probably glad to pay for the privilege. Animals always make good copy, especially if they're young and helpless. You can frequently find something a little more exotic than dogs and cats. In large cities, there are agencies that specialize in animals and can advise you on licensing. It's hard to top well-trained animals as a way to make your event a hit.

Demonstrations

On the more serious side of event publicity are protest-type demonstrations. They almost always draw press attention. Demonstrations are public gatherings and require the cooperation of public officials, some of whom may be the object of your protest. Reporters learned a long time ago to be wary of demonstrations staged for their own benefit rather than the public's. The outcome of a demonstration is rarely predictable, so, although they are your right as citizens, to avoid regretting your decision later, plan carefully.

After the Event

Make follow-up calls to the journalists and photographers whose cards you've collected. You might be pleasantly surprised at the coverage you get. The photographers may be happy to provide a couple of prints free or at cost for you to submit to newspapers and magazines for them. After all, they get paid, or at least credited, if you succeed. Write thank-you notes to everyone who helped. You'd be amazed at how often this little courtesy is overlooked.

SITE SEEING:

The following events have both national and local elements — don't forget to observe the publicity the sponsors are getting.

Avon Breast Cancer 3-Day Walk, www.avon3day.org. The epitome of a supremely organized and well-constructed event site. They get national attention all year long.

The Million Man March, Atlanta, www.millionmanmarch-atl.org. This event also received a lot of national exposure (and not all positive) in the various hosting cities.

World AIDS Day, www.avert.org/worldaid.htm. A great site for a great cause.

24

The Press Conference

It's 10:30 A.M., and you've called a press conference for 11:00. The caterer has set up a folding table with an urn of coffee, doughnuts, pastries, and little sandwiches. There is a stage in the rented hotel banquet room, and a lectern from which the president of your company will announce a merger. At the rear of the room are three folding tables for television camera operators to get the elevation they need.

You pace a bit, wondering if you've chosen the right-sized room. If there's too much unused space at a press conference, the momentum of the announcement is diminished. If the press is crowded into a room, there's a lot of discomfort. The president joins you.

"They did say they'd be here, didn't they?" she asks, and you assure her, for the fourth time this morning, that the press will come. They're always a little, er, late, ha ha. You ask the boss to go somewhere in the room because you don't want her greeting reporters as they come through the door. If they do. It's 10:45. Where the hell are they?

"Why do I have to leave? I'm not a movie star. I don't need to make a grand entrance." she says, in a way that questions your right to be one of the human race.

"It's better, that's all." You know the boss is thinking that the press would be here by now if she'd brought in an outside consultant. She is incorrect.

What would be happening if you had brought in a public relations firm is that you would have received another professional opinion on how to proceed with the merger's announcement. A press conference isn't always the solution.

At 10:51, the first member of the fourth estate, a reporter for *Software Saturday*, an influential online newsletter, arrives and heads for the refreshments.

"I'm starving," he says. "I knew you guys would have food. By the way, where is everybody?"

Freeze the action here and take a hard look at the situation. If the merger really is newsworthy, the press will soon arrive. If it isn't, you're going to humiliate yourself and maybe lose your job. Press conferences are not for the fainthearted. Maybe you should have sent a series of personalized releases to the private e-mail addresses you've collected from each of the media contacts who cover your company.

Keep the body identical but put the reporter's name at the top, maybe send them by messenger or fax as well as e-mail, and stay by the phone to answer the inevitable questions. The boss's day would be interrupted by the calls requiring her involvement, but she wouldn't be pacing around the lobby of the Hyatt at this moment, circling you like a tiger ready to pounce.

You stand convinced of your decision. This merger involves the livelihood of 500 employees, and you believe it's news. If the conference fails, you'll live with it, but you'll never be convinced that your instinct was incorrect. Sometimes, in dealing with the press, instincts are all we have.

Now let the action resume. Between 10:45 and 11:10, when the conference actually begins, a troop of reporters arrives. You receive a call from a television assignment editor who explains that the crew is just finishing a story nearby and will be right over. When everything is settled, you step up to the podium, tap the mike, adjust for squeaking feedback, and start to speak.

"Ladies and gentlemen, it's my privilege to welcome you on behalf of International Widget. Let me now introduce our president, Dr. Julie Ross."

Gone is Dr. Ross's I'll-have-your-hide look. She now looks trim, tan, well-tailored, and in control.

"Thank you, David. It is my privilege to announce this morning that Vidalia Digital International has joined with Phoenix Chipmasters in a merger agreed upon last week and finalized yesterday afternoon. Phoenix Chipmasters, as you may know, is the largest manufacturer of automotive audio software with a gross sales volume of 77.3 million units last year. Terms of the final agreement, as filed this morning with the Securities & Exchange Commission, are detailed in a report that Mr. Heifetz made available to you a few moments ago.

"There will be no changes in management or personnel. All Phoenix contracts will be honored according to their terms. I'll answer any questions you may have."

It's over in less than 45 minutes. You watch the boss field the questions you've anticipated for her. The press leaves, and your life resumes. The boss and you are pleased.

Getting the Word Out

A press conference is the release of a news story to a gathering of journalists who have been assembled for the sole purpose of receiving your information. It can be an informal conversation with representatives of two trade publications, or a statement to an auditorium full of reporters and television crews. Its purpose is always to disperse information to all interested journalists at once.

The following is a checklist for press conferences.

1. Press conferences are inherently last-minute operations, but you will never be forgiven if you leave anything out. The first item on the checklist, then, is make a checklist.
2. Don't confuse a press conference with a press party. One is the release of news; the other is a junket that gets little serious coverage.
3. Don't leak any information. You must remain as neutral as Switzerland until the moment of the announcement. Other-

wise, you might find coverage diminished when a news source breaks the story ahead of the announcement.

4. You must develop a carefully selected list of invitees. If the conference releases hard news, as most of them do, you don't want gossip columnists and feature writers from the Sunday supplement taking up space that should be allocated to other reporters.

5. While there are a number of ways to invite the press, the best method is probably a series of hand-delivered announcements followed up by telephone calls to the list of invitees to be certain that they know about the conference and to query as to whether they will attend. E-mail is fine if you have an online relationship with the journalist, but if you're making contact for the first time, you have no way of knowing whether this person is a proactive citizen of the Internet or a grouchy curmudgeon who still pounds on a typewriter and blissfully blows off his company computer advisors.

6. Morning conferences are best for most situations. Calling a conference for 10:00 or 11:00 A.M. allows the reporters enough time to file their stories.

7. Either have the event catered or provide your own coffee, pastries, mineral water, juice, and soft drinks. Wine and liquor are usually inappropriate for morning conferences.

8. Choose the right size room. If it's too large, someone will say, "At a press conference that drew scant attention . . ." If it's too small, you'll read: "The announcement was made in a cramped conference room at company headquarters." The room should be the right size for your estimated head count of attendees. Perhaps the most efficient method of balancing attendance with room size is to hold the conference in a hotel and discuss your expected attendance with a special events manager.

9. The cell phone is the lifeline of the press conference. Make sure you have yours charged and on and enough others ready in case a member of the press needs to make a call. It's a good idea to have someone with a cell phone at the back of the room taking calls. If it's a sizeable conference, make sure there are

enough telephones available in the conference room or nearby. Any conference center can set you up with as many telephones as you feel are warranted.

10. Keep your Web site updated during the conference, releasing the text of the announcement as soon as the rest of the press gets it. Post pictures (sound and video if feasible) with the text. Make sure phone numbers with live people on the other end are posted as well.

11. Allow for television's bulk. Make sure a room can be lighted, and darkened, if necessary. Can the satellite vans be parked? If there is a videotaped demonstration, be sure to have copies available for each attending television station in Beta or whatever format the assignment editors request.

12. Be sure to have plenty of heavy-duty extension cords and electrical outlets handy for the television crews. Camera operators prefer large and sturdy tables at the rear of the room so that they can shoot over the heads of reporters. If you have any doubts about the number of outlets needed, call in an electrician.

13. Sometimes the boss likes to ad lib beyond her prepared statement. Be certain the quips don't get out of control. The best format is a short formal statement, followed by a question-and-answer session.

14. Anticipate every possible question and go over each one of them carefully with the boss before the conference.

15. If possible, your company logo should fit on the front of the lectern over the hotel's name. Why should they get *both* the rent and the publicity? The lectern should be slightly elevated.

16. When you notify the wire-service reporters of the conference, you should also notify the Day Book editor in writing. This small step ensures that virtually every publicity source in your area will know about your conference.

17. The press usually arrives close to the appointed hour. Don't panic if they're a few minutes late.

18. Remember that a press conference is always in danger of failing. If a breaking news story such as a fire or a bank robbery

occurs, or the mayor has his own last-minute press conference, you may find yourself eating the pastries and wishing you'd become a dentist. Keep the list of likely attendees and their direct telephone numbers handy in case you have to call people. Keep your employers informed of your progress. If it looks as if your story is about to be superseded, tell the boss immediately. Don't stand around nervously hoping for the best.

19. Have someone posted at the door to greet the reporters and hand them a release detailed enough to contain the important facts, but don't make the dreadful blunder that most of the big PR firms and more than a few government agencies make at press conferences—providing a kit bigger than *War and Peace.* These people don't have the time.

Some love the action of a press conference, and some hate it. Wherever you stand, you'll certainly remember the morning for a very long time.

SITE SEEING

The Pentagon, www.defenselink.com. They have a daily press conference. Check them out.

The White House, www.pub.whitehouse.gov. You can see what the White House is releasing to the press today.

Hill & Knowlton, www.hillandknowlton.com. Handles a number of corporate clients.

Nokia, www.nokia.com. You can't run a press conference without a cell phone!

25

Trade Publicity

It's Friday at Caller One, and the executives are getting restless. They've had lunch and they have been paid, but they cannot leave for the weekend without their early copies of *Cell Phone Weekly*, the trade publication that defines their industry.

Theoretically, *CPW* (as it's called in the cell phone biz) comes out on Monday, with the next Monday's date imprinted on the cover. But no self-respecting executive in the field can afford to wait for the inside story on what's happening. Right now the mail room is late with the early copies, so assistants in cubicles are going online to see if the issue's been posted yet. Nope. *CPW*, like many magazines, isn't giving away what it can sell. The hot news comes out in hard copy first.

Finally, the van arrives at the door of the loading dock, and its driver is accosted by otherwise prim MBAs who serve as the company's junior executives. Their job of the moment is one of the most important tasks they perform all week, snaring *CPW* for their boss.

This ritual is repeated thousands of times per week. The intensity of the wait varies with the pulse of the industry and the competence of its trade publication. Some fields not only wait until Monday but even then remain passive. Others require immediate harnessing of the information flow and gossip in order for executives to function properly. There are "name" columnists unknown to the public, but in plastics, tool and die, broadcasting, or publishing, the sun rises and sets with them.

For some areas, a weekly publication is not enough. There are daily newspapers that are read ahead of any other publication. Furthermore, online publications—and the *online editions* of less frequent *print* publications—often update information on an hourly basis. Many of these online "trades" have editorial and publishing staffs entirely separate from their print counterparts. In other words, the *online* editor of *CPW* might think your company's palm navigator is the hottest thing on the market, while the cantankerous columnist, who still uses a typewriter to churn out his work for the *print* edition of *CPW*, thinks your gadget is not as great as the models coming out of Memphis.

Yet, trade publicity is often overlooked in planning campaigns. Clients who are willing to drop everything to do a backwater radio show, snarl when their PR reps sell them to influential industry magazines.

As in any publicity endeavor, your first task is to define your market. Which industries do you really want to meet and who in them has to know about your product or idea? And as long as you're looking into trade press, try to break your story out of the box. Yes, you might get a great report on your Palm Navigator 4 in *CPW*, but an interesting marketing campaign, a huge scholarship fund set up by your company, or a revolutionary management strategy could land you pieces in *Marketing Quarterly*, *Money-Givers Monthly*, and *Middle-Management Today*.

Even if you don't always reach the exact niche you'd aimed for originally, your boss will be thrilled when his buddy at the club compliments him on the genius reorganization he just read about in *DownsizeWeek*. Since the titles of the publications are so endemic to their purpose, you would be doing yourself a disservice to track down copies of all but the most influential among them.

Trade publications are often grateful for 8″ × 10″ or 5″ × 7″ photographs, printed and sent online or shipped on disc, if they relate directly to the industry served. In some cases, such as recreation, the subject matter need only relate to the people involved.

House organs are often overlooked as a publicity source. A *house organ* is a company publication, usually edited by one or two people who hire freelancers for graphics, copy editing, and editorial chores. The exceptions are multinationals or other large corporations whose in-house publications are often larger than your local newspaper.

You're probably going to find seasoned magazine professionals at the helm when you query house organs or trade publications, so maintain the same level of professionalism that you would apply if you were approaching *Time*. The person you're trying to sell probably worked there and left because no main-stream glossy could match the money and job security of a conglomerate. More to the point, this editor may still have friends at *Time*.

When approaching the trades with a pitch, remember that the editors know your field as well, if not better than you do. Don't try to fudge figures or sugarcoat a bad fiscal year with a fluff pitch. These folks always smell a rat, and a lame pitch that isn't backed up with solid numbers and stats can cost you your reputation.

Trade publications are easily located online, but it's also a good idea to thumb through them in the reference room of your public library. It could be one of the most profitable excursions you'll ever make. These people mean business.

SITE SEEING

Publishers Weekly, www.publishersweekly.com. It has the publishing industry covered.

Broadcasting & Cable, www.broadcastingcable.com. Check here if you want to learn what your television station manager is really thinking about, or know about programs long before you see them on the networks.

The Ford Motor Company, www.ford.com. This site will link you to Ford's internal publication.

Johnson & Johnson, www.johnsonandjohnson.com.   Visiting here can make you feel a whole lot better.

Equine Trade Journal, www.equinetradejournal.com.   Get back in the saddle and peruse articles on hunting, jodhpurs, and dressage.

26

Satellites

Your company finds that a competitor is going to release a version of ScamBot, the revolutionary security software that has been in development at your company for the past 18 months. They've called a press conference for tomorrow morning at 11:00. The boss is frantic. ScamBot was his idea, and he feels it was ripped off.

ScamBot moves through the World Wide Web at the speed of light, reading the codes on credit cards in its registry. It knows when fraud has been committed even before the card holder, and it tracks the address of the criminal, notifying the nearest police agency fraud unit or Interpol.

You suggest calling a press conference ahead of the competition, but even you feel that the haste and image of catch-up ball would be inappropriate. The boss is now kicking furniture. The time is 9:20 A.M., and you're not worried. You can't stop the competition, but you can use satellites to win the day.

You ask the boss how he'd like to see a feature on ScamBot on CNN tonight and maybe the nightly news of the four big networks as well. He says he'll do anything for you if you can pull such a thing off. He's so despondent that he promises you a Jaguar if the world knows about the ScamBot by tonight. You tell him they will but you'll need the cooperation of everyone in the top executive ranks of Supreme Software. There can be no hide covering and turf protecting today.

At 9:45 you've gone behind closed doors to make a couple of calls. What does the press actually *know*? All they seem to know is that the competitor's credit card security software is called "Rottweiler," as in the guard dog, and they're showing it to the world tomorrow. There's got to be a crack in this armor somewhere. You call a friend at the *San Jose Mercury News*, the Silicon Valley newspaper that has become one of our strongest voices in print coverage of all computer technology in America. Here you find the break you need. It's never about technology, always about human competition..

Your friend tells you that CNN got an advance look and shot some footage of Rottweiler for release after tomorrow's demonstration at the press conference. They'll probably put it on their financial network, CNN-FN, first, then run it on the main network and *Headline News* within the hour. This scoop leaves the competition stuck with "B-roll"—video footage with no sound track—that they'll have to edit. That gives CNN at least an hour lead even though, technically, they're not releasing their footage until the press conference.

CNBC's furious, just furious, says the reporter at the *Mercury News*, but the PR guy is just blowing off the press into a hellish maze of voice mail and the company Web site. And if that isn't bad enough, your contact hears that *USA Today* might also be getting the same advanced peek at the Rottweiler prototype.

"Either you do a press conference or you don't," your friend says. He's not happy with how they're handling this. Even though you know that the words "happy" and "reporter" do not easily link up, you listen sympathetically and coo in the right places.

Don't they know that the *San Jose Mercury News* has covered the Silicon Valley since the first geeks arrived from the East? Not that *USA Today* isn't up to it, but you don't go telling the *Mercury News* to take a number. Even Steve Jobs has the courtesy to call us first. The nerve of these Rottweiler guys. You tell your friend you will have something for him in about 15 minutes and he'll like it.

Now you call a contact at MSNBC, the joint venture between NBC and Microsoft whose coverage on technology is considered cutting edge. By going with her, you offer a release from the misery and score a television triple crown. You're going to get MSNBC, the combined cable and Internet network, the powerful CNBC cable network itself which invented financial coverage on cable, national distribution to over 500 smaller TV markets and cable systems, plus another 200 radio stations. How'd she like an exclusive and how soon can she get over here? You tell her to bring her Visa so we can code it and try to "steal" it. It will be great television.

NBC can go first on ScamBot, but as soon as they do, you've also got to offer a demo to the very unhappy CNN, probably for CNN-FN. When you play this game, you get people mad at you, but you've learned to live with it. Neither side can afford a grudge for very long.

Having secured the two principal sources of financial news, you've made sure they'll cover the world for you, including radio, but you don't want to leave it at that. You call your friend Josh at National News Uplinks, a satellite company used to working fast. You tell him you want two hours of satellite time this afternoon at two, and you want local technology editors in the top 10 markets called by his bookers and alerted for a special interview and demo feed. Yes, you tell him, you know he's tied up with a Barbie promotion for Mattel, but there's a rather large bonus that you will get approved quickly if he can get this done. He'll find a way.

The satellite producer is used to it. Every day clients call with some immediate disaster that has to be remedied by yesterday. They live in a world of tomorrow-may-never-come. They prefer 24 to 36 hours' notice, but this kind of request is not unprecedented.

Through the crack between the bottom of your office door and the carpet you see shadows of nervous footsteps. You know the boss and his entourage are in the outer office. You're thumbing through a Jaguar brochure. The phone intercom rings. The MSNBC crew is on the way.

The satellite people are busy notifying 380 commercial television stations and 1,500 cable systems that there will be an important feed representing a technological breakthrough this afternoon at 4:00. They spell out the satellite, transponder, and transponder number.

They then use another system to notify 2,800 radio stations that there is a news feature coming down on a revolutionary new security software system that will end credit card fraud online.

There are a number of sophisticated, computerized systems for reaching these outlets, and they all are in operation on a daily basis.

You accompany the boss into the company's Media Center and set up a bridge line that enables you to broadcast a video conference online to the company's major executives. It's a secure digital line that is almost impossible for anyone to monitor without the necessary codes. There's been a lot of nervous chatter about the Rottweiler press conference, and the boss offers assurances that everything's going to be fine for ScamBot, but you've advised him not to reveal what you're up to. Walls having ears is how ScamBot was compromised in the first place. You have to move fast now because, even though no one at the competition monitored the video conference, you have to assume a leak's under way.

The National News Uplinks crew arrives and tapes a demonstration of the ScamBot, which has been lighted and displayed against a satin backdrop in the Media Center. A producer takes notes and interviews your company president. Then the CNBC crew shows up, and the reporter is astounded when you reveal the intricacies of ScamBot.

The boss is asked to comment about the competing Rottweiler technology and he says he wouldn't presume to know, but he's sure that Rottweiler is interesting enough but the marketplace will prove that ScamBot is *the* cutting edge of Internet security technology. Never knock the competition directly. Kick them in the groin with faint praise.

They leave. Within an hour, they'll be on the air. You use the bridge line to the *San Jose Mercury News* and feed the demo material of the ScamBot, in time for their deadline. The *Mercury News* will have its exclusive around the world tonight. Next to arrive is a reporter from *Marketplace*, Public Radio's business program that is a favorite of the CEO.

If the Rottweiler people haven't heard that ScamBot's out of its cage, they will when these reporters call for a quote. No one's going to honor any request to hold this until tomorrow. In a little over an hour, you've lanced the competition by your knowledge of satellite technology.

It's only fitting that Time-Warner merged with Turner in the 1990s, because both companies pioneered the television, cable, and video revolution that began in 1975 when Time, Inc., started using satellites to beam Home Box Office into hotel rooms. At the same time, Ted Turner took a weatherbeaten UHF station in Atlanta and began beaming its signal around the world.

Today, through a mesh of live media interviews and the release of radio and television pieces in smaller markets, public-relations people have been able to form their own ad hoc networks. They broadcast feature material directly to stations and conduct follow-up surveys to report usage to clients. Typically, stations downlink B-roll footage and produce their own pieces around it. Radio satellite tours have also prevailed since the early 1990s, and all-news stations will accept audio to make their own pieces.

The PR satellite people rush to the nearest studio with "uplink" facilities, meaning that their finished reports can be transmitted to a communications satellite in orbit 23,500 miles above the equator. The signal is then returned to earth and picked up by the stations' "down-linking" receiving dishes. Satellite technology is expensive, clear, and efficient. Prior to satellites' elevation to widespread usage, signals were transmitted by high-fidelity telephone lines that were efficient but beyond anyone's budget for the type of project undertaken in the hypothetical case of the ScamBot. Let's continue with the day.

At 2:00, the boss sits down in the Media Center and starts talking by satellite to technology editors of television stations in the top markets—New York, Los Angeles, Chicago, San Francisco, Boston, Philadelphia, Atlanta, Dallas, Houston. The interviews are about five minutes apiece and are going well.

CNN, as predicted, is not happy, so they got 10 minutes and a promise of their own look at ScamBot as soon as they can get a crew to your company's headquarters. *USA Today* comes in at about the same time, demanding to know why they're playing catch-up to the much smaller *San Jose Mercury News*. The reporter looks at you quizzically, like maybe you have Attention Deficit Disorder. *USA Today* is *big*. The *San Jose Mercury News* is in San Jose and maybe that tells you something about priorities. Can you count, Rain Man? Do you know what our circulation is?

Gosh, I guess in the commotion to get on the air, I kind of went with my contact in San Jose. Sorry, won't happen again.

After that, you relieve the boss in the interview chair. There's no need for him to do the rest of the satellite interviews. He needs to figure out who to kill now that he's won. So you take over and talk to the smaller but still important markets—Salt Lake City, Las Vegas, Providence, Charleston, Tampa, Miami, Pittsburgh. Smaller markets receive B-roll footage, and the radio networks remaining unserved get audio, also by satellite. Tomorrow, you'll ask the boss to do a morning-drive radio tour to explain the ScamBot to Americans as they commute to work.

But you end up doing it, because the Rottweiler people decide to start a war by claiming they had the idea first and their lawyers are looking at your theft of it. So, of course, the boss needs to do *Today*, *Good Morning America*, and CBS's morning show in addition to live satellite pieces on CNN and CNBC on split screen with the CEO of the Rottweiler company.

By going with MSNBC, you've chosen a perfect portal to Internet news, and the Web is now buzzing with news of the ScamBot. You'll need to monitor Usenet for rumors and have company spokespeople briefed and ready to spend hours in key chat rooms and forums. Long after the ScamBot has passed its shelf life as a broadcast and print news item, it will continue to be major news online and needs to be treated accordingly. Be prepared to put out fires as soon as they start and to respond professionally and in a nondefensive manner.

The ScamBot and the scenario for its release as news is fictive, and slightly exaggerated in terms of the coverage an innovative technological advancement might receive. However, in biotechnology, where body parts are auctioned online and every year brings us closer to designer human cloning, the action moves faster.

And, of course, we all know that no *USA Today* reporter would be so ill-tempered as to call a company spokesperson "Rain Man" if he got scooped by the *San Jose Mercury News*. But the apparatus described, including satellite linkups with major radio and television networks and secure bridge lines for computer teleconferencing is in place and ready for you. Satellites and their usage are a vital part of every publicity person's arsenal of possibilities and becoming more so every day.

SITE SEEING

Target Video News, www.tvninc.com. Produces and distributes video news releases and public service spots, satellite media tours, and international event coverage.

Hospitality Television, www.hospitalitytv.com. Describes itself as a "distance learning company." Offers full production facilities, studio, editing suite, uplinking, downlinking, video conferencing, and more.

Planned Television Arts, www.plannedtvarts.com. In the biz since 1962, PTA is a major player in the media placement business.

27

Publicity Potpourri

Several publicity endeavors that probably fit more comfortably into the category of promotion are worthy of our attention because they are *hooks* to leverage exposure, especially online where discussion groups won't push anything unless it's relevant to their shared interests.

Speeches

A speech differs from a press conference in that the speaker is addressing a general audience rather than a group of journalists for the release of a specific story.

Conventional wisdom in publicity texts has been that we should speak whenever we can to spread the word on an idea. But speeches can be dangerous. Most people are better one-to-one than one-to-many, and if you're one of them, either don't speak at all or begin in very small groups.

Most speakers try to break the ice with a funny story. That can be a loaded revolver, because if it falls flat, your confidence will drop and the audience will drop you. The slightest betrayal of tentativeness will result in an awful moment when you're barely under way but can see people shifting in their seats or looking at their watches.

On the other side, however, you should know that a successful speech will make you feel like a Beatle in 1964. Or, Madonna in the

Material Girl video. Okay, Ricky Martin singing "La Vida Loca" at the MTV Awards. The crowd will lean forward, and you'll see people nod as you confidently rattle off your points. The question-and-answer period that follows the speech will further your momentum, as will the inevitable gaggle of well-wishers who will come to the podium when you're done.

There are many books and speech coaches for you to consult. Virtually all expert sources will advise plenty of rehearsal, even if you're one of those anointed souls with an ability to speak extemporaneously. In fact, most extemp artists got that way by hammering in their techniques through rehearsal. If you saw a professional lecturer in Phoenix on Monday and followed this speaker to Chicago on Tuesday, you would almost certainly see the same speech, complete with funny story, pauses, and inflections. The answers to the audience questions will even be the same.

Be certain that a release reaches the appropriate media sources well in advance to assure a good turnout, and, if you can swing it, try for a follow-up story.

Seminars and Workshops

Even if you're in the middle of Manhattan, you can get coverage for a workshop. It might come in the form of local cable and neighborhood newspapers, but it will be there if you pursue it. In a smaller city, you can promote on the local morning talk show, on radio, in the press, and to online discussion groups, especially if the event is free or available at minimal cost. If you're looking to walk away with a $5,000 fee, payable in advance, and you're selling investment packages as well, you'll find tougher sledding, but you can still do it.

Posters and Pamphlets

Benjamin Franklin and Thomas Paine used pamphlets successfully to influence history. You are not likely to get that far . . . but one never knows. As always, there are a couple of dangers.

The first is expense. As soon as your sense of aesthetics tells you that your pamphlet or poster just has to be in full digitized color against a rugged stock, you're going for broke and you're probably going to get there. Multicolored printed pamphlets require a delicate and time-consuming blend of tones and inks. The final result looks great, but the handsomeness is reflected in the cost. Printers tend to be very accurate in their assessment of costs, and you should consult with several before going ahead. Persuade an artistic friend to illustrate the master artwork that printers refer to as *mechanicals*. A mechanical is a completed design layout that is ready for reproduction by a printer.

Another pitfall is a potential brush with the law. Handouts litter, and the policeman won't necessarily be your friend if you distribute them in a public place. What usually happens is that someone takes your pamphlet and throws it away 10 seconds later. Instead, try to enlist the aid of established businesses to display a small handful of your pamphlets at a time. If the pile is too large, someone will take the whole collection. No one knows why, but it always happens. Maybe there are children in Europe starving for propaganda.

Posters are clearly illegal in most public places. The law is also with the property owner if you paste something on the side of his or her building. There are public bulletin boards in supermarkets and Laundromats, but they often aren't big enough for serious display of posters. Make sure you really have somewhere to place your posters before you give the printer a green light.

Writing

Your newspaper will always welcome a query if you have a flair for writing and wish to offer an article. Remember to query before writing and to begin with a clear idea of the word count. If they call for 500 words, don't give them 1,500 and assume they'll edit to suit their available space. They might just junk the piece.

You can take your cause beyond the local newspaper to magazines, Sunday supplements, newsletters, and other publications, on and offline. Even if you are not inclined to write, perhaps someone can organize your ideas on paper for you.

Besides the placement of articles, the value of a publication's letters column cannot be overstated. Most magazines welcome readers' letters.

You may chuckle at advice columns, but you don't see any shortage of them. These columns have been used to push products for most of the past hundred years. Throughout her career, advice columnist Abigail Van Buren, known to millions as "Dear Abby," could produce an unbelievable stampede for reprints of a medical study, a book, or a product she embraced. *Parade* magazine, the Sunday newspaper supplement, has an enormous readership, should you get a letter published.

Public Service Announcements

The Federal Communications Commission, even in these deregulated times, scrutinizes a station's response to issues in its community. The old Fairness Doctrine, which required broadcast stations to give equal time to opposing views of their editorial policies, has been replaced by small audio and video nuggets that show that the station is showing at least some regard for the community it serves. Call the station and ask about making a public service announcement (PSA).

The 1992 Cable Act and individual citations in FCC regulations lay out a whole picnic of community access and public interest options. Direct broadcast satellite (DBS) companies, for example, must carry channels that serve the public interest as defined by the FCC. If you have a genuine concern, write to the station and request an airing. Don't be surprised if you get it.

Parties

"I spent three grand entertaining those freeloaders and didn't even get a mention! Never again!"

Compared to the cost of a Web site launch party in a big city, that's pretty cheap. Probably the most classic mistake people make is expecting direct coverage from a party. If you're in a smaller community, you'll get your party on the appropriate page or perhaps even on television, but in cities there's just too much major news to allow for coverage of all social events. Parties can serve other, still valid, functions, however.

Attention is what you get for your money. Whether you're in San Francisco or in Centralia, Illinois, parties are common launch vehicles for new Web sites. Get the right socialite to host in a cool place and make sure there are a lot of local *glitterati,* including local talk show hosts, news anchors, and political leaders. There's one good way to get them there and all the pros know about it—pair your event with a decent cause and emphasize the cause.

The key here is to feel passionate about the issue. If you are bored by public radio but you notice that all the local celebs seem to bill themselves as "NPR junkies," you'll look like a jerk if you do a party after a long fund drive for the worthiness of noncommercial broadcasting. Instead, scan your own family history for the illness that took away a parent or a favorite relative and form a partnership with a local chapter. Get publicity, raise money, throw a party, modestly placing your own commercial endeavor in the background. Don't worry. You'll get credit.

But a lot of entrepreneurs just don't feel charitable in their formative years. Bill Gates and Ted Turner weren't known for their passionate support of causes when they were building their commercial empires, and, if you're in the building mode and do not feel comfortable about participating in a "worthy" cause just yet, fine.

Get a good room, do as much advance publicity as possible, and party down, dude. The press will attend and know what you're selling even if they can't write up the party itself. It is common experience for a reporter to say, "Michael, I'd like to talk to you more about this. Can you call me in the morning?" Or, weeks later you'll receive a call when a reporter is at work on a feature that applies to her beat.

The grand opening of an automobile dealership might not be considered news, but the owner might be interviewed later on the topic of the increasing value of used cars. And even if a reporter who attends your party does not call you for a story or even a quote, the hospitality you showed him almost always ensures a callback the next time you leave a message on his voice mail.

Parties don't have to be expensive. If you can coax either a business friend or a nonprofit organization to donate the real estate (e.g., a restaurant banquet room, a church activity center), you've immediately shaved hundreds off the budget. Friends who have specialty dishes can help with the hors d'oeuvres. But don't do anything that looks like a scrimp job. Don't run into a card shop and pick up an invitation that reads, "We're having a party at _____." Press people like name places, whether the name appears to be a fancy residence or a restaurant. If you are faced with a choice between renting a banquet room at a big-name restaurant at a discount or sending the press to Uncle Morris' Bar and Grill, go with the status or go without.

Printers will show you a variety of invitation options, and you can probably find a good one to meet your budget. Perhaps a friend who does calligraphy will make the master invitation.

All the rules in Chapter 23 apply to parties. Make sure you don't schedule on the date of a conflicting event, and make certain that your list is carefully planned to reach the press people you need. Journalists work hour by hour and might have a difficult time responding too far ahead of time.

With imagination and careful planning, you may find a party to be a valuable addition to your campaign.

SITE SEEING

The Washington Post, www.washingtonpost.com.   Covers all significant parties in the nation's capital.

Northlake Herald Journal, www.pioneerland.com/cgi-bin/ppo-newstand.   Check it out and see what's being covered in this smaller town.

The New York Observer, www.newyorkobserver.com. Covers every trendy Web site launch in the East.

San Jose Mercury News, www.mercurynews.com. Does a superb job of covering the Silicon Valley and its social life.

Professional Photographers of America, www.ppa.com. Need a photographer to cover your local event? Check out the yellow pages or this site.

National Speakers Association, www.nsaspeaker.org. Learn more about public speaking with this organization.

28

Going National

A no is as good as a yes," one publicist says to the other after the second drink of an expense account dinner at a four-star restaurant.

"Better still if it's a quick no," replies the colleague, and they both smile.

Their clients would want to boil these two high-priced dweebs in oil if they overheard this conversation about booking network morning television shows. The clients, however, would not be interpreting the shoptalk correctly. It's not that they don't work fiercely on behalf of the companies they represent; they are merely conversing in a shorthand that bespeaks the travails of the fastest lane.

The average major-market talk-show office gets plowed under with material and telephone calls every day. The network and syndicated daytime programs get *avalanched* beyond the comprehension of those who have not seen the daily parade of messengers, overnight delivery people, mail by the sack, e-mail so thick it clogs the system, faxes, birthday balloons for producers and hosts, and every conceivable gimmick to grab attention.

Nuts show up at NBC in Burbank demanding to see Jay Leno, as though he hangs out in the lobby just waiting to greet mothers with little girls who can sing "Tomorrow." African-American hosts are invited to scholarship fund-raisers in urban America so often that they would be unemployed if they accepted one thirty-second of them. After struggling against great odds to get their jobs, they're not thrilled to tell someone calling from a tiny Baptist church on the outskirts of Atlanta to "talk to my agent." But what choice to they really have? Jewish celebrities are asked to waive their $25,000 performance fees to show up at Bar Mitzvahs and Hadassah groups, while Catholics get pulled toward this or that diocese.

The parade of demands works against the program's own ghoulish time and energy requirements as too few staffers work to put out a show. Count the number of guests on *Today, Good Morning America, Oprah!, The Late Show With David Letterman,* or *All Things Considered,* to name just a few, and you'll find 15 or more interviews each *day.* Most of these slots are filled with newsmakers or "name" interviews, not because the shows are in love with them but because *we* are. If we all demanded to see more unknown talking heads, they would be there.

Thus, one should not be phenomenally surprised that people get the process backward. They think they can go on network shows and become famous. The reality is that you need to become well known in a particular area, pay some dues with other forms of publicity, and step up to national recognition. Then you'll be *more* famous. More famous is the key.

That is not to say that the network shows do not want you. Count the number of nonfamous people on *Today* and *Good Morning America* who managed to accomplish something magnificent or become embroiled in a local controversy. If you are hauled into jail for refusing to return a library book or if you stop a conspiracy to bomb your local high school, you'll be talking one-on-one with more celebrity hosts than you can count. But say, you didn't do any of those things. How do you go national with your campaign?

Chapter 30 will show you the directories you need to find a current list of national shows, their requirements, and producers. Once you get used to using them, the playing field is surprisingly level. Watch Oprah. Does she stack her shows with celebrity interviews? Not really. She has them, of course, but she didn't become the most influential talk show host in the history of broadcasting by listening to Bruce Willis talk about his love life.

Read *People*. Every issue has ordinary individuals who accomplished something extraordinary. How do they find these folks? The main office may be far away in Manhattan, but the magazine survives by keeping a watchful eye on trends, wherever they occur. You may be assured that there's a *People* correspondent, probably freelance, scanning the publicity in your area.

"The stringer network is very important to *People*," says former senior editor Landon Y. Jones. "In every major city, we have people who do not work for the magazine but contribute to it. They send in clippings that are taken so seriously that I would say at least three or four stories per issue originate in this fashion."

Choose any national publication—*USA Today, Time, Newsweek*, or a major metropolitan daily such as *The New York Times* or *The Washington Post* which syndicate their articles nationally, and you'll find a constant monitoring of local news. The Internet facilitates the search. If you're making publicity locally, you're probably being observed and you may one day get a call from one of these publications.

The best thing to do first is gather information. Check out the sites of your targeted national media. Check the masthead of the publication you want, and you'll find a wealth of information directing you to the editor you want. Some publications want you to query with a Web site posting while others pay close attention to personal notes.

As we mentioned in Chapter 17, a recommendation from an NPR member station does not guarantee you a booking, but it may get you to the attention of the right producer. If you look under the hood of the network, you'll find that there is no monolithic booking entity called "National Public Radio." *Talk of the Nation* is as independent of *Fresh Air* or *Morning Edition* as it is from your local cable system.

And how many fresh voices do you hear on *Morning Edition* every week? Lots. They're on live with Bob Edwards, on tape reading their thoughts as essays, or responding to pieces through a special line the network has set up for it. One would venture a guess that noncelebrities have a better shot at getting on than movie stars, although there's plenty of room for them as well.

A quick scan of the NPR Web site will give you a thumbnail idea of the kinds of topics the hosts prefer. Yes, they can all interview Yassir Arafat or the 97-year-old gospel singer still hitting the high notes at the First Baptist Church of the sleepy southern town. But dig deeper. What's the preferred terrain of the hosts? Robert Siegel of *All Things Considered* likes the professorial issues—the transition from the Eurocentric ethos of the last century to the multiracial culture of the twenty-first, and what's going to happen before the turf is conceded. Linda Wertheimer and Susan Stamberg are also bookish, but I'd say lighter.

Scott Simon seems to have more fun on the air than most public radio hosts. He moves easiest from Baltic tragedies to, say, obscure hit records and other issues of popular culture. Liane Hanson favors puns and word play. Bob Edwards, as anyone who ever listened to NPR for more than an hour knows, goes for hard news and has a particular weakness for sports, while Alex Chadwick is a guy you'd picture going down the Colorado River on a raft. Noah Adams, a Kentucky native, has a deep-rooted interest in rural poverty.

I use NPR as an example because it is universally coveted by publicists. Oprah may be the highest possible goal for a book or entertainment publicist, but she's out of reach for many. Everyone wants to get someone on NPR. But a common complaint is that producers there miss topics that would be perfect for them if only they'd dig a little more.

A visit to NPR reveals the other side of the complaint and a very assertive counter-argument. The network might not be poor any longer, but it *is* understaffed. Your brilliantly worded pitch letter or e-mail is clogged in the pipeline, but there's a way out. Producers at NPR say that publicists simply don't understand their system. They feel deluged by aggressive pitches from people who clearly have never listened to the programming. They don't know who Robert Siegel *is*, let alone his preferred topics. Worse, they don't have a clue as to the difference between shows.

But those who do know these differences and consistently pitch the right guest or topic for the right segments, develop strong relationships at NPR. The lesson applies to all national media. Check it out, understand the flow of the programming, and spend time with the Web site. Don't just scan it—stay awhile and you'll begin to develop a keen sense of the program's culture. Once you know that, you're on the way to going national.

Oprah Winfrey believes so firmly in reclamation after personal hardship that it's hard to imagine any segment without such a theme. But that does not mean she doesn't sometimes seek lighter fare. But if you're not thinking inspiration and change through conflict, you're out of luck. Her producers do read their e-mail and listen to voice mail. But if they don't call you, bag it and go on to something else. You can't pick a topic like weight loss, race, or inspiration and assume she's going to drop everything and say, "Get that person on the phone." A more common response would be "We've kind of done that show. Unless there's something really new . . ."

I can tell you one thing that won't work. Do not try to get Oprah's attention by bombarding every security guard, make-up person, her longtime boyfriend Steadman Graham, her personal trainer, her cook, or her limo driver with catchy material. Several years back, it worked when the publicists at Warner Books tried it with an inspirational book called *Simple Abundance*. Since then, the idea has gotten, shall we say, tedious around the production office.

Prime time news magazines such as *20/20*, *Prime Time Live*, *Dateline*, *Sixty Minutes*, *Sixty Minutes II*, and their legions of imitators are heavily influenced by human interest stories they find online and in the local press. In recent years, they represent a growing trend toward interactive media fusion. *Dateline* partners with *Court TV* and invites viewers to vote online regarding the innocence or guilt of a defendant. They're also wide open to straight-in queries, especially at their Web sites.

"We look for a news story, a real news story that can stand up to thorough substantiation by our staff," says Don Hewitt, the founder and longtime executive producer of *Sixty Minutes*. Hewitt is the gruff Old School prototype of the ink-stained journalist come to television but he's hardly a throwback. Several generations of producers who have followed in his wake feel that the old rules of journalistic scrutiny are the barriers of democracy.

Yes, you can go on the *Today* show or its competitors by dressing up as a kumquat and writing a love poem if you're willing to stand outside the network's studio at dawn. But there are better approaches that you'll find on their Web site. Try writing or e-mailing the producers, or, better yet, come to favorable attention from the folks at your local NBC station and let them pitch you. That way you can sleep late.

Can you get on the Howard Stern Show without taking off your clothes? Not easily, but it's possible. One Boston security consultant was wise enough to understand that Howard does not cotton to the usual "protect your home from burglars" segment. He offered to come into the studio and knock someone senseless with a stun gun—a legal, if bizarre, approach. He got a plug in for the products he was pitching and spent days taking orders. And, he had a magnificent hook for going on every morning show in the country, assuming that his sidekick didn't turn into a raving lunatic.

A friend of mine is a master at getting books plugged on the show and was thrilled when he got a trivia quiz on the air. However, Howard is Howard, and the segment didn't quite go as planned. Instead of Howard opening the book and running questions by Stuttering John and Robin, the segment he scored was "Homeless Jeopardy." His bosses were not happy.

Getting David Letterman or Jay Leno to book you as a guest is difficult because their shows are about celebrities. But, if you have something a little offbeat, you can e-mail the producers and get a phone call or have a product plugged on a "desk segment."

Going national can also be a serious and heartrending experience. Weekends on talk radio are brimming with possibilities. Cancer survivor Selma Schimmel has a national show for fellow cancer survivors on Sundays thanks to the foresight of New York's WOR radio, a superstation heard around the country by satellite. There's also a show for people who are HIV positive, and many other specialized radio broadcasts.

Bloomberg has niched itself in the business community with hundreds of opportunities for business-related topics that can carry your message to millions in premium time. And, if you book a new product on Public Radio International's *Marketplace,* you can be assured or reaching many of the highest rollers in business.

In 1995, AudioNet pioneered the inevitable merger of the Internet and radio by streaming Dallas station KLIF online. Five years later, as Broadcast.com, the company was audio server for over 500 stations. At the same time MTV Interactive purchased Imagine Radio, the originating source of listener-determined radio programming, and created Radio SonicNet. The upshot is that the hundred-year-old idea of "tuning in" is dramatically changed. As new technology creates better sound than FM, we'll be creating not only our own music on CDs, but our own menu of radio programming. Sites such as www.discjockey.com offer music from any decade from the 1940's on.

In the late 1990s, KBON in Eunice, Louisiana, began developing a small but global following online with its blend of blues and cajun music, while those who wanted to hear the Latin beat at its original source logged on to jb.fm in Rio. WHRB at Harvard University in Cambridge, Massachusetts, went global with the music marathons that it had long broadcast during reading periods before exams. And talk radio weighed in with yadayada.com.

Soon, everything you do will be national and international. The idea is to do it right and make it count.

SITE SEEING

National Public Radio, www.npr.org.   Lurk before you leap
Dateline, www.dateline@msnbc.com.
KCRW, www.kcrw.org.   A pioneer in public radio as well as Web-
casting.

The Today show, Today@msnbc.com.   Because of the NBC and
Microsoft partnership, *Today* and other programs put a lot of
broadcast content online. An excellent site.

Howard Stern, www.koam.com.   Hey, you never know.

KBON, www.kbon.com.   See what the fuss is about in Eunice,
Louisiana.

29

Publicity at Work

The public be damned," said Cornelius Vanderbilt at the height of publicity's sleaziest hour. Between 1865 and 1900, when Vanderbilt expressed that touching sentiment, the railroad interests spearheaded a movement to use the press as a vehicle to gain support for their expansion. Truth was not considered an especially useful commodity, especially when an editor might be induced to juggle the facts for, say, $200.

Enter the Muckrakers, a group of reformist writers whose ranks included Upton Sinclair, Ida Tarbel, and Lincoln Steffens. They used their skills to further favored causes of their own, usually at odds with the industrialists. Sinclair's *The Jungle*, for example, exposed the horrors of the Chicago stockyards and stands as a sound historical example of persuasion's just side.

Foundations of Publicity

The early twentieth century introduced Ivy Lee, a gifted and influential publicist whose work gained him folklore status even in his own time. Lee, who represented John D. Rockefeller, crusaded for a policy of industry keeping the public informed, a canny but startling posture in the Robber Baron era. His 1906 lobbying to the press on behalf of the Anthracite Coal Mine owners, and a much-commented-upon "statement of principles" released that same year, portrayed his clients as tough but paternalistic architects of an era that would make America great.

Conditions in mines were treacherous, and it did occur to many that something was wrong with putting children to work full-time in the sweatshops, but romantic reveries associated with that period of "rugged individualism" persist, thanks in part to Ivy Lee. He was also the twentieth century's premier image consultant, changing public perception of Rockefeller from tyrant to a twinkly figure who had a shiny dime for every kid who crossed his path.

Propaganda was an innocuous word used to describe the flow of information until after World War I, when the Allied nations fought with the Germans to influence world opinion. In 1917, the U.S. Committee on Public Information was set up by Congress under the leadership of George Creel. Ideas, it was postulated, are weapons.

In the same way that it is difficult to look at a yellowed photograph of a great-grandparent and feel the personality of a long-dead human being, it is hard to imagine the enormity of this assumption. Sure, philosophers had said it for centuries, but now a Congressional Committee was meeting to use words like "nerve gas." A few opening shots from our side:

"The war to end war."
"The war to make the world safe for democracy." (We're still selling military deployment with that one.)

This was, of course, pabulum compared with what the Nazis, Fascists, and Communists were up to between 1939 and 1941, when they proved to the world that keeping up with the propaganda Joneses was an imperative. Every country scrambled to beef up its internal public-relations apparatus.

In business, we were also learning a few tricks. Shortly after World War I, Elliott White Springs, a former Air Corps ace, caused widespread controversy when he developed a print advertisement for his line of Spring Maid Sheets. An Indian maiden was pictured on a bed in a desert. In the background, a brave looked very satisfied. The cutline: "A buck well spent on a Spring Maid Sheet."

Aside from the obvious breakthrough of the effectiveness of sex appeal in advertising, Springs conveyed a couple of important publicity lessons:

1. All successful publicity is ultimately transmitted by word of mouth.
2. An ad can be used to start a publicity campaign.

Radio boomed during this period. Every manufacturer fought for its share of the market and attempted to convince the customer that all radios were not alike. General Electric's Clyde Waggoner arranged for the weekly broadcast of a radio program from the South Pole by Admiral Byrd himself, making sure the world knew that GE and its excellent equipment had orchestrated this superior feat of technology.

Publicity and public relations boomed between the world wars. Businesses, emaciated by the Great Depression, hired consultants to bolster impoverished images, while movie studios, theatrical producers, radio and other enterprises drummed up business in the heyday of the stunt. Thumb through any news magazine of the period and you'll find flagpole sittings, high-wire acts, skywriting, contests of every type, exhibits, and many other gimmicks pegged to specific promotional causes.

Radio programs were branded to their sponsors, and the product had a way of appearing throughout the show. Rudy Vallee hosted the *Fleischman Hour,* while Edgar Bergen (Candice's Dad) and his famous ventriloquist's dummy Charlie McCarthy had a Sunday night program known as the *Chase and Sanborn Hour.* Bromo Quinine was as much a part of radio's Sherlock Holmes adventures as Dr. Watson. Performers plugged their shows with appearances on other programs, a practice that continues today.

Fred Allen and Jack Benny met on the air for a March 14, 1937 "feud" designed to publicize their respective network radio shows.

This mock battle froze the nation with one of the largest audiences in radio history up to that time, second only to one of President Roosevelt's "Fireside Chats." Roosevelt used radio to sell his New Deal program and soothe a nation suddenly out of work. Many historians see these informal, one-way radio conversations as one of the greatest acts of political leadership in the twentieth century.

Unfortunately, the power of radio did not go unnoticed by any number of fortune tellers, bogus physicians, marriage counselors, and other snake-oil hucksters. These con artists would show up in a town, buy a half-hour of radio time, give a superpitch, and invite listeners to attend a lecture or meet them at a prearranged point of sale. Others would simply go on the air, fabricate case histories of miracle cures, and invite people to send in a mere dollar for the elixir that would do it all. John Romulus Brinkley, the "goat gland man," was typical of the genre that inspired the Communications Act of 1934, when the FCC was born.

Demagogues found pure gold in those airwaves. Father Charles E. Coughlin, a Michigan priest and outspoken right-wing social critic, spoke to CBS audiences of 30 to 45 million a week and drew no fewer than 50,000 weekly letters to his Shrine of the Little Flower in Royal Oak. When CBS demanded the right to read his text before letting him on the air, he simply set up his own network with the contributions he received. He'd have loved the Internet and today's communications satellites.

Newspaper columnists dominated the era. A mention on Walter Winchell's Sunday night radio broadcast ("Good evening Mr. and Mrs. America and all the ships at sea . . .") was enough to make a book a best-seller. A "publicity story" in Hollywood parlance came to mean a piece fabricated for fans. Mickey Rooney "dates" Judy Garland.

There were also "rumor mills" for word-of-mouth publicity. These were specialized publicity firms that clients hired to start rumors about their companies, or, on the dark side that eventually rendered them illegal, to start talking negatively and falsely about the competition. Practitioners of this dark art would walk into crowds in pairs and start talking loudly. Sometimes it took and sometimes it bombed, but the company always got paid well. Their descendants today work the online chat rooms, legally we hope.

Television

The Golden Age of Television was a godsend to publicity as press agents scurried to peddle their clients' wares on the new medium. Everywhere you looked in those days, you found plugs. In the early fifties, everyone wanted to be on *Texaco Star Theater*, known in history as *The Milton Berle Show*. Not all of the era's quiz and game shows were rigged, but they all were pitched by cigarette-smoking, cocktail-swigging publicists.

You Bet Your Life, a popular quiz show with Groucho Marx, was on the surface a zany interchange between the host and everyday contestants, with the occasional intrusion by a duck whenever a "secret word" was mentioned. Contestants were chosen for their ability to play off Groucho, and the press agent who could provide such a person was usually rewarded with a nice plug.

If you got a refrigerator pushed as a gift on *The Price Is Right*, or a washer and dryer on *Queen for a Day*, you could be assured of a growing clientele. Talk showed up early with late-night shows like *Broadway Open House*, the forerunner of the *Tonight Show*. Anyone pushing an upcoming movie opening, play, a product, or a book showed up on the show. The greatest of all variety shows was *The Ed Sullivan Show* starring a moody, New York newspaper columnist who was about as telegenic as a toad in short pants.

But no one, it seemed, missed his show. From Woody Allen to the Beatles, Sullivan had a knack for spotting the next big thing in America. No one's done it since. Sullivan was a Family Values guy who was fond of referring to snarling rock musicians as "nice boys," and so influential that even the Rolling Stones changed the lyrics of "Let's Spend the Night Together," to "Let's Spend Some Time Together," to accommodate his bow to his mainstream American audience.

Sullivan guests often came from managers and publicists who visited his office daily to pitch. He was a great trader of favors, and he did his cronies a big one by creating a segment where he'd gesture toward the audience and give a plug.

"Before we bring out Señor Wencas and the dancing bears from the Moscow Circus, I'd like to say hello to Arthur Schlesinger Junior, whose new book is called–uh–uh–A *Thousand Days*. Arthur Schlesinger Junior, everybody."

And the author would stand up and take a bow. Hey, if the guy could get Mick Jagger to change his lyrics, he could get a historian to stand up and smile on national TV.

Jack Paar was the only straight man to host *The Tonight Show*, so he often played to his own strength by talking with authors like Alexander King. JFK and Nixon dropped by to pitch their bids for the presidency. Paar was so popular during the 1960 presidential elections that he broadcast *The Tonight Show* live from JFK's inaugural. Martin Luther King, Jr. made his first appearance on *Meet the Press* that year.

In the 1960s and 1970s, touring authors and entertainers, including Redd Foxx, Jackie Mason, Joan Rivers, Gore Vidal, Jacqueline Susann, and Truman Capote pushed their wares on a staple of all publicity tours for over 25 years, the afternoon movie. Every major market had at least one big one, often featuring a popular giveaway franchise called *Dialing for Dollars*. The guest would reach into a fish bowl, pull out the name of a viewer, usually a housewife. During the next movie segment, they'd interrupt the film to cut to the celebrity making the call and chatting amiably. If the viewer knew the password, and the amount of the jackpot, she'd win the dollars.

Eldridge Cleaver, Gloria Steinem, Abbie Hoffman, Jerry Rubin, and Betty Friedan, angered by the Vietnam war, sexism and racism in America, all ended up pushing their books on *Dialing for Dollars*. By the mid-1970s, the franchise had branched out to weekend programming and a new incarnation called *Bowling for Dollars*. It was my pleasure to send several Watergate felons who published books to make their pitches at middle American bowling alleys.

The Pulitzer Prize–winning historian David McCulloch got his start as an imposter on *To Tell the Truth*, and Harold Robbins, the steamy best-selling novelist who sold more fiction than any human being alive at the height of his fame, was marched to the Ed Sullivan theater to be introduced before the bears came out.

Syndicated shows like *The Mike Douglas Show* and *The Merv Griffin Show* blended entertainment and quasi-serious talk. Programs like *The David Susskind Show* and *Donahue* talked more seriously. And in Baltimore, a young news anchor named Oprah Winfrey was paying her dues on local television. By the late 1980s, she was the unquestioned queen of daytime television, and if she felt like it, she could dominate prime time as well.

Today, publicity is an interactive mesh of radio, cable, satellites, the Internet, and whatever comes next, usually all at the same time. The Richmond Savings Bank of Vancouver, British Columbia, is Canada's third-largest credit union. When a survey indicated that a full 15 to 20 percent of bank customers were unsatisfied with their banks at any given time, Richmond jumped in with a campaign to capture that market. It created a campaign for a fictitious "Humongous Bank," whose motto was "Our Money Is Your Money."

Richmond also developed a logo for Humongous, jingles, and a Web site. Through an integrated blend of humorous advertising and a publicity campaign around the site launch, Richmond positioned itself as the Big Bank alternative. Three days before launch, the local press received an invitation with a large H, informing them that an event was imminent that would stun them. The next day, they received an invitation from Humongous with no reference to Richmond Savings, save for a contact number.

While it might not play in New York or LA, this campaign was an astounding success in Vancouver. The largest television station in the market did a three-and-a-half-minute feature on the site for its evening news, and soon the site had nearly 40,000 visitors. Unaided recall of Humongous leapt from 3 to 18 percent, and with help respondents to surveys indicated a recall response rate of 88 percent.

Probably the key lesson here is that Richmond staffers didn't just hang out and say, "Hey, let's have some fun. Hard research indicated a huge gap in the marketplace, and they were creative and humorous enough to create a campaign to steer the market into their bank, which they did in droves. In a short period of time, nearly 500 visitors to the site had completed the "Contact Us" form, indicating that they enjoyed the site and might be willing to switch over.

If people think you're a little whacked, you may be on the track to a great promotion. When I visited Michael Dell at his corporate headquarters in Austin, he told me that people thought him clever when he started selling customized computers out of his college dorm room in 1983, but when he decided to give up his premedical studies to do it full-time and take on IBM, they probably figured he'd sow some wild oats and then come to his senses. After all, he was a bright young man. He could have been a *doctor.*

Such is the nature of ideas. Anyone who ever spent a day around books could have told Jeff Bezos that the Internet really isn't the place to sell them. They're a retail item. Fortunately for Bezos, he didn't know that. And one of the wackiest ideas imaginable is selling *cars* online. What kind of a lunatic would even try such a thing?

In 1994, DealerNet introduced the Virtual Showroom, where auto shoppers could browse at home, choosing from a variety of models and prices. To launch the site, DealerNet offered to give away a new Nissan and soon learned how strong the virtual market is. The promotion tore through the Usenet newsgroups like an Oklahoma twister in June. The word spread from online to off as newspapers, magazines, radio, and television programs took notice. Today, it's hard to imagine a major car dealership without a well-designed site.

In October of 1999, the Encyclopedia Britannica, beleaguered by an 80 percent drop in sales of its print encyclopedia over the past decade, learned a grim lesson about site launches. Sales may have been down and the door-to-door sales force a thing of the past, but the Encyclopedia Britannica is a blue chip brand name. But when it launched its new Web site, britannica.com, it drew such a stampede that the site went down for nearly a month until switching to a much stronger server. While they tried to figure out where they fit into e-commerce, there was one thing they weren't worried about. People know who they are and like what they do.

The Blair Witch Project will endure for years as the ultimate example of the Internet tail wagging the mainstream media dog. The film didn't start any hype fires at the 1999 Sundance Film Festival, but a fledgling company called Artisan Entertainment saw commercial possibilities in this mockumentary about three young filmmakers who disappear while looking for a witch in the Maryland woods. Artisan paid a million dollars for the worldwide rights to the movie, including sequels. As things turned out, that's a deal comparable to what the settlers paid for Manhattan.

The campaign Web site, www.blairwitch.com, blurred reality with police reports of the missing filmmakers and a history of the cursed woods. The campaign also included a "documentary" on the Sci-Fi channel, shown extensively before the film opened. Within weeks, the site was viewed over 30 million times, and *The Blair Witch Project* soon soared to a $75 million box office bonanza for a film that cost about $60,000 to make and $15 million to market.

Though *Blair Witch* seemed to come out of nowhere and invent Internet marketing with the creation of this instant urban legend, it followed years of online promotion, first by independent film makers, then by Hollywood.

The online promotion for *Men in Black* was under way a full year before its release in the summer of 1997. In chat rooms and on message boards, fans received word of aliens and strange accounts that could be found at the film's site, *www.mib.com*. *Toy Story* and *Pocahontas* were other early successes online.

But not everything in Hollywood is magic, especially when a site isn't ready for its hype. In a famous gaffe, Apple and Paramount formed a partnership in the mid-1990s for a Web site for the Tom Cruise movie, *Mission Impossible*. Paramount assumed that Apple, whose products are displayed in the film, would be the perfect company to design a user-friendly, high-impact site. They probably were, but it just wasn't in sync with the millions of dollars the studio spent on advertising and promotional appearances by the film's cast. And when it did go up, its use of Netscape 2.0 and plug-in software programs was too complicated for most surfers, including eight or nine million AOL and Prodigy users.

The lesson for a modern movie studio is the same as it was for Ivy Lee. Publicity abhors a vacuum. It is a team player. To do its job, all other elements of promotion and distribution must be in place. When all is said and done the whole ball of wax—radio, print, television, satellites, cable, and the Internet are about getting one human being to talk to another about your idea.

SITE SEEING

Media Life, www.medialife.com.   An excellent look inside modern public relations.

TV Industry, www.tvindustry.com.   Look at their feature articles on television.

Fast TV, www.fasttv.com.   A service to local television that makes programming available worldwide. Lots of interesting television shows and links.

Parrot Media Network, www.parrotmedia.com.   Provides online information for media people about the freight-train-paced broadcast/cable/web/print machinery.

Swart Advertising, www.swartad.com.   A leading creator of marketing campaigns for television shows. Their site reflects their leading-edge position. It will tell you a lot about the TV industry, and who's playing and who isn't.

Windows Media, www.windowsmedia.com.   A guide to online radio and television programming.

30

Directories: Your Uncles in the Business

You don't need a network of high-powered media contacts to garner several millions of dollars worth of publicity, but you do need reference texts. Even the smallest public library offers some of these volumes, and it can usually procure others for you if it is wired to a regional system, as most libraries are. If you're planning a tour, or any large-scale regional campaign, the purchase of one or two of these books is highly recommended. You can get most of them either online or in hard copy with e-mail updates.

There are no rights or wrongs, except that it is an immoral waste of time to attempt a campaign without some of these texts. Think of them as the springboard to your own personal database of contacts. They name names, cite audience and circulation figures, provide the direct extensions of hosts and producers and tell you who likes e-mail and who doesn't.

You'll find out everything you want to know about *The New York Times* or CNN, who's who this year at NPR, and which topics they favor. Browse, test drive, and choose for yourself. The books are like cars in that each has a feel, a mood, a suitability to your temperament. Most publishers put out a whole line of texts tailored to the niche you want to pitch.

Here are several traditional favorites to get you started.

Infocom Group

Publicists often glaze over and smile rhapsodically when they talk about their "bulldogs." Some, of course, are referring to pets. Most are referring to an indispensable line of texts published by:

Infocom Group
159 Hollis Street, Suite R2
Emeryville, CA 94608-2008
510-596-9329
www.infocomgroup.com

The *Bulldog Reporter* is a twice-monthly, eight-page newsletter that provides up-to-the-minute information on media personnel, beat changes, in-depth interviews with media people, and contact listings.

If I had the resources for only one directory for a campaign, it would be Infocom's *The National PR Pitch Book: The Insider's Placement Guide to the Most Influential Journalists in America*. The editors warrant that they have contacted all 27,000 media sources in the Business and Consumer edition. They also offer to research any contact you find outdated and get back to you within 24 hours with updated information.

The *Pitch Book* has more information on pitching *The New York Times* than even people who work there know about. NPR? They make perfect sense of it. Syndicated columns or specialized national radio shows are a snap. Not only do they give you the producer's name and phone number, but the anchor's as well.

Infocom puts out a number of other directories and shorter volumes for targeted publicity—*Top U.S. Business Media, Pitching The Wall Street Journal*, even the *Insider's Guide to Justifying the PR Budget to Management*.

Bacon's Information Inc.

Bacon's takes a more matter-of-fact approach to its information gathering than Bulldog, but the guides are packed with so much useful information as to be considered the industry standard by many working publicists. There's *Bacon's Radio Directory, Bacon's Magazine Directory, Bacon's New York Publicity Outlets, Bacon's TV Cable Directory*—anywhere you want to go, there's a *Bacon's* guide to take you there.

332 South Michigan Avenue
Chicago, IL 60604
312-922-2400

Editor & Publisher

Since the late nineteenth century, E&P has covered newspapers and is today a great source for two very strong, but overlooked media; online editions of the offline press and weekly newspapers. For years, the familiar red-and-white *Editor and Publisher Yearbook* was a fixture in every PR office in America. Today E&P has kept up with the times and broadened coverage to include Webzines and other forms of Internet journalism. Get it online, offline, at your library, or if the bucks are very tight, beg last year's material from a local PR firm. But use it.

11 West 19th Street
New York, NY 10019
212-675-4380
www.mediainfo.com

Contacts: The Media Pipeline
for Public Relations People

Like the Bulldogs, *Contacts* comes in a number of different forms. Their newsletter is superb and highly recommended.

500 Executive Boulevard
Ossining, NY 10562

914-923-9400
E-mail: Contactpr@aol.com

Hudson's Guides

Hudson's just puts it out there and you do the rest. They've always been easy to read and access.

2233 Wisconsin Avenue, NW
Washington, DC 20007
202-233-4904
www.daybooknews.com
www.minutepage.com

The Broadcasting and Cable Yearbook

The *Yearbook*, a broadcasters' bible, is irrelevant to most publicists in major cities but invaluable for local publicity in small communities. Many small libraries stock it or have online access. The *Yearbook* lists every radio, television, and cable system in the United States and Canada, and tells who runs them, what networks they carry, and what kind of special programming they provide for their audiences.

Once you know how to use the *Yearbook*, you can get hundreds of interviews not listed in other directories just by calling or e-mailing a station and asking questions. It has helped me find excellent interviewers on short notice and saved me from having to turn in anemic tour schedules hundred of times over the years. I consider it the ultimate publicity Saint Bernard.

245 West 17th Street
New York, NY 10011
212-645-0067
www.broadcastingcable.com

BPI Media Services

Excellent guides, newsletters and online services.

1515 Broadway
New York, NY 10036
212-536-5263

New York Publicity Outlets, Metro California Media

These folks in rural Connecticut doggedly cover some of the toughest booking streets in the country with the accuracy and panache that comes from having been at it for a very long time. Great references. I wouldn't book these markets without them.

PO Box 1197
New Milford, CT 06776
800-999-8448

Two Essential Online References

If you're planning to work online, there are two books you've got to consult, both of which have been invaluable to me, both in putting this edition together and in daily practice:

Public Relations on the Net by Shel Holtz (Amacom, 1999). Easily the best book written to date, not only on the intricate proliferation of new media and what it means to the everyday practice of public relations, but to the big picture of measurement of campaign results, online rumor management, use and misuse of corporate sites, and the lessons we can all learn from the experiences, good and bad, of those who went before us as the Net grew into a revolutionary social force.

Publicity on the Internet by Steve O'Keefe (John Wiley & Sons, 1999). O'Keefe is my kind of publicist, on or offline. He plunges in at full throttle on behalf of his clients, poking fun at himself for the mistakes he's made and sharing the wisdom he's picked up from years of being flamed and maimed online. O'Keefe has figured out the combination to the safe and he passes it along without esoteric language or condescension. I wouldn't click a mouse without this book on my desk.

Index